D0206193

The Origins of the Cold War

Caroline Kennedy-Pipe

palgrave
macmillan

First published 2007 by
PALGRAVE MACMILLAN
Houndmills, Basingstoke, Hampshire RG21 6XS and
175 Fifth Avenue, New York, N.Y. 10010
Companies and representatives throughout the world.

PALGRAVE MACMILLAN is the global academic imprint of the Palgrave
Macmillan division of St. Martin's Press, LLC and of Palgrave Macmillan Ltd.
Macmillan® is a registered trademark in the United States, United Kingdom
and other countries. Palgrave is a registered trademark in the European
Union and other countries.

ISBN-13: 978–0–230–53550–3 hardback
ISBN-10: 0–230–53550–X hardback
ISBN-13: 978–0–230–53551–0 paperback
ISBN-10: 0–230–53551–8 paperback

This book is printed on paper suitable for recycling and made from fully
managed and sustained forest sources. Logging, pulping and manufacturing
processes are expected to conform to the environmental regulations of
the country of origin.

A catalogue record for this book is available from the British Library.

A catalog record for this book is available from the Library of Congress.

10 9 8 7 6 5 4 3 2 1
16 15 14 13 12 11 10 09 08 07

Printed and bound in China

185095694

The Origins of the Cold War

Contents

Acknowledgements

This book has been a long time in the making, though a relatively short time in the writing, and it is a pleasure of finishing it that I can finally say thank you to those who have helped along the way.

First, thank you to all those friends and colleagues for their comments on papers, lectures and talks I have given over many years. Mick Cox, John Dumbrell, Mark Kramer and Geoff Roberts while not necessarily agreeing with my interpretations have proved friendly if robust critics.

I have also had the benefit of the comments of colleagues after lectures I have given at Leicester, Warwick, Aberystwyth and St Andrews and at various meetings of the British International Studies Association. My own students at Sheffield have been a great source of insight and commentary and the graduate researchers, most particularly Andrew Mumford and Thomas Waldman, have provided levels of advice and support far above the call of duty (especially since I was supposed to be commenting on their work, not they on mine!).

There are other debts. My publisher Steven Kennedy has, as ever, proved to be a supportive, helpful and constructive editor who has really engaged with this project. Randal Gray has edited the text with his usual precision. Clive Jones and Nicholas Rengger have given me advice on chapters and proved to be, as always, valuable friends. Pauline Kelly, Colin McInnes, Donna Lee, Neil Collins and Justin Morris carried the burdens of office in BISA with me; and largely because of their help and support I was able to write this book.

Fritz Stern has argued that the historian must serve two masters, the past and the present. Our present seems troubled. At the beginning of this century we are preoccupied with the threats posed by terrorism, ideological enemies and the instability of what seems to be a new era of anxiety. This book attempts to encourage students to look at the past, at the origins of the Cold War, to understand it and perhaps to extrapolate from those early years of post-war turmoil some understandings for our own time.

CAROLINE KENNEDY-PIPE

Introduction

> It is the Dead who govern. Look you man how they work their will upon us … why man, our lives follow grooves that the dead have run out with their thumbnails. Melville Davisson Post, *Uncle Abner, Master of Mysteries* (1918)

This book is an attempt to accomplish two things. First, I want to reflect on the origins, evolution and initial character of the early years of the Cold War and to provide a clear account for students and the general reader of how the struggle between Russia and the United States erupted after the end of World War II. A second task (see Chapter 7) is to examine how these Cold War years, the events, the personalities and the crises might inform our understanding of international relations more generally.

Many scholars, from different academic areas, have offered insights into the origins of the Cold War. Some are referred to and discussed in the following chapters. There are quite literally thousands of books and articles exploring the very many different dimensions of international politics between 1945 and 1962. We have books and articles which address not just the political dimensions of the relationship between Russia and the United States but the economic, the military, the nuclear, the cultural and the personal ramifications of the struggle. Detailed monographs exist in abundance on the character, impact and legacy of the leading figures in Cold War history. We are all familiar with some if not all of the accounts of the great dictator Joseph Stalin, the British Prime Minister Winston Churchill and of course President Franklin Roosevelt (e.g. Freidal, 1952; Montefiore, 2003). There is scarcely an event or a crisis that has not evoked its own scholarly debate or even a so-called school. Here, we might think of the fierce clashes

1

between historians over the issue of who or what was responsible for the actual breakdown in diplomatic terms between Russia and the United States in 1945.

When we think of Cold War history and especially accounts of its origins we look to the work of 'traditionalists' (that is the early commentators on the conflict), such as George F. Kennan who saw clearly that the outbreak of the Cold War was primarily the responsibility of Stalin and the drive for Soviet expansionism. Writing in the 1940s and 1950s and literally responsible as an official within the State Department for the making of American foreign policy, Kennan believed that the United States had no choice but to emerge from isolationism and protect the Western world in both Europe and Asia from the threat of Communism (Kennan, 1947).

This so-called traditionalist school dominated our understandings of the origins of the Cold War right up until the 1960s. And many of its ideas still have purchase today. We cannot and should not ignore the breathtaking scale of Stalinist ambition in creating a Soviet empire after 1945 – the occupation of Central and Eastern Europe and the desire to compete with the United States. Equally we cannot and should not be blinded to the very great brutality that Stalin's regime and that of his successor Nikita Khrushchev visited upon the peoples of Eastern and Central Europe. In that sense George Kennan was correct that here did indeed lie a threat to liberty and certain versions of justice and human rights.

Yet perhaps the central flaw in the traditionalist version of Cold War history was, and is, to place too much emphasis upon the figure of Stalin. In this version of events, American politics was merely reactive and defensive to the dynamism of its Communist foe and especially the charismatic figure of Stalin.

This version of the origins of the Cold War was challenged in the 1960s by the so-called revisionists. Associated primarily with the American historian William Appleman Williams and his Wisconsin school, they offered an alternative explanation of the origins of the Cold War. Williams claimed that the fault for the breakdown should be placed firmly at the door of President Harry S. Truman and the demands of American capitalism. The United States sought a Cold War in order to promote a new international economic order, secure markets in Asia and Europe and maintain prosperity at home (Williams, 1962). American economic and nuclear strength combined quite literally to leave the USSR out of these new post-war arrangements. Soviet strategies are treated more sympathetically and part of the story is that after the death of Roosevelt in the spring of 1945 and given the anti-Communist nature of his successor, Harry Truman, there was actually little that the Soviet leader could do to promote cooperation.

Although immensely controversial as an interpretation, not least because of the negative critique of American politics as essentially selfish, this explanation became quite fashionable and remained important, along with other so-called leftist versions in understandings of the Cold War for well over a decade. Of course all debates about history must be seen in the context of their own political landscape and it was no coincidence that as American armies were increasingly embroiled in Vietnam, these revisionist scholars saw in the origins of the Cold War, a tragic and failing path of American foreign policy after 1945 that led seamlessly to the quagmire in Indo-China.

In the 1970s yet another version of Cold War history began to emerge – this time characterized as neo-revisionism and led by John Lewis Gaddis. While remaining confident that Stalin and his authoritarian system was guilty for the outbreak of confrontation, Gaddis pointed to the labyrinthine nature of the origins of the conflict and the many mis-steps, misunderstandings and misperceptions on all sides in the months after the end of World War II. Some ground was conceded and some mistakes by American leaders admitted to by the neo-revisionists in their dealings with the Soviet Union. Indeed a rather more fragile and less confident America is depicted by Gaddis as successive presidents struggled to come to terms with the changing shape of global politics and the burdens of acting in a superpower role.

As Gaddis pointed out the United States was not a confident power in 1945 and actually had to reshape many of its domestic priorities and institutions to cope with the demands of competition with the Soviet Union. There was a price to pay – which was not just financial – for eternal vigilance, the alliance with the West European states and a global policing role. In this version of events, the United States was a somewhat reluctant superpower (Gaddis, 1972).

In the foreground to all these versions of recent history lay the very real shadow of a nuclear confrontation, a nuclear accident (which did actually occur in 1986 at the Chernobyl reactor in Ukraine) and the misery and poverty of those in the developing world who were embroiled in the many conflicts that formed the overall shape of the Cold War world. In 1945 the US atomic bombings of Hiroshima and Nagasaki changed irrevocably the nature of potential threats and beckoned in a new age of national security or, rather, national insecurity.

Debates over the outbreak and origins of the Cold War were further fuelled after 1989 by the release of documents from not just the United States but from Russia and the states of Eastern Europe. These documents were seized upon with alacrity in the hope that they would allow us to finally 'know' in the words of John Lewis Gaddis the truth about the origins of the conflict that dominated world politics after 1945 (Gaddis, 1997). The so-called 'new' history of the Cold War has though turned out to be not very new at all: articles have merely justified the American Cold War stance and heaped what appears to be endless blame on the dictator Stalin for his actions and behaviour. This type of critique is a sign of our own times and our own preoccupation with the threats posed by dictators, especially those dictators in possession of weapons of mass destruction.

So what more can this book add to the debates and our understanding of those years of turmoil and anxiety, and what might we as students of history draw from this past? The book opens (Chapter 1) by considering the themes and trajectories which formed the backdrop to the Cold War, paying particular attention to the ideological dimensions of the conflict as well as the geopolitical aspects of military security. In the contemporary world we are all aware that military security may coincide with economic and resource security, not least over the issue of commodities such as oil, as we see in the wars in Iraq. But I also want to underline the power of ideas in international history and their role in the origins of the Cold War.

Ideas mattered in the Cold War in different ways. First, the emergence of the idea of Communism in Russia after 1917 provided a startling and striking alternative to capitalism. The utopianism of Karl Marx and Vladimir Lenin seemed to have some success in eradicating corrupt monarchy and providing a new form of social equality. The call to arms made by the rebellious Bolsheviks unnerved Western European elites and provided American leaders with much food for thought. As we will go on to see, American politicians were perplexed by the appeal of Communism and sought from very early days to prevent the promotion of a Soviet-style Communism both at home and abroad. Woodrow Wilson, the Democratic President at the time of the Russian Revolution, made little secret of his dislike of authoritarian forms of government. Here we will explore what I term the 'dictator question' in American politics and the preoccupation of successive US administrations to eradicate dictatorships, well those that do not serve the priorities of Washington.

Communism quickly came to represent a powerful alternative mode of politics to that of democracy and – as we will see throughout this book – ideological threats, or the perception of ideological threats, really mattered when competition broke out between the USSR and the United States. Western leaders treated the emergence of Communism after the Russian Revolution of 1917 much as they have treated the threat from radical Islam since the events of what is now known as '9/11'. 'Communism' was the great Other of the twentieth century as much as it now appears that Islam or certain variants of it will be for this new century. Furthermore, the ideological challenge of Communism was perceived by Western leaders such as Wilson to exist as much within 'our' own societies as it did outside them.

Ideas also mattered on another level. Ideologies such as Communism or Liberalism provided people with ways of navigating the rocky plains of human experience and political elites with justifications for organizing their societies. Some Russians – inexplicably perhaps to us – cried in their gulags when the news came that their brutal dictator, Stalin, had died. Soviet leaders had developed a national political culture based on a romanticism of the past and a fear of capitalism. Stalinism had provided a form of comfort during the years of war as a focus for the building of a Soviet nationalism. American (and European) political elites also found Soviet ideology useful in constructing their own anti-Communist narratives and policies. To manage the Communist threat was vital for Western leaders, but anti-Communist ideology and Cold War structures provided cohesion, and some might argue a useful sense of purpose, for state building especially after World War II. Again ideas/ideologies provided ways of organizing and, in the Soviet case, disciplining society.

Here I will not disagree with those scholars of the traditionalist school who have pointed to the central role of Stalin in the making of the Cold War. Though I do not believe for a moment that a single man can make history, human agents, that is people, certainly matter in politics and the dictator and his successors were central to the construction of Cold War politics. As we will see below, debates still rage about the supposed incompetence of President Roosevelt in the Allied World War II conferences which set out to organize the post-war settlements.

General thematic concerns and a survey of the important ideas and issues in Cold War historiography give way to the more specific focus of the next four chapters. Chapter 2 looks at the origins of the Cold War and the ideological and geopolitical conditions of the 1920s and the 1930s. I will show how interdependent these two aspects of the period were. In particular the context of Revolution in Russia and how its enemies interpreted the changes in the country was central to the violently fluctuating geopolitical and economic instabilities of the 1930s. Fascism flourished in these conditions; but so too did Communism. Russia was, after the Revolution, excluded from the League of Nations and left on the periphery of international affairs, free only to conspire with a defeated, revisionist and increasingly authoritarian Germany.

However, it is also worth noting that Communist ideals and the Communist system attracted many liberals in the West as presenting a different and superior pattern of politics. Authors and poets made their way to the Kremlin to speak to the dictator about his political visions and ideals.

In contrast the United States, after its engagement in World War I, chose to reject President Woodrow Wilson's vision of a new world order, eschewed diplomatic relations with the USSR and retreated into a form of isolationism away from the affairs of 'Old Europe'. Preoccupied by the Wall Street Collapse of 1929, democracy did not seem to be in robust shape. It was the challenge of authoritarianism in the shape of Germany and Japan (not, it is worth noting, the USSR) which required America's re-engagement in international politics. The assault on American property and people at Pearl Harbor in 1941 propelled a massive shift in US behaviour and the country's entry into the war. The events of 1941 are now often compared to the tragedy of 9/11 and there is a symmetry between the reactions of the White House in 1941 and 2001, not least in the perception that global politics had changed for ever.

Chapter 3 focuses on the impact of World War II and the issues and players that shaped the Cold War. In particular I will look at the interweaving of the ideological and geopolitical in the context of a growing sense of distrust and fear felt by the wartime Allies even as Germany, Italy and Japan were defeated. Here the American experience of surprise attack at Pearl Harbor is examined. The tactical alliance (the Grand Alliance) with the great dictator, Stalin, is seen to be a key theme as the United States sought to reshape a new world order. Here too I stress the point that wartime experiences were instrumental in shaping great power politics after the war had ended. Stalin expected, indeed demanded, that after the massive sacrifice of men and resources during the war years the USSR would be rewarded in numerous ways. It was after all on the Eastern Front that Hitler had been defeated. The figures for Soviet losses are quite simply staggering. The country lost something like one-eighth of its population during the struggle with Fascism (Roberts, 2006). Some 25 million people perished, two-thirds of them civilians. Little wonder that Stalin believed that territorial gains as well as massive reparations were due to the Kremlin after victory.

Here too we examine the negotiations which took place over four years of war and will focus on the great power summits between Roosevelt, Stalin, Truman and Churchill held in Teheran, at Yalta and at Potsdam. It is worth noting that Western diplomats who came into contact with the Soviet leader were impressed by his personal charm, his wit and his diplomatic sophistication. This was despite knowing full well the nature of his often bloody regime. Anthony Eden, the British diplomat and later prime minister, who met the dictator, noted that he found it hard to reconcile Stalin the man with blood dripping from his hands with the urbane character he actually encountered. We will examine the charge made against Roosevelt that he failed to read the dictator correctly and was duped by him into permitting the Soviet occupation of gallant Poland. Roosevelt it appears to some was incapable of dealing in an adequate manner with the dictator and is still criticized in many quarters for his inability to negotiate a post-war settlement which would have installed democracy throughout Central and Eastern Europe. His successor Harry S. Truman has in terms of historical reputation fared rather better. His supposed toughness, backed by a new nuclear arsenal, is claimed by some to have had a more positive impact on Soviet behaviour (e.g. Graubard, 2004). In Chapter 4 I will argue differently: that a new world order along American lines was not preordained and that the United States after 1945 lacked confidence, if not conviction, in the early years of confrontation with Stalin and the USSR. Why this should be after so many years of study remains a central puzzle. Why did the United States, the greatest military power – a true superpower – take so long to outrun a tortured and illegitimate state such as the Soviet Union? For was the United States, after 1945, not the more desirable power in the eyes of much of the world? Surely, it is no coincidence that when faced with a choice between Communist power on the European continent or an American commitment to the expansion of liberal values Western statesmen were quick to align with Washington? Or is it the case, perhaps, as I hope to illustrate, that liberal states, such as the US, that commit themselves to wars, world wars, cold wars, even wars on terror, can often find themselves compromising their own standards and values and hence undermining a domestic confidence in their chosen role?

Part at least of the American story in the early years of the Cold War is the reluctance to actually change the Republic into the type of 'garrison' state deemed necessary to wage long-term 'war' in the international system. For some critics of Cold War politics it would have been preferable surely to stay away from the rotten politics of Old Europe in the isolationism of the North American continent without compromising domestic norms through membership of international institutions and alliances. In other words a post-war consensus for the conduct of the Cold War was not evident within the United States.

Chapters 5 and 6 continue these themes and demonstrate that democracies are sometimes uncertain in their actions especially when confronted by what appear to be very powerful and committed enemies. Democracies do not usually seek war or confrontation. However, after 1945, the United States saw its own economic prosperity and sanctuary hinging on the control of certain regions and certain allies. In that sense part at least of the revisionist version associated with the importance of a new international economic order appears accurate.

We also 'now know' that the Soviet Union and the Soviet bloc was economically and politically fragile and that under Stalin's successor, Nikita Khrushchev, it limped from one brutal crisis (for example Hungary in 1956) to another. Yet it is worth stressing that this was not how the USSR appeared to observers at the time. Soviet politics certainly looked brutal; but it was, for policy-makers in Washington, a dictatorship of vast geostrategic reach and strength, and with its nuclear weapons a dangerous opponent of the liberal version of politics and was determined, or so it seemed, to have access to Japan and the resources of the Middle East.

Dictators are always economical with the truth. We 'now know' the full extent of Khrushchev's deceptions during the 1950s; but it is not, and was not, easy to discover the reality of closed societies. We need only think about how little we actually 'know' even now about the 'hermit kingdom' of North Korea. Perhaps those present at the birth of the Cold War were too taken with the rhetoric of Communism to perceive the reality of Soviet society, especially as the Cold War developed. There were changes in the Soviet bloc under Nikita Khrushchev and he was not a dictator in the mould of Stalin. Yet this seemed to make no difference to American policy-makers who by the early to mid 1950s were wedded to a style of Cold War politics and a form of statism in the international system. This explains, at least in part, why, even when rebellions occurred east of the Iron Curtain in 1953 and 1956, the United States was not prepared to intervene on behalf of those rebels hungry for democracy.

In some ways this was understandable. There was fear of an unknown reaction from an ideologically driven and now a nuclear foe. As John F. Kennedy remarked of the 1961 construction of the Berlin Wall, 'a wall is a hell of a lot better than a war' (Beschloss, 1991: 278).

All of these events and processes come to a head with the October 1962 confrontation between the United States and the USSR that the world knows as the Cuban Missile Crisis. In a very real sense, one might say of this event as Winston Churchill had famously remarked about the final Battle of El Alamein and its impact upon World War II, that the Cuban Missile Crisis did not mark the end of the Cold War, it did not even mark the beginning of the end of the Cold War, but it did perhaps mark the end of the beginning of the Cold War. Accordingly the crisis in Cuba is the last major event with which we deal in this book. After this confrontation, the Cold War as a 'structural' aspect of international politics was, as we shall see, largely set. The missile crisis was the type of crisis which had threatened to unfold ever since 1945 – direct confrontation between Washington and Moscow that promised to escalate to a full nuclear exchange.

The resolution of this crisis along peaceable lines was testament to a degree of diplomatic skill on both sides, by Khrushchev and Kennedy, as well as perhaps an overriding level of fear over the possible exchange of nuclear weaponry. It also marked the manner in which future major 'Cold War Crises' – the Middle East Crisis of 1973, the Soviet Invasion of Afghanistan in 1979, the row over NATO nuclear deployments in the mid 1980s – would be confronted.

Overall, this book argues that a proper recognition of the past could teach us much. We might, for example, recognize that we are mistaken in assuming that there is an entirely new character to the threats/anxieties and fears which currently face the West and seem to dog our everyday lives. Understanding the origins of the Cold War will not in my view help us fight the 'war on terror'. Nor will it help us to structure responses to the future ideological and geopolitical struggles of the twenty-first century. Yet a study of those early years of the Cold War might help us understand some of the errors or missed opportunities made by previous generations. For example, not seeing more clearly the fragility of the Soviet state or understanding the attempts to transform the Soviet system in the 1950s away from the bleakest level of tyranny. The study might help us to understand the strengths and weaknesses of our own type of society when it is under threat.

As such, the following questions, I think, continue to resonate down the years from Stalin to now and so we might find it worthwhile to ponder them as we look at the Cold War. Are dictatorships/authoritarian states capable of change from within? Are all foes really as robust as they seem? Do we/should we engage with authoritarian states or should we isolate them? What duties might we have to help those who rebel against authoritarian structures? Should we continue to take the American commitment and the sacrifices of its own people in preserving peace for granted? Do we appreciate exactly how our liberties are compromised in any ideological confrontation? Is security really worth the costs in liberty that some think it requires? The final chapter will think through some of these questions in greater detail.

I do not suppose that this book has all the answers – though it hazards some suggestions as we proceed. But if the book contributes to a better appreciation of how central these questions are to understanding the current trends in the politics of the international system – and how central to understanding them the history of the Cold War is – than I, at least, will be more than satisfied. Ultimately, the task of understanding the Cold War, and learning from it, is a task for all of 'us'; in liberal states and in others. This book will I hope appeal to a general reader seeking to make sense of why and how the Cold War occurred when, as I argue, no one really wanted it to. This in turn might help us to think about how the contemporary confrontation that seems to be growing almost daily might be understood better, and how we might avoid the mistakes of the last century at the beginning of the present one.

1

Cold Wars: Themes and Trajectories

The Cold War seems to have receded from our memories much more quickly than we might have expected. For many, it is now almost impossible to understand how the Cold War framed practically every aspect of life for over four decades from 1945. With scholars and practitioners now concentrating on the threat from Islamic extremism and the apparent multiple threats posed by radical terrorism, the significance and character of globalization, or the multifarious threats posed by global environmental change, the Union of Soviet Socialist Republics (USSR) and its alleged threat to dominate the Western world through the spread of Soviet-style Communism (a threat which never successfully materialized) has a quaint, almost fusty air about it – like meeting a dimly remembered yet once very formidable maiden aunt.

There are many reasons for being concerned about this state of affairs. In the first place, the old adage that those who do not remember their history are doomed to repeat it might be cited; and the first step to remembering history lies in studying it. Naturally, over the last half century there has been a vast amount written on the history of the Cold War, but it is astonishing how quickly much of that literature – once considered central for the student of international relations as much as for the diplomatic historian – has vanished from the reading lists and, indeed, from the general set of assumptions that govern our behaviour.

A second reason for concern is that the Cold War has not, of course, 'gone away'. Rather, it has become submerged. But like geological formations, once the surface crust of the contemporary breaks, the layers that underpin it are visible once again, and if we cannot properly recognize them we may misdiagnose the likely effects. Yet to recognize them we must know what it is we are looking for, and for much of the politics and international relations of the twentieth century that means looking for the traces of the Cold War and its legacies. Any contemporary student of Russia and its relations both with the United States and with its own former empire (now its 'near abroad') hardly needs to be told this.

A third reason lies simply in the (one would have thought) obvious fact that it is the Cold War that has shaped much of the reality of the contemporary world at every level along with many of the assumptions both explicit and implicit that go to make it up. We are currently deep in a conflict that is centrally concerned with whether or not it is possible to 'deter' aggression (say from terrorist groups or dictators) and which uses the possession of, or the possible possession of, 'weapons of mass destruction' as an effective *casus belli*. Yet almost no references are made to the literatures that created the contemporary concept of deterrence or to those figures who established 'deterrence theory' as the primary logic of force in the latter part of the twentieth century. All of them wrote in the context of the Cold War and, indeed, the technology about which they wrote, if not a product of the Cold War, was only properly thought through during it – and some might say has not been thoroughly thought through yet. To seek to understand these assumptions without understanding the history and nature of the Cold War is, I propose, a gigantic exercise in futility.

Naturally, it is equally true to say that there are dangers in letting the experiences of the Cold War overly shape our contemporary concerns, since the world is different now. That is true. Yet those who accused the West – or the United States – of remaining too bound to the legacy of the Cold War in the early 1990s perhaps underestimated the possibility of the opposite very quickly becoming true, as I suggest it has. In any case, even if we wish to transcend the experience of the Cold War, we must understand what those experiences actually are; otherwise we may mistake them.

This chapter outlines three key resonances of the Cold War for our own time; three reasons, in other words, for taking the Cold War seriously, even if our primary interest is the international relations of the contemporary period. It will then move on to argue why the distinctively historical questions about the origins of the Cold War are themselves still central to our understanding of it and thus to the use we might make of it for understanding our contemporary world. Finally, I will try and say something about the relationship of history to broader questions of international politics as a precursor to the 'pragmatically chronological' chapters that follow. Before any of this, however, there is a need to say something about the historiography of the Cold War itself, as a way of setting up these concerns.

Debating the Cold War: Historiographical Thoughts

Where to start? Surely, a good place is with the term itself. As with most aspects of the Cold War, there are multiple possible origins for it. As Fred Halliday points out (Halliday, 1983) 'Cold War' was a term used by Muslim historians in the fourteenth century to describe the opposite of a 'hot' war which involved an actual engagement with the enemy to one which did not involve direct military conflict, and there are many other possible sources as well. However, in its modern context, it owes its existence and popularity to one of its earliest and most prescient analysts, the American editor and author Walter Lippmann.

The occasion for Lippmann's use of the term – he himself said that he had picked it up from one used in Europe during the late 1930s to describe Hitler's war of nerves against the French (Steel, 1980: 445) – was his critical reaction to George F. Kennan's celebrated 'X' article in the journal *Foreign Affairs* (Kennan, 1947). Lippmann was so critical of Kennan that he devoted 14 successive columns of his celebrated 'Today and Tomorrow' column in the *International Herald Tribune* to refuting it, a collection that was then published as a book under the title *The Cold War* (Lippmann, 1947). Given the history of the Cold War, a history we will come to trace in a moment, it is perhaps worth quoting Lippmann's most pointed denunciation of what he considered the errors of Kennan's containment doctrine. Lippmann was convinced that 'confronting Soviet power at every point where (it) shows signs of encroaching' was sheer folly and would lead to disaster. 'The History of Diplomacy', Lippmann said, 'is the history of relations among rival powers which did not enjoy political intimacy and did not respond to appeals to common purposes. Nevertheless there have been settlements'. And in perhaps the unkindest cut of all (in a rebuke to a man who was, after all, still a serving diplomat), Lippmann continued acidly: 'For a diplomat to think that rival and unfriendly powers cannot be brought to a settlement is to forget what diplomacy is all about' (Steel, 1980: 445).

Ironically, of course, over time Kennan came round largely to Lippmann's view. But by that point, so to say, the die was cast. The ideological elements in the Cold War, those elements that Lippmann most distrusted, had already taken on a life of their own: as a trajectory of persons and events that we will see repeated many times in the various stages of the development and evolution of the Cold War.

But if the Cold War was difficult enough for professional commentators like Lippmann and Kennan it has proved even more problematic for the diplomatic or international historian. Investigations of the Cold War rested on at best half of the evidence. Historians had until recently no access to the Soviet side, let alone to the Chinese version(s) of the Cold War (see Westad, 1988). The bulk of what was written concentrated on an Anglo-Saxon account. In terms of the historiography of the Cold War, this narrowness was understandable as those historians or analysts seeking to come to terms with the Soviet story had to work primarily with US sources or at best with a mixture of Western archival sources, Soviet official sources and, for the few rather more adventurous, theories of Soviet behaviour. The dearth of Soviet sources in particular was always a concern for the historian bold enough to venture into the terrain of post-war Soviet foreign policy or international history. Some historians wisely issued caveats over the nature of the historical investigation and some dissuaded graduate students from venturing into such uncertain territory.

There were other problems with studying the Cold War before it ended. It was, after all, a continuing 'process', and shifts in the political, cultural and (perhaps specifically) the ideological climate of superpower confrontation necessarily affected historical endeavours. If all history is, as Benedetto Croce asserted, in fact some form of contemporary history, then the evolution of thinking among historians about the Cold War demonstrates this perfectly. To illustrate this, a brief tour of the historiography of the struggle, that is traditionalism, revisionism and post-revisionism, is useful.

The 'traditionalists' working during the beginning of the post-war period sought to portray the Soviet Union as inherently expansionist and as the key source of the Cold War (Kennan, 1951, 1961). It is not, with hindsight, in any way curious that the revisionists, led by William Appleman Williams (Williams, 1962) but working against the backdrop of the US military involvement in Vietnam, should have sought to portray American foreign policy as 'guilty' of fuelling the Cold War through economically exploitative expansionist motives. The interpretation of the United States as a 'greedy colossus' searching endlessly for raw materials and foreign markets radically shifted the parameters of the debate over American history in a period when many scholars were doubtful about the conduct of contemporary US diplomacy. Post-revisionism, a child of the 1970s, is equally a product of its time and the détente period. While not excusing Soviet behaviour, the post-revisionist emphasis upon the bureaucratic complexities of American foreign policy attempted to point to a more complex and multifaceted network of reasons for the Cold War. Even so, the preoccupation with assigning 'guilt' or responsibility for the origins of the Cold War remained a feature of many historical works (Cox and Kennedy-Pipe, 2005).

This rush to judge has not been removed by the end of the Cold War, and some of the finest scholars have not refrained from using 'new' evidence, however slight, to bolster earlier claims. Within the new evidence, however, there is reassurance for some that they had been correct all along in their assessments of Soviet policy. Revelations over Stalin's involvement in the origins of the Korean War for example provide the 'hard' evidence for some judgements made many years ago by analysts such as Malcolm Mackintosh (Mackintosh, 1962). John Lewis Gaddis is in this respect probably among the more gallant of the international history community in openly acknowledging that some (but by no means all) of his earlier judgements about the Cold War were in need of revision (Gaddis, 1997).

The limited access to archives during most of the post-1945 period could and did, if not distort notions of the Cold War, certainly and understandably lead historians in certain directions. For example, the access to post-war British sources led some to proclaim an English school of Cold War history in which the War could be understood not through the establishment of American hegemony but through the careful nurturing and tutoring of the

Americans by the British in the harsh realities of the new post-World War II order. While there is little doubt that British opinion was indeed influential in certain essential areas, not least in the issue of Germany and in the foundation of the North Atlantic Treaty Organization (NATO), it is also the case that the stories from the British archives were and remain only one part of a diplomatic and historical equation.

This is not to say that the new archival evidence is not compelling in its own way – it certainly is on the Soviet and Chinese sides. Not least is that the evidence that we have points in the Russian case to a rather fragile type of superpower. Evidence, for example, of Soviet military capabilities point to the flawed nature of certain Western assumptions about Moscow's strength during the early Cold War period. Recent interviews from former members of the Communist Party, in addition to the data from the archives, point to an inherently more precariously and technologically challenged military power than most Western experts had believed. The state of discipline within the Soviet Army (as the Red Army became in 1946), the problems of morale, the need for constant internal vigilance and the struggle for technological innovation are all now part of a new story of the Soviet Union which emphasizes relative weaknesses, not massive strengths (Kennedy-Pipe, 1998).

We are also now aware of the manner in which Soviet nuclear programmes twisted and distorted the economy and the ecosystem, depriving ordinary Soviet citizens of the benefits of consumer goods and health for many years. We also now have a much clearer picture of the terrible toll token on different ethnic and religious groups as Stalin sought to control unruly peoples in the early years of the Cold War.

If the Soviet Union was indeed a rather fragile superpower with more limited capabilities than has been assumed, Soviet weakness was compounded by an inherently uncertain set of relationships within the Warsaw Treaty Organization and the wider Communist world. We 'now know' of the tensions that dogged the Kremlin in its relationship with the satellite states. In many respects one of the more telling pieces of new evidence from the archives in Moscow indicates that the Soviet crushing of Hungary in 1956 and Czechoslovakia in 1968 was not so much the behaviour of a self-confident superpower as the reaction of a nervous ruthless power fearing a loss of control in Eastern and Central Europe and feeling itself pressured into action (Kramer, 1992).

The idea of some form of monolithic Soviet bloc has lost much of its resonance as scholars working throughout Russian and East and Central European archives unearth new evidence, if not of simple resistance within Eastern and Central Europe, then at least of a more complex package of interactions between Moscow and the peripheries. Wilfried Loth, for example, has provided new accounts of the manner in which the East German leadership during the 1940s had their own views about paths to socialism, while the evidence from Poland, Hungary and Albania and Romania or China certainly does not point to a trouble-free relationship or alliance on the Communist side (Loth, 1998; Zubok and Pleshakov, 1996). Recent work also points to Marshal Tito as a not inconsiderable thorn in Stalin's side.

Perhaps most importantly the new evidence alerts us to the importance of ideas and ideologies during the Cold War. Studies of the new evidence from the archives, for example on the decision-making undertaken by Soviet leaders, underline the enduring importance of ideology in the making of Moscow's foreign policy. Historians have long debated the influence of Marxism–Leninism on the making of Soviet foreign policy and the origins of the Cold War itself. Some have tended to dismiss ideology as an input into the making of the Soviet worldview, implicitly adopting a realist perception that pragmatism and interest were not ideas that dictated the Kremlin's external strategies. The new evidence from Russian archives demonstrates that ideological considerations were indeed determining factors in Soviet conduct. Marxism–Leninism, for example, had a profound effect upon both the nature of regime and the perceptions and preoccupations of Russian leaders, justifying the rule of the Communist Party and the maintenance of an elite to lead society. This legitimating function meant that any modifications in ideological thinking could and did exercise a profound impact upon the domestic political system. Again this was aptly demonstrated even before the death of the great dictator Stalin in 1953 when some of those around him attempted to modify the more extreme aspects of Soviet doctrine.

In the early years certain sections of the Soviet leadership were at key points governed by a Marxist–Leninist notion that a crisis of capitalism could paralyse the Western powers and allow for some manoeuvring by the Kremlin. In terms of Third World strategy, at least some of the Soviet leadership continued to believe that socialism could provide a sustained and successful model of development, thus aiding Soviet ambitions. Yet new evidence also points clearly to disputes between Tito and Stalin on the future orientation of socialism in Europe and to a far more complex set of calculations behind Mao's relationship with Russia and indeed the external world (Zhang, 2000).

My point here is that ideologies, ideas, and how states are organized matter. International historians have questioned the very notion of the state itself through a variety of work which examines questions such as how states organize themselves, how power is organized within the state, the sources of state power, and how these factors have impacted upon the making of foreign policy. Here, ideas and concepts widely used by social scientists, such as bureaucratic politics and the use of psychology in decision-making, have provided avenues of exploration (Allison, 1971). Historians have always been aware of the complexity of understanding just what goes on inside foreign ministries and international institutions. But traditionally diplomatic historians have been somewhat guilty of collapsing the state into the archives and thereby equating the 'state' in a simplistic manner with the 'bureaucracy'.

So, despite Gaddis's firmly ironic 'We Now Know' in the title of his impressive survey of the Cold War, there is also an awareness that while many important details of the story of the Cold War have been filled in, the revelations of the archives on their own do not bring us any closer to some of the bigger questions of the Cold War world. Not the least of these is why the USSR, given its inherent fragility, managed to survive and compete for so long. What role did ideas and ideologies play in the Cold War world? How did the Cold War affect those 'outside' its diplomatic framework, for example Soviet nuclear workers, Soviet Jews, American Communists, and how should we 'now' understand the framework of the struggle?

As I go on to suggest, works such as Fred Inglis's book *The Cruel Peace: Living through the Cold War* (1995) and Abbott Gleason's *Totalitarianism: The Inner History of the Cold War* (1995) represent new ways forward. For example, Gleason's book, in which he traces the emergence, evolution and implications of a concept – totalitarianism – that clearly affected Western understanding of international history and international relations, offers a rather different interpretation of the former than can be found simply within the archives or indeed through concentrating on diplomatic or state history.

It should, of course, be noted that some broadening of the agenda of both historical studies has already taken place. Zara Steiner, in an important article 'On Writing International History: Chaps, Maps and Much More', published in *International Affairs* in 1997, traced the evolution of international history as a discipline. She highlighted the way in which, for much of the twentieth century, diplomatic history has broadened out away from reliance upon the 'annales' to a livelier and more vibrant subject concerned with more than the mere behaviour of statesmen (there were few women) and diplomats. More crucially Steiner also pointed to a greater willingness on the part of the international historian not only to broaden the historical 'canvas' but also to interact with other subjects and disciplines: most notably those of anthropology and sociology but also that of international relations. For a number of years the respectable international historian would have had little truck with the 'goings on' in international relations, even though many international historians had consciously or unconsciously adopted a form of realism as methodology; but, as Steiner argues, international history has in some respects developed out of all recognition from the style of diplomatic history, and Cold War history has already benefited from the expansion of the menu of history. For example, the work of David Holloway on Stalin and the Soviet atomic weapons programme, *Stalin and the Bomb* (1994), demonstrates just how important constant technological innovation was to those who made foreign policy during the Cold War.

Holloway's work has also had another noticeable effect. As he explains, within the USSR itself, the demands of the Soviet nuclear programme had an immense impact on the lives of those engaged in the work of mining uranium and building the atomic programme. Many of those involved in the construction of Soviet nuclear plants, for example, were drawn from prison labour, and the conditions in which they lived, worked and died were brutal (Holloway, 1994; Hunt, 1992). Christopher Andrew has also unlocked a hidden side of the Cold War through various works on the intelligence services of both the United States and the Soviet Union. This 'hidden' side of the Cold War points to a broadening of the agenda of its international history (Andrew and Mitrokhin, 1999).

Yet, historians of international affairs can only benefit from a continuation of the broadening of such a trend and, more controversially, less reliance on wholly archival work. Indeed, despite Steiner's identification of a broadening in the historical agenda there is still little real dialogue, and this seems especially marked in the academic communities of the United States, between international historians and international relations scholars. John Gaddis has described this estrangement as a 'Balkanization' effect: he means that near neighbours do not 'talk' to each other.

The main reason for the lack of dialogue is the shape and methods that mainstream international relations theory has taken since the 1970s. Principally it has been preoccupied with the debate surrounding Kenneth Waltz's theory of international politics which had emerged by the 1980s as the predominant theory. (The debate between neo-realism and the liberal internationalists subsumed theorizing throughout the decade but neo-realism and liberal internationalists shared the methodology and the commitment to systemic analysis.) Waltz argues there have been two ways of conceptualizing the international system. The first he calls reductionist, which 'reduces' the properties of the system to the properties of one or more units of the system (the character of states, for example). The alternative is what Waltz terms a truly systemic model where the properties of the system are wholly deducible from its own character. Once systemic theory is chosen, one of two ordering principles must be asserted – hierarchy, where there is clear structure of authority running from top to bottom, or anarchy, where no such structure exists.

By definition, thus, the international system is anarchic. This creates a neo-realist synthesis and a theory which concentrates on the character of that system (anarchy) and on the only thing that neo-realists hold to matter in the context of anarchy – the relative capabilities of the unit. From this flows the characteristics of neo-realism, the inevitability of the balance of power and the irrelevance of the character of the units because of the need for all units to be, in Waltz's phrase, 'functionally undifferentiated' (Waltz, 1979).

This theory and its manifestations have been widely criticized since 1989 for the failure to explain adequately the balance of power during the Cold War and to predict its sudden end. For example, it has been argued that one of the striking aspects of the new evidence from the archives is how obvious the asymmetry in power between the two sides of the Cold War actually was (Wohlforth, 2000). There was, as we now recognize, a striking disparity in raw power between the two superpowers, but to accuse Waltz of missing this 'power differential' is in many respects to miss the point of his theories. Yes, the USSR was hugely inferior both economically and militarily, but this did not matter to those addicted to the study of neo-realism.

Criticism that neo-realism failed to predict an end to the Cold War system, let alone a peaceful one, should indeed be regarded as a major failing for those parts of the discipline that claimed a predictive ability. In itself, though, it is not a major criticism because neo-realism does not seek to predict the behaviour of individual states at any given time, only the logic of individual relationships. So strictly speaking this criticism of failure to predict cannot, at least in terms of Waltz's views, be upheld. However, this does not mean that neo-realism can simply be 'let off the hook'. Any theory that purchases such immunity from criticism by retreating to the level of abstraction is vulnerable on other grounds: not least simply because when theories become so abstract and formulaic they become meaningless; and if they cannot tell us about the Cold War it means they have nothing to offer in terms of explanation about the events that dominated global politics for almost half a century.

William C. Wohlforth, one of the most influential of the American scholars working in Cold War studies, has argued that part of the problem with using international relations theory, particularly the ideas of Waltz, to address the period is that international relations theorists simply do not care about the archives and that they would not in any case be persuaded by the new archival evidence (Wohlforth, 2000). This point is correct but in many ways irrelevant. It is perfectly valid to point out that theorists do not take history as seriously as a diplomatic historian would like, but really such a criticism does not get us further than recognizing Waltz's theory as simply ahistorical. As long as neo-realism remains dominant in international relations theory there cannot be a dialogue between international relations theorists and international historians that will be of any great significance.

Many historians have long accepted the notion of an anarchic state system. Some, for example A. J. P. Taylor in *The Struggle for the Mastery of Europe 1848–1918* (1954), worked within the idea of an anarchic international system but without using the language recognizable to international relations. Waltz in one sense simply systematized what some international historians – such as Taylor – had been saying for some time. But there are intriguing signs that historians are beginning to use various aspects of international relations theory to more effect. Historians such as Paul Schroeder, for example, are adding to our conception of how the international system might be interpreted. Although Schroeder (1994) is sceptical about certain facets of Waltz's neo-realism as a whole, he is convinced by specific parts of systemic theory and believes that international historians should test the ideas of Waltz against historical case studies.

In this sense, Schroeder's notion that states might take advantage of the international system has something, as noted below, in common with the agenda developed by constructivist theorists of international relations, and, in so far as Schroeder's work is rooted in elaborate historical processes, might be said to carry the argument further than international relations theorists have so far done and point to the way in which theory and history can be successfully combined.

As Schroeder argues, there are many misunderstandings (perhaps wilful) of the tasks of the social scientist and those of the historian, especially the historian of international affairs. Political scientists for example sometimes claim that historians seek to understand and explain without theoretical rigour and that the historian is concerned with the details, the particular and the narrative. The criticism often levelled by the social scientist at the historian is that he or she merely arranges dates and events in a chronological order, allowing the facts to speak for themselves. There are, not surprisingly, few historians who would or could agree with such a (mis)perception of their pursuits.

Partly though, as Schroeder points out, there is a problem with the way in which the use of 'narrative' has been narrowly and perhaps wilfully misinterpreted by some, if not all, political scientists. At least part of this problem is the fact that the idea of narrative in historical writing is complex and debated. Its use in Schroeder's own work for example is hardly similar to its use by Hayden White, who is basically concerned with the structures of historical consciousness and the forms of historical representation. The key to narrative in his work is what he terms 'emplotment' (White, 1975), that is the ordering of events into a meaningful structure. One international relations scholar, David Campbell, uses White's notions in his book *National Deconstruction: Violence, Identity and Justice in Bosnia* (1998) to argue that the best way to confront any event, such as the violence in the former Yugoslavia, is to examine and disrupt the master narratives that have been used to explain or account for the event – those of the actors, those of the interveners and those of the observers, and to use this exercise to deconstruct the problematic ethno-political questions.

In this context it is not whether one agrees with such a use of narrative methodologies but that such an approach inevitably foregrounds questions of historical knowledge and representation. The significance of this is that narrative is clearly a crucial aspect of historical work, but there are potential overlaps, as Campbell has demonstrated, between these historical concerns and at least some of the issues which are central to international relations theorists.

This is simply to emphasize that there are overlaps which as yet have not been properly explored by either side and that historical debates, such as those about narrative or about the international history of concepts – for example totalitarianism – are central to different aspects of international relations theory and are not just systemic aspects.

During the Cold War, for example, Gleason's point was that totalitarianism had what we might term a prehistory as well as continuing implications, and that it is a term with resonance from at least the mid 1930s to the 1990s. Gleason's argument, if correct, suggests strongly that both the theory and the practice of international relations depend at least in part on regime type and ideological justification for state behaviour. Here is a historical argument, which would produce serious doubts about Waltz's third image systemic approach. In this vein, the study of ideas or studies of intellectual history supplement more traditional archival history and provide quite clear links to the work of those engaged in international relations theory.

I have argued that historians need to focus not just on the archives but on the bigger ideas, ideologies and theories of international behaviour. Here, of course, Steiner's robust defence of how much international history has already moved away from its narrow diplomatic focus is worth noting. Perhaps historians are indeed beginning to see woods and not just trees. Yet a dialogue with international relations theory is in many ways imperative if we are to understand the bigger questions of the Cold War. While we might 'now know' in greater detail the story, or some of the diplomatic activities of the period, there is still a need to examine ideas, ideologies and how the international system began to operate after World War II.

Taken together, these reflections offer a conspectus – a kind of methodological preliminary – of what this book aims to achieve, which is to take the literatures of the origins of the Cold War and develop them in ways in which we can gain both a greater sense of understanding of the phenomenon itself and also a sense of how relevant its lessons are to our conditions now. Before moving on to look more specifically at the Cold War, and how the book is structured, it is necessary to say something about the subject's contemporary relevance.

The Cold War and the New Wars on Terror: Three Resonances

This book argues that the Cold War has clear contemporary resonances and that it does so in three main ways.

First, there is a compelling parallel between the origins of the Cold War and the new war on terror in the fact that, in both cases, the United States reacted to an ideological threat which it saw as threatening both its material power and its values, a threat which it also perceived to have potentially global reach. Horrendous though the attacks of 9/11 were no further such terrorist attack has yet been carried through successfully on the soil of the continental United States (Cox, 2002). Yet al-Qaeda's version of 'fundamentalist' Islam was perceived to be a potent threat to the American way of life, to the values that found expression in that way of life and to the US position in the world. In that sense Islamic extremism has replaced Communism as the supposed threat to the American Republic. It was Richard Neustadt who once famously proclaimed that it was the fate of the US not to have an ideology but to be one. In that context, in the twentieth century, the US has tended to be in the forefront of those who respond to other ideologies that might challenge what we might call the 'American Ideology'. Soviet Communism was perceived as doing this, as is radical Islam.

Second, just as the current war on terror has effectively produced a new framework for the conduct of American foreign and security policy so did the Cold War. Radical Islamic terrorism has in fact replaced Communism as the defining security issue for America both at home and abroad – notwithstanding the very real other prominent security threats that the US faces, at least in the medium to long term. In addition, there are any number of similarities between the way in which the United States waged the Cold War and the manner in which it is now attempting to counter the challenge from al-Qaeda. The US has since 9/11 reshaped its foreign and national security strategies to deal with the terrorist threat, creating new institutions and alliances (US Government, 2003). Washington has dedicated its formidable arsenals to a war on terror and the defeat of those groups which wish to unseat America. This energy is similar to that exercised by policy-makers in the 1940s and 1950s. Just as now, during the early years of the Cold War policy elites in Washington perceived a range of threats, created alliances and sought to reshape global politics to protect American interests.

There is no denying that the US feels imperilled by the terrorist attacks on its soil and assets (Halper and Clarke, 2004). The comparisons between Pearl Harbor and the attacks of 9/11 as both starting a new age of American politics have been made many times (Ferguson, 2005: 62). Yet, these historical parallels require considerable investigation, for on the surface they are more than a little odd. Should the al-Qaeda attacks really be taken as equivalent to a 'war' launched by another sovereign state? It is in some ways understandable that policy-makers use historical analogies to understand the contemporary environment. After all, both 9/11 and Pearl Harbor represented an undermining of all that US leaders had sought to avoid since the foundation of the Republic. Apart from the audacity of America's enemies, both the Japanese assault and the terror attacks were testament to intelligence failures, to a degree of complacency and, most dangerous of all, to the inability to read international politics correctly. After Pearl Harbor, just as after 9/11, there was a grim determination on the part of US leaders not to be caught unprepared again. Perhaps most importantly of all, these leaders responded to external threats through the expansion of the military and the construction of a new type of patriotism at home (Falk, 2002; Gaddis, 2004).

Yet, a better if duller parallel to 9/11, rather than Pearl Harbor, is the beginning of the Cold War and the identification of Russia as the enemy of the US. Not least, the Pearl Harbor analogy is rather unwise because Japan was as it turned out crushed in a relatively short time (under four years) and a complete victory by the US and its allies was clearly achieved. Japan was subsequently transformed by occupation and re-education. It does not appear likely as I write this that any such fate will befall al-Qaeda.

The third way in which the Cold War still has contemporary resonance is the extent to which both understanding it and understanding the war on terror depend upon our being able to link together the ideological and material elements of politics and international relations. There is a tendency among many contemporary scholars to privilege the material over the ideational; this has been a hallmark of so-called neo-realist scholarship at least since the late 1970s. But it has not been confined to 'realists'. Many liberals have argued, implicitly, if not always explicitly, for a primacy of a power and interest approach. Even those approaches within the academy that have most persistently argued an alternative line that – as Alexander Wendt has famously put it – 'anarchy is what states make of it', sometimes seem to suggest that all you have is the material with some 'bolted on subjectivity' – to use Fred Halliday's dismissive phrase.

But trying to understand something as complex as the Cold War suggests very powerfully that it is in the relations between the ideational and the material that the real trick lies; only by trying to understand how these facets entwined and interpenetrated can we really start to see the outlines of the explanations that will help us: either in the case of that era or in more contemporary times.

The Cold War as History

Needless to say, these musings on the contemporary resonance of the Cold War should not obscure what, as I suggested earlier, is a serious attempt to revisit its origins and some of its central themes. One cannot think of the resonance of the Cold War to our own time at all unless we take the period seriously itself as an instance of history. And there are plenty of puzzles that generate real and important questions, whether or not they contribute anything to the understanding of our contemporary position; and it is a bad scholar of international relations who forgets that sometimes the most important questions are the purely scholarly ones and not ones likely to yield anything of particular relevance for today. For example the emergence of the Soviet Union as a 'threat' seems odd, at least in part, given the fact that the United States and Russia had been allies. From 1941 to 1945 the two countries cooperated closely in the effort to defeat Japan and Germany. Indeed, there was a tremendous admiration for the Russian people and their military achievements within both the United States and Britain. What, therefore, was it that happened so that, by 1946, Stalin's Russia had become international public enemy number one? (Kissinger, 1994: chs 16 and 17). In short, why did American (and British) policy elites change their minds about Russia?

This question is all the more puzzling since by the end of World War II the United States was the greatest military (including the only nuclear) and economic power on earth. It really had little to fear from Russia (as, in real terms, is also the case with al-Qaeda). The USSR was deeply wounded economically by the war (Beevor, 1999). We are now familiar with the sheer horror of the war for the Soviet people, and even though in 1945 the USSR emerged victorious it had paid a huge price. So too did Britain and France, not least in terms of their national financial plight but also in terms of an inability to project influence throughout the colonial world they had created. There was in 1945 no other power that could rival the United States in terms of economic, industrial and technological power. So what did American policy-makers fear? Well it would appear it was not just Soviet strength but the potential of Soviet ideology/ideas. This potential was regarded as vast and especially difficult to manage in the context of the collapse of the British, German, Italian, Dutch and French Empires.

But if we return to January 1945, there seemed little real indication that the Grand Alliance would fall apart as rapidly as it did. Although the USSR no longer exists, we should not forget the potency of what I term the 'Soviet myth' for US policy-makers. (I use the term 'myth' to convey the idea that the USSR was never as powerful, coherent or logical as Western policy-makers believed or said that they believed it was.) The ideology of the USSR was certainly a threat to the ideologies of the West, quite explicitly so, but in 1945 there seemed little intention with Soviet Russia – exhausted by the greatest and most terrible war in its history – to turn that ideological challenge into a military threat. On the contrary, as we will see, Stalin actively wanted to pursue a continuation of the Alliance. This made sense. A ruined economy, a devastated population, and a fear that Germany would become resurgent were all reasons for the Kremlin to seek to continue some form of rapprochement with the other great powers.

What is interesting was the inability of the American leadership to treat the USSR as a normal power once the Cold War had taken hold. One of the questions explored in this book is why this was. First, there was the problem of dictatorship and Stalin in particular. We will return to the peculiar nature and perceptions of the Soviet dictator in Chapter 2. One point though worth making here is that having studied Stalin for many years, our views of the dictator are coloured by what we came to know of him after the process of de-Stalinization. But during the war years and their immediate aftermath the personal qualities of this man were highly regarded. Those foreigners who met 'Uncle Joe' were clearly taken by him. We live now in an era when certainly the Bush administration is adamant that there is a potent axis of evil of dictatorship and that this has to be dealt with in an exceptional way through isolation, sanctions and/or military actions. But Stalin himself was viewed at least initially with some sympathy, and his view of Russia's need for a security buffer was not one that many officials on the American or British side disagreed with. As we will see, some diplomats favoured the division of Europe accordingly.

This does not mean that there is not a very long tradition within the US polity of viewing tyrannical regimes with unease, and there was on the American side a growing exasperation with the negative response of the Kremlin to the creation of new and democratic structures in Eastern and Central Europe. All of this I will suggest was tolerable just so long as balance was maintained on a regional basis in Western Europe. The American response came, not so much I suggest to the extension of Communist rule in Eastern and Central Europe, but to the potential for hurt to be extended into Western spheres.

This led to a strategy of containment and the downgrading of diplomatic tools by the United States and its allies. During the Cold War period after 1947, 'traditional diplomacy' and the balancing of power became something of a 'lost art' and power politics of the purely nuclear variety dominated strategic and diplomatic thinking. This is because in many ways the United States had achieved its objectives, at least for the 1940s – stability and reordering.

Here it is also worth thinking about why the United States failed or never really tried to exert diplomatic pressure on the Soviet presence in Central and Eastern Europe. This is odd, not least because many of the states subdued by Communism did at least have non-authoritarian traditions and democratic inclinations. Yet, it was in Iran during the crisis of early 1946 that the Americans responded robustly and with the threat of force to the possibility of a permanent Russian presence. This is important because it points to something interesting, which is that the United States did not in the early Cold War years have a 'plan' to be the main opponent of Soviet interests in every nook and cranny of the globe. The US, at least initially, wanted to stop Western Europe falling to Communism and protect key sites such as Iran, Japan and Germany. The role of the global superpower, therefore, as the book demonstrates, emerges incrementally and with little confidence in the early stages.

This incrementalism can be explained by the changing nature of the international system. It is of course quite unusual for historians of diplomacy to engage with the international relations literature on 'structure'. But let me try here. The world quite literally changed in and after 1945. We are used to thinking about that change in terms of the European balance of power. In 1945, with Germany destroyed, with France and Britain fatally weakened, there was a power vacuum in the heart of the continent. Many states and societies, wracked by war, struggled to find order either domestically or in the international sphere. What became apparent by 1947 was that there were only two great powers capable of instigating order, militarily, economically or politically. These were the US and the USSR.

What this book tries to demonstrate is that the emergence of bipolarity and the vacuum of power in Western Europe meant that both powers faced each other for the first time. This was literally true in Germany and Central Europe where armies converged to divide up previously hostile states. There could be no old-style balancing of power because states had so few options for balancing.

It was this framework that to my mind made Russia an 'exceptional' (not super) power and that this led to an inability on the part of Western elites to understand the fragile and fragmentary nature of the USSR and Soviet control in Eastern and Central Europe. The

American reaction to the 'loss' of China to Communism in 1949 added to the anxieties among Western political elites of the early Cold War era. It is also the case that the Communist threat was perceived as so potent that it might 'catch on' in the United States. Just as President Harry S. Truman passed a raft of legislation to aid the shaping of the US Cold War, George W. Bush has adopted and adapted a range of emergency legislation. Perhaps we should remember that debates over how far civil liberties could be eroded in the fight against terrorism are not new.

But perhaps one of the interesting features of the post-war years is the lack of confidence in the ability of US power to exert or project influence in the global arena (Gaddis, 1972) – in this respect this book marks a departure from some of my other work which might be regarded as having too much of a revisionist colour to it. In part this uncertainty arose from a genuine hesitancy in American politics over the future of the US position from 1945. There is a longstanding debate over whether the United States has been histor-ically an isolationist or an interventionist power. I suggest that these categories retain explanatory power after 1945 as the US did in fact reject isolationism, although it would continue to command attention in some quarters.

In 1919 the American public rejected President Woodrow Wilson's great creation for global peace – the League of Nations. There was a less marked ambivalence in 1945 about the United Nations (UN) project, certainly in the US. This marked a clear break with the past and to my mind signalled the end of isolationism. There was also clearly by 1947 a desire to provide for the security of Western Europe through institutions which could prove robust against Communism. And of course, as Fred Inglis has argued, a 'fear of Communism ran deep in American Culture and the frames of feeling opened up by world war needed another suitable enemy ... The Soviets fitted the frame perfectly. Gloomy, suspicious, dreary in appearance, reliably brutal in action, they fitted every caricature that was drawn of them' (Inglis, 1995:438).

The Importance of History to International Relations

Also of course the problem of creating a new world order loomed large. We are familiar with the debates over the design of a new world order at the end of the Cold War and the struggle by President George Bush Senior to enunciate a new vision of global politics, but there was a similar set of dilemmas for all policy-makers with the demise of Hitler's Germany and the reconfiguration of international relations. On all sides there were differing ideas and ideals about mitigating future war, economic order and the future of colonies. These were powerful issues and, as this book attempts to show, it was not a foregone conclusion that Russia would be the isolated player it became after 1947.

Antagonism and future isolation arose precisely because Russia was perceived as posing a threat not just to US interests but to the stability of the new international order organized by Washington, and influenced to a lesser degree by London, after 1946. There was in short a clash of ideas and ideologies about the making of the new international order and not just about national interests. In this respect those historians who regard themselves as carrying the traditionalist banner have presented a powerful case for the need for containment. Not just the nature of Russia itself but its ideology and expansionist tendencies meant that there was little choice but to contain and control Soviet expansionism. From George F. Kennan through to a new generation of those who study the Cold War, there were few other realistic options for Western policy-makers. I pause here to simply highlight the similarity to the aftermath of 9/11, for the United States not to have sought vengeance on the architects of the attacks on Washington and New York is not a scenario that it is easy to imagine.

It is also the case that the struggle was not a simple one between the two sides. Some historians have been rightly critical of what they have seen as the exclusion of other powers from debates over the Cold War. There is after all quite a powerful British school which emerged and Britain did have input into ideas of world order and the framework of politics which emerged. During the war years there was what we may regard as a very traditional pattern of politics in diplomatic terms. The British were certainly crucially important in the alliance dedicated to defeating Hitler and drawing up plans for a Europe in the post-Hitler age. During these war years, though, there was little sense on either the British or the Russian sides that the shape of alliance politics was preordained and that America would emerge permanently from splendid isolationism. Britain actually played a powerful role in war diplomacy, yet there is little doubt that its authority receded rather rapidly after the summer of 1945. Specifically the decline of Empire and the British inability to project onto the international arena in its traditional role left a gap in terms of European politics. I suggest that that gap still exists today.

Despite all the talk amongst politicians, academics and others about Britain as a special partner to the US (this was especially a trademark of the Labour Prime Minister Tony Blair), this role was neither preordained nor seen very clearly by British policy-makers during the war years (see Dumbrell, 2006). Indeed, British diplomats had held out hopes that prolonged cooperation with Russia rather than 'specialness' with the Americans might provide a new balance of power on the Continent. In fact, there were relatively few hopes and many anxieties over the future path of US foreign policy in the minds of British diplomats. However, I argue that by 1946, because of the crisis over Iran and a series of threats to areas of Europe, most notably Greece, the British had reassessed the Soviet threat and pinned their hopes on the United States.

In Washington there was no great desire for an ongoing multi-lateral commitment to its 'friends' in Western Europe. There was anxiety, however, with the commitment and ability of some of the European states to get themselves organized along democratic and financially secure lines. This feature of US politics in the early Cold War years runs counter to many revisionist accounts of the period. This is not to say that the US did not accrue advantages from engagement in the economies and politics of Western Europe but that certainly there were those on the American side who felt a degree of impatience at having to shoulder such a huge burden when the US had its own urgent domestic demands (Baylis, 1997). The lure of hegemonic power and all that entailed for American domestic institutions was debated hard in policy and public circles.

As it turned out the Americans had their own ideas about and responses to the crisis in Europe and the emerging Soviet threat. In part at least this was to eventually but not inevitably refashion Western Europe as an extension of liberal American hegemony and to safeguard liberal values against the possible incursions of the Russians and Communism. As we will see in Chapter 4, through the Marshall Plan of 1947 onwards the Americans ensured the vibrancy of economic and political life. Whatever critics, and there have been many, now make of the Marshall Plan it was greeted with massive enthusiasm in Western Europe and indeed in parts of Central and Eastern Europe. Revisionism has painted the gesture with rather dark colours but this later interpretation and selfish perception of US behaviour takes perhaps not enough account of the struggle over American foreign policy at home in 1946–47.

In this respect, the Marshall Plan was a turning point since Stalin's effective self-exile from the construction of a new liberal international economic order effectively sealed Russia's later economic fate. While I have no doubt that the architects of the Marshall Plan sought to exclude Russia from the scheme by setting terms which were always going to be unacceptable to Stalin, this it seems to me was a crucial decision not for the Stalinist elites but for the ordinary peoples of Eastern and Central Europe. In this respect, perhaps the tragedy of the Cold War was the consigning of many millions of people to lives which were harsh, certainly by our own comfortable standards. This raises the perennial issue of judgement in international relations, which is how the many can be sacrificed to safeguard the liberty of a few. I am labouring the point here that any balance of power including the current one necessarily asks and perhaps fails to find adequate answers to these questions.

Perhaps it was the coincidence of the collapse of empire, the invigoration of the US economy and the extension of Soviet power which caused worlds previously kept apart to collide. Or perhaps, as I hope to develop, we can move to a rather different interpretation that sees ideological overreach, international structure and the breakdown of the balance of power in Europe (and perhaps most of all the relations between them) as having been the major contributors to the Cold War. But, of course, the proof of the pudding is in the eating. We shall have to examine the development and evolution of the Cold War and see.

As I said earlier, my hope is that this book provides both a greater understanding of aspects of the Cold War – of how Stalin's Russia emerged as the 'Other' in international politics – and the contemporary relevance of that process. However, I also argue that even as the Cold War emerged the seeds of its own destruction were embedded in the arrangements of international politics. Not the least of these was that although all the great powers acquiesced in the arrangements for Eastern and Central Europe, they also knew that the problems of Soviet 'control' were profound and that populations unwillingly co-opted may prove unruly over time. I will also seek to prove that international structures shift and change. Thus I hope to add to our contemporary thinking about the contest between Russia and America but also to reflect on how we should understand the past; and in doing that we might also, perhaps, understand better our options in the present.

2
Casting Long Shadows: Revolution to War

The roots of the Cold War lie in the events of 1917 and the long shadows they cast on the politics – both material and ideational – of the 1920s and 1930s. At the same time as World War I continued to unfold with its unremitting sacrifice of human life, its multiple personal tragedies, the ineptitude of the generals and the inability of any one side to decisively prevail, a new sentiment was expressed – a new vision of human life and of global politics. In Russia, the Bolsheviks seized power and in a clear challenge to liberal democracies encouraged workers everywhere to overthrow the shackles of their bourgeois states. This was a startling turnaround for Russia. In August 1914, thousands of Russians had gathered in St Petersburg to welcome the outbreak of World War I in the expectation that war would bring about a rapid Russian victory. Political elites were convinced that a successful war in Europe would solidify Russian imperial power abroad and at home. But by 1917, millions of Russians had been killed and wounded, the Russian Imperial Army was near defeat and enthusiasm for war waned. The Russian economy faltered, prices rose and the cities were short of food. People gathered in the streets of the capital to protest against Tsar Nicholas II. He was forced to abdicate and a provisional government was established but was then overthrown by the Bolsheviks.

The Bolshevik agenda was clear for international politics: peace must be immediately agreed, self-determination as a principle must be enshrined and classless societies must be established in a world without war. These new societies would transform the lives of working people. The agrarian classes would have land, the industrial worker access to the means of production and women would be emancipated from the drudgery of marriage and domesticity. The ruling classes would be overthrown by the march of the irrevocable laws of history eventually, but by violence and revolution where necessary.

This chapter attempts to assess both the background to, and the consequences of, the Russian Revolution in the context of the struggle for global supremacy that took place after another terrible war, but which that revolution foreshadowed. To do this, we need to consider both the impact of the Revolution on Russia itself, as well as its impact on European and world politics; and we must bear in mind, as the last chapter made clear, that that impact was as much in the realm of ideas and visions of a future state of being as it was in the realm of hard politics. For many, in the 1920s and 1930s, and indeed long after, the Revolution's promise was something they would hold to. It led those, like the Cambridge University spies in Britain, to betray their country and, eventually, to abandon their life for one in the home of the Revolution. For many others it remained an inspiration that the reality of life in the Soviet Union – or the actions that the state undertook – would only gradually loosen.

Perhaps the longest of the shadows that the Revolution cast was an ideological one. But to understand just why and how it cast such a long shadow we must understand the manner in which the ideological challenge of the Revolution was blended with the politics, international politics and context of the interwar period. As I noted in the first chapter, it is this relational character that is perhaps the most important and interesting aspect of the story of the Cold War and which is present from the beginning of the story. Only when we have seen this, can we begin to see, albeit perhaps indistinctly, the shadows it cast on the Cold War, and indeed on our own times. That is what I shall try and do in this chapter.

Russia and the Revolution

Despite the promise of transformation, the Bolsheviks were to be disappointed with the response of ordinary people; disillusionment with war, poverty and oppression did not lead to revolution throughout Europe. In December 1917 when the Bolshevik Leon Trotsky appealed to the people of those states at war with Russia to rebel against their own governments and to join the Revolution, he met with a half-hearted response. The Bolsheviks pinned their hopes on revolution in Germany. Tsarist Russia had entered the war against Germany in August 1914 but the Bolsheviks now hoped that the German people would rise up against the Kaiser (Service, 1997). Germany remained at the centre of Bolshevik planning for revolution. But the Bolsheviks hopes were not realized, and the Germans actually advanced far into Russian territory where they met with little resistance from Bolshevik forces whose numbers had been depleted when peasants had deserted the army and rushed home to share in the break-up of feudal estates (Acton, 1990). Revolutionary ideals based on the ideas of Karl Marx and so keenly pursued by the Bolsheviks did not evoke popular support even in Russia itself. In what was to become one of the defining features of modern Russia, there was much to be feared for the revolutionary project at home (Carr, 1950).

We perhaps need to be reminded that the Bolsheviks were at this point very much a minority grouping in Russia with approximately 4–5 million adherents out of a population of some 140 million (Gooding, 1996: 165–6). The Bolsheviks and their ideas were opposed by rival political factions such as the Mensheviks, the Socialist Revolutionaries, and the Monarchists. These opponents raised the standard of opposition to Lenin and formed the White Armies to oust the revolutionaries. (The White label appears to have been used to contrast with the 'Red' label.) Initially the volunteer army was small, consisting of some 4,000 men, mainly former army officers. Two years later it had grown into an army of 100,000 volunteers, with nearly half of its number drawn from the Cossack population (Robinson, 2002: 1–15).

So, in 1917 and 1918 the Bolshevik project remained a troubled one. At the end of 1917 the Bolsheviks controlled only a narrow tract of land between Petrograd and Moscow. With the fall of Tsar Nicholas II, many parts of the Russian Empire took the opportunity to break with the centre and declare independence; Finland did so and collapsed into civil war. The Whites in Finland were helped significantly by the Germans and pushed the border with Russia back almost to Petrograd. Within Russia, the Whites looked to the Western powers for aid and encouragement to fight revolution. Bolshevik ambitions threatened to collapse altogether under the pressure of opposition and the war. By early 1918, rather than creating a new social order, ignominious defeat for Russia loomed large in the war with Germany, thus threatening all hopes of a new political order. Vladimir Lenin, one of the architects of the idea of revolution, actually argued that Russia would have to accept the humiliation of an immediate settlement with Germany. He therefore advocated a 'separate peace' so that the revolutionaries could concentrate on stopping the enemies of the Revolution at home before exporting it abroad.

The idea of an armistice with Germany provoked considerable controversy among the Bolsheviks. Nikolai Bukharin argued that a peace with Germany would be a humiliation. Joseph Stalin eventually sided with Lenin in advocating peace. He argued that the Bolsheviks could not expect at this point for revolution to overcome nationalism in Europe and that the German presence would merely strengthen the counter-revolution in Russia. After vigorous debate with other Bolsheviks, Lenin agreed to the Treaty of Brest-Litvosk which was signed on 3 March 1918 and signalled, at least for the time being, the end of the Russian attempt to subdue Germany. Under the terms of this agreement, Russian power receded and the Bolsheviks were forced to give up Ukraine, Poland, Finland, the Baltic states as well as a piece of land along the border with Turkey. Lenin himself described the agreement as an 'obscene peace'.

It became from this point on an ambition of Russian leaders to reclaim these lands, not just out of pride but because these territories yielded many valuable raw materials, were home to ethnic Russians and contained rich industrial infrastructure. No less than 32 per cent of Russia's cultivable land was lost, as was some 27 per cent of its railways and 89 per cent of its coal mines (Gooding, 1996: 166–7; Lenin, 1964: 442–6). The 'reclaiming' of these territories became a matter of importance. It is also the case that although historians often ignore the impact of geography upon history, they do so at their peril, especially in the case of Russia. All subsequent discussions in the early Cold War age over borders arise precisely from the desire of the leaders of Russia to expand on the periphery, make good any territorial losses, protect the approaches to the homeland, and in diplomatic terms to negotiate from a position of strength (Carr, 1950; Figes, 1996; Mazower, 1998).

Lenin was, through this 'obscene peace', quite simply buying time. Ironically, given his very long-term vision of global politics, immediate pragmatic considerations prevailed. But this had to be the case. There were still multiple threats to the Bolsheviks, both internal and external. Not only were the Germans a force of occupation, but a large cross-section of the Russian population still opposed the forces of Revolution. Brest-Litvosk itself had caused the fragmentation of the ruling coalition. The Socialist Revolutionaries had resigned from the government and encouraged attacks against the Bolsheviks. By the summer of 1918, a vicious civil war was being waged, and Lenin vowed to destroy both the Socialist Revolutionaries and the Mensheviks. In November 1918, Vice Admiral Alexander Kolchak, the former Black Sea Fleet commander and one of the leaders of the Whites, proclaimed himself ruler of Russia taking power in Omsk, Siberia – this claim was recognized by the Allied Control Council in Paris.

Most pressing for the Allied Powers was the danger of a Russian–German axis arising from the deal done at Brest-Litvosk. It was this strategic nightmare that caused the British, the French and the Japanese to urge that the Allied forces should militarily intervene and re-establish an Eastern Front in Russia. President Wilson initially prevaricated over intervention by American troops (Knock, 1992). He was only too aware that his allies were motivated not just by a desire to see Germany defeated but by a set of considerations which were designed in his view to protect imperial preferences and, certainly in the case of Japan, by a desire to annex parts of Russia.

However, Wilson was finally persuaded to deploy troops (some 5,000 to Archangel in the so-called Polar Bear Expedition to North Russia and 10,000 to Vladivostok on the Pacific) when Czech soldiers travelling along the trans-Siberian railway became locked in conflict with the Bolsheviks. The Czechs took control of that region of Western Siberia; to save the Czechs and to gain hold of Siberia the decision to intervene was taken. An Allied presence also of course meant that the Germans had fewer chances to exploit resources within Russia and could not just concentrate their attention on the Western Front. This intervention should have helped the forces of the Whites, but it actually strengthened the cause of the Bolsheviks who pointed to the nature of the Allied powers wishing to defeat revolution. The longer-term legacy of the intervention was that it proved, if proof was needed, that the imperialist aggressors had not changed their stripes (Robinson, 2002).

However, Russian perfidy over the separate peace shocked the Allies. Woodrow Wilson was also dismayed by the type of regime that was emerging in Russia. The Bolsheviks had dismantled the Constituent Assembly, which had been at least a form of rudimentary democratic body, and revolution threatened to construct an authoritarian state in Russia. As John Lewis Gaddis has argued, American politics always reflected a deep distrust of concentrated authority.

The ending of World War in November 1918 marked a descent into political and social chaos for states throughout Europe and Russia. In a somewhat eerie anticipation of the winters which would follow the end of the next world war, 1919 saw Europe crumble into turmoil as famine, flu and unemployment spread. In Russia itself some 300,000 people died. Disease was the grimmest of reapers: two million people died from typhus and typhoid (Danilov, 1988; Husband, 2000). Not for nothing did the opening of the Soviet anthem begin 'Arise, ye wretched of the earth'!

The European peace settlement saw a defeated Germany loaded with reparations, responsibility for the outbreak of conflict and isolation in the international arena. There was, as so many historians have remarked, little sense of justice demonstrated here: world war surely had more complex origins than simply German ambition. The peacemakers at Versailles, though, having exacted their price from Germany, watched as the Russian Civil War ended in victory for the Bolsheviks and what appeared to be an emboldened agenda for the spread of Communism. There were a variety of reasons for the failure of the White forces to defeat the Reds. One was the disparate nature and ambitions of the counter-revolutionary groups and hence their lack of coherent military planning.

A second reason for failure was the attitude displayed by the Whites towards the indigenous people – the peasants. Many of the Whites sought to return to the old ways of ruling and this reinforced a growing view that the peasants were the natural allies of the Reds. The Whites were also notorious in the areas they held for the bribery and corruption which characterized their administration. In Ukraine, the Whites were infamous for their harsh treatment of the Jewish population (Heretz, 1997; Robinson, 2002).

Perhaps most importantly of all, the Whites suffered a huge blow when the Allied forces withdrew from Russia. This left White leaders such as Kolchak militarily exposed and he eventually surrendered to the Communists. The Reds had also eventually proved more than a match for the Whites in military terms and Leon Trotsky, who had proved on occasion an inspired military commander, had overseen much of the Red Army's success. Military success in civil war by November 1920 was not yet replicated in the international arena. In 1920, the Bolsheviks also faced the challenge of a Polish invasion of the Ukraine. Trotsky and Stalin led a summer counter-offensive deep into Polish territory but were decisively defeated on the outskirts of Warsaw. The subsequent Treaty of Riga in March 1921 ended the Russo-Polish War until a new round began in 1939.

The Bolsheviks, however, did not cease to contemplate and experiment with the export of revolution. With the end of war 'Soviets' sprang into existence in Berlin, Munich, Warsaw and Riga. In March 1919, the Comintern (Communist International) was established in Moscow. Its mission was to ferment revolution abroad. The Comintern targeted Germany but the uprising of 1919 in that country proved rather a dismal affair, while in Hungary, where a Communist leadership had actually emerged, success proved to be short lived and Bela Kun's rule rapidly collapsed. Comintern officials though held out great hopes for revolutionary change in the East and in 1920 at the Congress of Toilers of the East, held in Baku (on the Caspian), it was decided to try and take the Revolution to British India, Malaya and to the ports of China. It was only in China though that there seemed to be hopes that Communism could flourish in a bid to counter the imperialists and the warlords. In the 1920s, though, even this hope for revolutionary change was dashed when the Communists were ruthlessly suppressed by Chiang Kai-shek, with a particularly vicious massacre on the streets of Shanghai in 1927.

These abject failures to promote the Revolution or Communist influence abroad brought home to the new leaders of Russia that there were perhaps few immediate opportunities abroad. The priority therefore became to secure a period of peace, a breathing space to strengthen the regime and to stave off intervention by the Great Powers. In concrete terms this meant the acceptance of traditional European state diplomacy, recognition of state boundaries and non-intervention in the affairs of other countries. Ironically these revolutionaries now had a tremendous interest in traditional diplomatic norms. In short, there would be a period of peaceful co-existence with capitalist states, which Lenin hoped would reassure other nations that Russia was peaceable and would allow for a period of reconstruction in Russia with the help of Western technology.

Lenin's successor, Joseph Stalin (Iosif Vissarionovich Dzhugashvili), also hoped to build the Revolution at home with a strong Soviet state, with revolution eventually being exported, but not just yet. That the Revolution abroad was still to be promoted was a critical caveat. The acceptance of diplomatic norms but still with the pursuit of revolution was to sour relations between Russia and the United States for decades to come. After 1919, the Politburo (the ruling body) sent large sums of gold, roubles and dollars to America through various individuals. The colourful American Communist journalist John Reed, who had the rare distinction of interment in the Kremlin walls when he died in 1920, and whose life later became the subject of Warren Beatty's 1981 film *Reds*, received some 1,008,000 roubles in 1919–20 alone (Rosenstone, 1990). The obvious contradictions of the Soviet position were clear certainly to Western diplomats who eschewed recognition of the new regime or its inclusion in the newly formed League of Nations – a body designed by Woodrow Wilson to prevent future war and aggression.

Competing Visions after World War I

The Bolshevik vision of a future Communist society was, however, not the only new vision on offer after the war. Woodrow Wilson too offered a competing vision of global politics that ran counter to that of Lenin (Dukes, 1989; Knock, 1992). It was clear that this was a clash of ideological visions over the future of international politics. This was apparent both in 1919 and would again become clear in 1946. Wilson had come to believe that the only way to safeguard Europe was to promote self-determination, democracy and economic prosperity along a liberal model. While Russia might have been lost to Bolshevism, the rest of Europe had in his view to be spared through the adoption of American-style economies and the eradication of poverty. Communism might prove attractive, but to Wilson's mind, a liberal vision of politics could not fail to be preferable (Bobbitt, 2002; Mead, 2001).

Some observers could not see how the Bolsheviks could have any popular appeal given the savagery of their rule in Russia. Lenin had imposed a rule of iron on the territories under Bolshevik control and had even established a secret police unit (called the Cheka, which was later changed to the NKVD – the People's Commissariat for Internal Affairs) which had proved ruthless in hunting out political opponents. As one commentator, Volkoganov, has remarked, in Russia terror was not something dreamt up later by Stalin (Volkogonov, 1998: 102). In many areas the NKVD had meted out a brutal and summary type of justice; and after 1918 its powers were further expanded. American diplomats were therefore fairly confident that Bolshevism would eventually collapse within Russia. What troubled Americans was not so much the existence of authoritarianism within Russia but the commitment to the spread of Communist ideas into other states in Europe and Asia and perhaps into the United States itself.

This was a somewhat puzzling position and one which ran deep throughout twentieth-century American politics: namely, to see the manifest flaws in Communism but still to believe that this doctrine would appeal to a society such as the United States which for all its flaws was probably the most open in the world. Was this indicative of a lack of confidence in the robustness of democratic structures? Or was the fear of the spread of Communism the product of a very specific set of domestic circumstances. In truth, fear of Communism appears to have arisen from a combination of insecurity and social/economic upheaval at home. This American response to the turmoil in Russia after 1917 foreshadowed many of the attitudes which would become apparent in the events of the early Cold War years (Caute, 1978).

Wilsonian liberalism was not the only challenge to the revolutionary ideologies of the Bolsheviks, however. Very quickly after World War I, the revolutionary left was challenged by an equally powerful force from the right. Beginning in Italy in the aftermath of the war fascism very quickly gained a considerable following in Europe. Benito Mussolini came to power in Italy in 1922 and established the first 'Fascist' regime. From the beginning fascism shared a good deal with its revolutionary cousin to the left, perhaps most especially the ambition to make men anew and not to tolerate any opposition to the official state ideology. Here we see the origin of the notion of 'totalitarianism', a term originally coined by the Italian journalist and critic of Mussolini, Giovanni Amendola, and developed by the house philosopher of Italian fascism Giovanni Gentile (Bracher, 1985; Gleason, 1995: 13–20). In the 1930s fascism was to take a still more powerful (and more sinister) form with the emergence of National Socialism in Germany. But here too the revolutionary aims of the ideology were explicit and ambitious: nothing less than the creation of 'a new kind of man, a new kind of state, a new kind of world'.

The result of this was that the world of the 1920s and – especially – the 1930s became dominated by the ideological struggles of these competing visions of world order and in important respects it was the Russian Revolution that was the originating cause; it was as a bulwark against Communism that fascism often defended itself and appealed to others, and on these grounds also that fascists often offered an accommodation with liberalism, and in many cases it would seem liberals shared the sentiment (Bracher, 1985).

Perhaps the climax of the ideological confrontations of the interwar period came in Spain when the Republican (and broadly left of centre) government was challenged by the alliance of ardent Nationalists, romantic, if sometimes extreme, Catholics and neo-fascist 'phalangists'. The resulting civil war became a kind of microcosm of the ideological and more general divisions of the 1930s with the liberal governments of Britain and France reluctant to get involved but with both the Soviet Communists intervening – in part through the 'Comintern' or Third International group of communist parties that Lenin had established in 1919 (and which Stalin was to dissolve in 1943) – and with troops from fascist Italy and Nazi Germany both intervening on the side of the nationalists. The Spanish Civil war became an ideological cause célèbre for many in the liberal world as well, and much of its history – and the legends that surrounded it – became central for both World War II and the emerging Cold War of the late 1940s (Preston, 1993; 1996).

If Karl Dietrich Bracher is correct to see the twentieth century as the 'Age of Ideologies' – and it is surely true that he has a very strong case for so doing – then the central fulcrum of that age must be the 1930s and the pivot on which that turned was the Bolshevik Revolution and the responses to it. This is not laying at the door of the Revolution blame for what rightly lies elsewhere. The Russian Revolution did not 'cause' the rise of fascism, the Spanish Civil War or World War II, but it did create much of the 'framing' for the way in which the politics of the 1930s evolved. In that respect, as a number of writers have pointed out – it is the real beginning of what Eric Hobsbawm (1994) was to call the 'short twentieth century'.

Perhaps a final point to note here is that, given the centrality of ideology to the politics of the interwar period, it really will not do simply to dismiss it as epiphenomenal, as rationalist international relations (IR) theory would. Perhaps one of the more enduring legacies of the Cold War in terms of its general impact on the field – as I will try to show – is that constructivist IR theory is right to say that ideas *do* matter even if one does not always agree with individual constructivists about *how* they matter (Kratochwil, 1989; Wendt, 2001). It will certainly be my argument that the ideas element of that era matters very much indeed, not necessarily as a matter of causation – the Cold War was not 'caused' by ideological rivalry – but certainly as a matter of the framing of the conflict and its implications.

Mixing Ideology and Power: The Geopolitics of Revolution and Counter-Revolution

The fact of the very real ideological responses to the Russian Revolution (and indeed advocacy of it) did not banish more traditional concerns from European and international politics. Indeed, in many respects it simply deepened them. The ideological crisis was woven into the tapestry of interwar politics and international relations at every level, but there were many other threads, all central to the weave. In the first place, the spillover from the Revolution continued to worry many in Europe and beyond. In the United States, for example, the Labour movement had grown increasingly powerful during 1914–18. There had been a number of strikes during the war over working conditions. Wilson had actually supported organized labour and had looked for peaceful outcomes between workers and business owners. Yet his support did not continue when strikes closed down factories which produced the materials needed for the war effort. The President wanted the war to end before working conditions were addressed.

When war did end, many workers went on strike for higher pay. Some two million workers went on strike in 1919 alone. While many simply demanded higher pay, others called for a radical restructuring of the economic system with a greater control of industries such as the railroads by government. The demands for centralization or what we would call nationalization evoked concern in some parts of business and government that what organized labour really wanted was a greater concentration of business in the hands of government – could it be that the Russian example had inspired such demands?

There was in these years political unrest within the United States. Radicals staged a series of bombings, strikes and parades on May Day 1919. A bomb exploded in the home of a senator and another was planted outside the home of the Attorney General, Mitchell Palmer. In Boston, even the police went on strike (Haynes, 1990). This naturally led to a spate of criminal activity as thieves took advantage of the lack of policing to break into shops and homes.

Such radicalism, though, was countered by a rich vein of patriotism and conservatism. Groups sprang up to defend the United States from the Communist menace, and during the so-called Red Scare, red flags were actually banned in 28 states (flags seem to have special meaning in the rituals of both the Soviet Union and within the United States). The Attorney General, Palmer, decided to take action and he prevented coal miners from striking, while ordering a series of raids to arrest 'leftist' leaders. He also expelled a number of foreigners suspected of Communist activities, and a unit was created in Washington tasked with the hunting down of subversives (Haynes, 1990). An anti-Communist coalition, if we can use that phrase, saw an eclectic range of people bounded together. In this coalition there were religious groups which objected to the Bolshevik disdain for religion, some who objected to the emancipation of women under Communism and all that that might suggest for traditional Christian values, and yet more who saw the creation of a classless society with the centralized control of business in Russia as a troublesome example (Leffler, 1994: 14–15).

In short, what was immediately apparent was that Bolshevik/ Communist ideology did not sit well with American values at home or abroad. The competition and advocacy of which values could best organize society was to persist and it is here that the ideological seeds of the later Cold War were sown. President Wilson and his immediate successors would not and did not recognize the regime set up in Moscow, ostensibly because of its lack of democratic credentials, but equally because of the manner in which the Communists attempted to promote revolutionary ideas abroad.

The Bolsheviks had hoped for better; Lenin specifically wanted trade and commercial links with the United States and was more than willing to allow American firms to operate in Russia. Despite the promises of a new society in Russia, the abject poverty of the country was breathtaking to observers and in 1922 there was a major effort by Americans to distribute food to prevent starvation. Herbert Hoover, who led one of the campaigns to provide food and was certainly no friend of Communism at all, argued that humanity demanded that ordinary Russians not be left to starve to death (Hoover, 1952). Again this is a rather odd feature of the relationship between Moscow and Washington, that although American leaders saw the absolute poverty underlying the Soviet experiment they knew that there was, despite the economic fragility, tremendous potential within Russia, not least in terms of material resources and peoples. It was this potential coupled with Communist ideology that would emerge as a concrete threat for American leaders at the end of World War II.

Yet Russia was not, at this point, a central focus of American attention. There were other battles being played out in domestic politics over the future shape of US foreign policy. Not the least of these was the fierce debate over Woodrow Wilson's brainchild, the League of Nations. His idea of an international body dedicated to preventing aggression and war in the international system had run straight into opposition from the Republican Party. Specifically Article X of the Covenant of the League meant that members were obliged to take action including that of military force should that prove necessary to deter aggression. The rejection of this idea by many Americans, not just Republicans, signalled at least temporarily that the US sought not to underwrite the workings of an international organization (Small, 1996: 52–5). But the rejection of the League did not signal an end to American engagement in the international arena. The limitation of armaments, especially naval forces, international trade arrangements and the working of international capitalism preoccupied those in Washington. President Hoover himself was also clear that there were ideological threats that clearly might undermine US interests abroad and demand a vigorous response (Jones, 1992: ch.1; Knock, 1992).

In this context the interwar period can be seen – to use a famous football metaphor – as a game of two halves. The 1920s were a period of relative geopolitical stability with the 'new international structure' that had emerged from World War I – especially the League of Nations – settling into a reasonably optimistic shape. Yet the 1930s were a period of huge geopolitical instability with the rapid decline and then, finally, collapse of the hopes that the Versailles settlement – and its working through in the 1920s – had engendered. The question, in essence, is what had created the shift?

In part, the answer is obvious: the financial crisis of the late 1920s and the early 1930s. The 28 October 1929 crash on the New York Stock Market seemed to prove correct the Communist predictions that there would in fact be a crisis of capitalism. The crash not only affected the United States, Germany and Japan but for many intellectuals it discredited the workings of capitalism and, consequently, fascism gained many new supporters, as did Communism (Eichengreen, 1970; James, 1988; Kindleberger, 1973).

It is easy to lose sight of the admiration that many in the West had for the newly formed USSR (Union of Soviet Socialist Republics) (established on 30 December 1922 and the constitution ratified in 1924); an admiration that took many decades for some on the left wing of politics to shake off! Soviet Russia seemed a bright and shining example of a successful society organized along egalitarian lines. The Hungarian author Arthur Koestler, outraged by the injustices and hypocrisy of the capitalist states and ruling classes, initially believed that the USSR was immune to such deficiencies before dramatically changing his mind (Koestler, 1940). Indeed by the 1930s many in the West regarded the USSR and its achievements with a degree of awe. This of course seems odd to us; we are now so used to tyranny as shorthand for evil that we cannot cast our minds to an era when admiration and even affection was bestowed on the man who had succeeded Lenin: Joseph Stalin. He replaced Lenin as leader and then elevated him to the status of what we might call a cult. The reverence for Lenin and his teachings became a feature of Soviet life that all citizens and schoolchildren grew up with. There is a parallel here to the manner in which American schoolchildren relate to Abraham Lincoln or George Washington, although the political context is obviously very different (Lane, 1981: 258).

Dmitri Volkoganov (1998) has not been the only one to identify that Stalin's Russia and its system held a certain fascination for many left-wing intellectuals and some ordinary people in the West.

This is a theme taken up by Martin Amis in his work *Koba the Dread* (2002). Talking about a night in London at a political meeting at Conway Hall, Amis and his wife had gone to listen to the Hitchens brothers Christopher and Peter discussing the European Union. Amis recounts that Christopher Hitchens when recalling his past in the building said that he had spent many an evening in it with 'an old comrade'. This evoked 'affectionate' laughter from the audience. As Amis asks, why did the idea of an evening with a comrade supportive of a barbarous regime such as Stalin's seem worthy of laughter. As Amis writes 'It is of course, the laughter of universal fondness for that old, old idea about the perfect society'. Such it appears was the lure of the Soviet experiment for the chattering classes. (Does it in fact still remain?)

Many foreign writers during the 1930s upheld the myth of Stalin the genius, a man who had created socialism in one country. Despite the barbarity of the regime, it appeared to many people not to have the obvious failings and inequalities of capitalist societies. Others, such as H. G. Wells, who himself favoured some form of world government, were rather disappointed when having met with Stalin discovered the cynicism of the great dictator. In a rather interesting interchange recorded for posterity, the leader of the USSR in conversation with Wells, rebuked the author with the words, 'You, Mr Wells, evidently start with the assertion that all men are good. I however do not forget that there are many wicked men' (Stalin and Wells, 1937).

Stalin, however, even as he exploited the naïvety of some of his admirers abroad and as he constructed a new form of politics within his own country, knew that dangers lurked throughout the international system, not least from a resurgent Germany and an ambitious Japan. In the 1920s, Russia had been something of an outcast in international politics and had through the Treaty of Rapallo on 16 April 1922 reached a pragmatic diplomatic and economic understanding with the other outlaw state – Germany – over military and technical assistance. This allowed for the exchange of technologies some of which had military applications, and many of which had been forbidden to Germany under the terms of the Versailles Treaty. The German–Soviet alliance, reinforced by the 1926 neutrality treaty, held together until the election of Hitler.

Yet, the Soviet leadership still feared foreign intervention. Much of Soviet politics during the late 1920s was an attempt to build an internal consensus based on the idea of a readiness to withstand foreign intervention and conflict. There were many public displays that demonstrated the supposed readiness of the Stalinist state to stave off invaders and the attention of the capitalist powers. In 1929, for example, the events put on in the Parks of Culture and Rest during the mass public holidays were designed to mobilize civilians around the issue of preparedness for war (Lane, 1981: 173–6). The militarization of the civilian population was apparent in the formation of Komsomol (Young Communist League) regiments and the mingling of soldiers with civilians on holidays. At a higher level, in a bid to stave off the obvious ambitions of the new German leader, Adolf Hitler, Stalin sought alliances. Maxim Litvinov, his Foreign Minister, was tasked with forging collective security arrangements and with trying to construct alliances to counter the threats from Tokyo and, after 1933, from Hitler's Germany. In 1931, the Japanese had moved into Manchuria and created a puppet state. Moscow held out the promise of a non-aggression pact with Tokyo. At the same time Stalin strengthened Soviet forces in the East and tried to pressure Chiang Kai-shek, the leader of the nationalists in China, to oppose Japan. By late 1931 the Soviet leadership was characterizing the emerging crisis in Manchuria as the important problem in foreign policy.

These geopolitical threats augmented and made far worse the sense of crisis and instability already created by the Wall Street Crash and the ensuing Great Depression. And it was hardly accidental that at the same time the major state in the system was paralysed by depression at home – caused by the crash – and irrelevance abroad – caused in large part by the decision in 1920 to opt out of the league. In this context it is perfectly reasonable to claim – as Kenneth Waltz might – that the multipolar character of the interwar system exacerbated the risk of conflict – because it multiplied the possible number of 'conflict dyads' (Waltz, 1979) – but only if the perceptions and fears, ideational as well as material, are factored in.

The structure of the interwar system was, in any case, very fragile. A new system working without a clear hegemon and where security was technically the responsibility of a new organization, but where the main players in that organization were still pursuing their own interests, was always going to be unstable. The powerful sense of both ideological and material grievance nursed by a recovering Germany – nurtured powerfully after 1930 by the resurgent Nazis – connected with the territorial clauses of the Treaty of Versailles. The so-called war-guilt clause (which laid the blame for war simply on Germany) and the reparations provisions, which had been partly responsible for the inflation of 1923, caused great resentment. On top of that there was a rising power in the Far East itself smarting under the refusal of Versailles to include a racial equality clause and anyway ambitious for territorial and imperial gains at the expense of the old European imperial powers. Given this potent brew, it is hardly surprising that the second half of the period was so unstable. In the diplomacy of the interwar period, structure and agency are both to the fore and each reinforces the negative aspects of the other; a vicious circle of hostility, fear and suspicion was the almost inevitable result.

Henry Kissinger, in his celebrated study *A World Restored* (1999 [1954]), argued very convincingly that the world after the Congress of Vienna peace settlement was a relatively successful one for a hundred years because the settlement made a real attempt to include the defeated power, France, into the settlement as an equal and an ally. It therefore choked off, for a long time, the emergence of what Kissinger called 'revisionist' revolutionary powers and thus stabilized the system. Versailles can in this sense be seen as the 'anti-Vienna'. It created two powerful revolutionary powers in Germany and Japan (Wilson also offended Italy at Versailles) and made no attempt to involve or placate perhaps the most dangerous long-term revolutionary power of all (the Soviet Union). And the most powerful potential balancer in the system played no part in it, until it was virtually too late.

The newly elected American President, the Democrat Franklin Delano Roosevelt, thus faced a daunting series of domestic and international challenges. He needed, after the shock of 1929, to construct a new consensus at home. His 'New Deal' programme heralded a novel and controversial period in American politics. Aware of Japanese ambition Roosevelt opened formal diplomatic relations with the USSR in 1933 (Leffler, 1994). There were sound reasons for this, many were economic but many had to do with geography. The US too feared Japan and its ambitions in Asia, but also sought new markets. The authoritative Red Army newspaper, *Krasnaya Zvezda*, commented that recognition by the United States would subdue the Japanese and that American power would tilt the correlation of forces if not in favour of the Soviet Union then at least in favour of the status quo (20 November 1933).

The shadows of revolution though still lurked between the two powers. So much so that in return for diplomatic recognition, Litvinov had to pledge not to promote or encourage political disruption in the United States. Both leaders appeared to fear domestic opposition to their agendas although for very different reasons: Roosevelt had to face re-election in 1936 and Stalin potentially the betrayal of those around him. This fear never left the dictator and in part explains his behaviour throughout the 1930s. A certain madness appears to have engulfed him and he ordered the murder or exile of those he considered enemies of the state. Soldiers, poets, politicians were all exterminated at will. A reign of terror of almost unimaginable proportions operated at Stalin's behest. Few escaped and many confessed. Torture was routine in a bid to obtain confessions (Montefiore, 2003: ch.17).

The show trials of 1936–38, during which many leading Bolsheviks were accused of treason and a plot to kill Stalin, were widely reported in the international press and of course at home. Opinion was divided over the spectacle on display in Moscow. John Dewey the American philosopher published a report tellingly entitled 'Not Guilty' but the US Ambassador in Moscow, Joseph Davis, in his book *Mission to Moscow* (1941) accepted the verdicts as accurate.

What was so peculiar though was that, even as he knew the danger lurking abroad, Stalin ordered the destruction of the top echelons of the Soviet military command. Approximately 90 per cent of the highest army commanders were purged, all of the admirals and some 90 per cent of corps commanders (Woff, 1997: 361–2). The irony of course was that the real threat to Stalin and his regime lay with Germany.

Stalin, ever fearful of Hitler, brought the USSR into the League of Nations and the agenda of the Comintern was adjusted for cooperation in the creation of the Popular Fronts – that is anti-fascist alliances. This began in France during 1934 in the face of what seemed to be a relentless upsurge of right-wing politics. It was made official policy at the 1935 Comintern Congress. The Popular Fronts were not taken seriously by the Great Powers and both Britain and France remained cynical about Soviet motives. Trotsky commenting from exile famously quipped that given the control of the Comintern from Moscow, Stalin had managed to turn the vanguard of revolution into the border guard of the Soviet state.

Roosevelt, himself a prisoner of domestic circumstances, remained somewhat aloof from the gathering storm clouds in Europe. His 'New Deal' ambitions remained controversial and divisive at home and he was accused both of sympathy with Communism abroad and of allowing the penetration of US institutions by Communist sympathizers (Black, 2005).

Stalin was disappointed with FDR and even more so with the British and French after the betrayal of the Czechs at the Munich meeting of September1938 when the British Prime Minister Neville Chamberlain famously, if wrongly, declared that the strategy of appeasement of Hitler had brought 'peace in our time'. The Munich meeting was one to which Stalin was not invited. Given the Western strategy of appeasement (itself a respectable diplomatic strategy at the time) of Germany and Hitler's making it clear that Russia could escape attack, well at least temporarily, Stalin took the opportunity to cement the Molotov–Ribbentrop Non-Aggression Pact with Germany in August 1939 (Roberts, 1995).

The infamous Nazi–Soviet pact left Britain and France isolated. This had clear implications for the United States. Roosevelt saw clearly that the Axis had to be defeated – so that the US could prosper politically and economically. It could not survive in a world run by Hitler, Mussolini, General Tojo (politically influential from July 1940 as War Minister) and Stalin. Roosevelt, though, whatever his public persona, never doubted that Hitler and not Stalin was the threat to the balance of power in Europe and that Japan threatened the balance of power in Asia. In Europe, he chose to maintain relations with Moscow while trying to isolate Hitler. He therefore did not sever diplomatic relations with Stalin when the Red Army invaded Poland nor when the USSR attacked Finland and seized the Baltic States in 1939–40. This was in his view a form of pre-emptive self-defence – surely a phrase that has an uncomfortably familiar ring to it as I write in 2006.

After the fall of France in June 1940 American officials began a series of lengthy negotiations to sustain relations with Moscow and to keep open channels of negotiation. Stalin was in no doubt that the fall of France was a strategic disaster for the USSR, as he argued when told the news – France should have fought better: 'Hitler was sure to beat our brains in' (Montefiore, 2003: 341).

Later, the failure of the French in 1940 to at least hold out longer against Germany would colour all of the dictator's feelings about what France could expect in any post-war settlement. In the meantime, Stalin reorganized the Soviet command in the Far East and signed a treaty with Tokyo to fend off an attack by Japan but failed to arrange the defensive forces in his Western territories to face surprise attack. Fortified positions remained incomplete and troop lines were too thin. Washington actually alerted Stalin to evidence of the impending Nazi attack, as did a great many other sources, but this information was ignored. In June 1941, Hitler attacked Russia and the balance of power in Europe and Asia changed irrevocably.

Reflections

This chapter has tried to show how, on several fronts, the conflicts – both ideological and material – of the 1930s in particular can be traced to the Russian Revolution and responses to it. Such a claim, of course, is not new. But what perhaps is less well appreciated is how much the patterns of the politics of the 1930s sets the scene for what comes later, both in World War II, but also in the emergence of the Cold War itself in the mid to late 1940s. The suspicion, even fear, of Bolshevism in the 1920s partly explains the appeal of fascism and the reluctance of the liberal Great Powers to oppose fascism until it was nearly too late.

A similar trajectory is visible in the Cold War, one which led to the Western powers embracing many unsavoury regimes as allies because they were 'anti-Communist' – a policy to receive a formal defence as late as 1979 with the publication of the American politician Jeane Kirkpatrick's much quoted essay 'Dictatorship and Double Standards' followed by her book (Kirkpatrick, 1982). At the same time, the Cold War period shows the same blending of the ideological and the material that we saw in the 1930s (and perhaps see again today). It is simply not the case that we can say one or other of these two forces was 'more important' than the other. Both ideational and material factors – and their relations – were central to the shape that the 1930s took.

Finally, the argument shows again how interdependent politics within societies and international politics are: to try and separate them out is to fail to fully understand the deeply interpenetrated character of all human political life. In war, as in peace – if indeed we can see the 1930s as a period of peace – that fact applies, as we shall see in the next chapter.

3
Wars and Empire

So Stalin had got it wrong. The man revered as a prophet and a genius had failed to read Hitler correctly. The German attack of 22 June 1941 seemed to prove this beyond any doubt. Hitler had in strategic terms got the better of his Communist 'ally'. Stalin had, in the short term at least, apparently miscalculated. This, in spite of all the evidence warning of a German attack, both from his own intelligence services and from diplomats in the West trying to help him (and of course themselves). Even those individuals around Stalin brave enough to tell the Soviet dictator what the Nazi tyrant planned were seemingly not believed. This blindness, combined with the effects of the purges carried out on the Red armed forces, meant that Russia was ill-prepared for the German onslaught. Historian and analyst Dmitri Volkogonov has written that Stalin's miscalculation was of such vast, catastrophic proportions that it is hard to find anything comparable in history (Volkogonov, 1998: 119).

In this chapter I will try to show how the birth of the Cold War was prefigured in the decisions taken at the heart of the greatest war in human history, and how the ghostly tendrils picked up and emphasized in the previous chapter slowly began to solidify around the conditions that would generate the Cold War, once World War II was over. There is no suggestion that this represents an 'inevitable' course of events: human beings made the history and, as always, they could have made it differently. Nonetheless, as I emphasized in the Introduction, understanding the course of events depends upon seeing the manner in which agents and structures, ideology and material power, blend together. Here, the blending took place in the cauldron of war.

The tendency in discussions of World War II is to focus on the enormous scale of the conflict, on the protean and sometimes appalling character of the actors and on the sheer destructiveness of the conflict. There is also an obvious tendency to focus on the war, that is to say the military aspects of the war, at the expense of the political and ideational ones. All of these tendencies are understandable and some are almost inevitable, but it is worth remembering that, as David Stevenson's study of *The First World War and International Politics* (1988) has emphasized, the politics of the war was, if not separate from the waging of it, at least separable from it.

Not that the waging of the war did not take up a huge amount of time for governments; but certainly after the first two or three years, the governments of the Allied powers became as much concerned with the world *after* the war as they were with *winning* the war itself. And it is in these concerns that we shall find both the echoes of the debates of the 1920s and 1930s and the shadow of the crisis of the late 1940s.

The Impact of Operation 'Barbarossa'

There is a debate about Stalin's reaction to his own terrible error over Hitler; some reports speak of the dictator suffering a nervous breakdown at the news of the German attack. Others report a terrified man scared that those around him would punish him for his miscalculation. Yet more stories depict a man, although depressed, ultimately in command of the situation (Overy, 1997: 73). Most of these accounts appear to overstate or even misread Stalin's reactions. New evidence demonstrates the dictator was indeed shocked in the aftermath of invasion but more by the inability of the Russian military to repel the Germans than by the actual fact of Hitler's perfidy (Roberts, 2006).

What the dictator had not foreseen was the German advance deep into the Russian homeland, even as far as the approaches to Moscow. Very quickly, much of the Ukraine had fallen and agricultural land, peoples and materials were in the hands of the Germans and their allies. The impact on the Red Army was initially, at least, devastating. Some three-quarters of a million Russian troops perished. The situation was such that some historians have argued that Stalin considered an 'obscene peace' such as Brest-Litvosk

(Roberts, 2006). Stalin actually was more resolute than perhaps he has been given credit for. The Soviet dictator, the Red Army and the Russian people after invasion rallied in a manner which earned huge admiration among the peoples of the West. Hitler had indeed won numerous huge victories but he had also failed to achieve any of his key objectives: Moscow, Leningrad and the industrial Donets Basin had not been taken. The Red Army although heavily damaged had not been obliterated.

The sheer resolve of the Soviet peoples in the wake of the German advance caused even those with grave doubts about the nature of Stalin's rule to applaud the war effort. We should not though forget the dreadful brutality inflicted upon those who did not perform their duty on the Soviet side. Executions were commonplace. As Stalin explained in a radio speech on 3 July 1941, 'there was no room for whimperers or cowards, for panic-mongers and deserters' (Overy, 1997: 80–1). In June, martial law was imposed throughout the western parts of the Soviet Union and a labour conscription law mandated that men and women should work some eight hours a day constructing defences such as anti-tank traps, trenches and artillery emplacements. All leave and public holidays were cancelled. During the second summer crisis, on 28 July 1942, Order Number 227, 'Not a step back' (in Russian '*Ni Shagu nazad*!') was issued to ensure discipline within the ranks of the Soviet forces. Officers were not to order retreat – to do so would be regarded as treachery. As Geoffrey Roberts has pointed out, 'blocking' groups were placed behind wavering divisions to ensure there could be no movement away from battle (Roberts, 2006) All those who surrendered or were captured by the Germans were traitors to the motherland (Overy, 1997: 158–60). This resulted in the execution of 13,500 retreating soldiers on the Stalingrad front alone. (This order was not made public until 1988.)

Stalin himself recovered from the initial shock of German betrayal and negotiated with the British and the Americans over aid for the war effort. FDR offered Lend-Lease in August 1941. (Lend-lease was the name of the programme through which the US supplied the allied nations with war materials.) After the Japanese surprise attack on the US naval base at Pearl Harbor in December 1941, the American President lost no time in bringing his forces fully into the war against Germany, Italy and Japan. The trauma of the attack on the naval base and the losses (some 2,343 people were killed) shocked the American people in a manner which, perhaps, we can understand after witnessing the reaction to the tragedy of 9/11 (Andrew, 1995; Gaddis, 2004). Popular sentiment enabled Roosevelt to rally popular opinion for the war effort and to silence the voices of isolationism. On 11 December Hitler gifted FDR Germany and Italy's declaration of war. As the President argued in a radio and newsreel speech, which has been invoked many times since the events of 9/11, the day that Pearl Harbor was attacked was one 'destined to live in infamy' (Graubard, 2004: 281). With the subsequent entry of the United States into the war against fascism, the Grand Alliance was forged.

Stalin immediately pressed his new Allies to relieve the terrible military pressure upon the Eastern Front: he needed some form of Second Front to open up in Western Europe. This issue for Stalin became one of many tests of faith in his counterparts Roosevelt and Winston Churchill. The issue of the Second Front was one that would dominate all meetings between diplomats right up until 1944. In 1943, conferring at the Casablanca conference in Morocco, Roosevelt and Churchill agreed on an Allied invasion of Europe to relieve the Red Army. They chose to attack Europe from the South, through Italy, which surrendered in September 1943. For the Soviet dictator this operation was a mere sideshow and he continued to press for another Allied invasion, preferably one in France. When the three leaders finally met in late November 1943 in Teheran, the capital of Allied-occupied Persia (after Stalin's first journey by aeroplane), the British and the Americans unfolded their plans to launch the cross-Channel military operation and open the Second Front.

Stalin was clear that once Germany was defeated it would pay a high price for its invasion. In the meantime, Hitler was clearly the enemy that Stalin wished to concentrate upon and he made it clear to Western diplomats that although Japan had to be subdued, and that Russia would be engaged in that war too, the defeat of Germany was the priority. What was seared in the mind of the Soviet dictator was the damage done by the Germans to his state and of course the betrayal by Hitler. At the moment we are preoccupied by the casualty rates of our soldiers in modern wars, such as the Iraq war, the sheer scale of devastation to the Red Army and civilians in the Soviet Union defies imagination. Richard Overy, the distinguished military historian, has placed Soviet war losses at approximately 25 million dead (Duffy, 1991; Overy, 1997: 288).

Melvyn Leffler has powerfully argued that historians of the Cold War should not lose sight of the enormity of the Soviet war dead. He places the Soviet casualty figure at some 27 million and explains that this number is important in explaining later USSR security needs and Soviet mentalities over the post-war settlement. Leffler points out that in what is perhaps the most important account written in the new Cold War historiography, the *We Now Know* monograph written by John Lewis Gaddis, that most eminent of Cold War historians, actually accords only one sentence to the wartime losses of the USSR (Leffler, 2000: 47). This is quite an omission. I note that, in his impressive book on the American presidency, one distinguished scholar talks of the losses at Pearl Harbor as 'huge' (Graubard, 2004).

The use of one sentence by Gaddis to describe Soviet losses in this war is an important understatement because, as Leffler goes on to argue, much of the new evidence actually shows that Stalin was preoccupied by the revival of German (and Japanese) power and their potential to inflict further damage. Stalin drew from the experience of occupation and invasion of the USSR from the time of the Revolution onwards that because Germany could not be pacified it must be defeated and subdued as it was in 1918–19: but this time on a permanent basis. In this quest the Soviet dictator saw clearly that American military and economic strength would be required for any post-war occupation of either country. This was evident to Stalin because, as we saw in the last chapter, the fall of France had proved beyond doubt the military ineptitude of Paris. It therefore became of paramount importance to Stalin, regardless of ideological differences, to seek cooperation with the United States over any peace settlement. The Russian warlord did not want confrontation with Roosevelt; rather he sought military alliance, economic aid and understanding of the geopolitical requirements for the future security of the USSR. In this bid to build a cooperative relationship with Roosevelt, the Soviet dictator was pushing at an 'open door' as the US President had come to believe that he could, through a combination of personal charm and diplomatic finesse, win over 'Uncle Joe'. (This tag was one given to Stalin by the American media during the war years. It was not a name that apparently impressed the dictator.)

Roosevelt and Stalin: Another 'Brutal Friendship'?

It is perhaps worth stressing that international politics, like all politics, is misunderstood if it is seen simply as the clash of material interests or even of ideas and ideologies. Material interests have to be expressed, ideologies articulated; and human beings do the expression and the articulation. Human relationships, thus, form the core of politics at any level, whether those relationships are conflictual, or cooperative. At the level of international politics, it is often said that individuals count for little against large impersonal forces or social structures. Yet it is a thesis well born out by the history of the Cold War that individuals and their relations do matter; more, perhaps, than just a little, and especially at certain moments.

Sir William Deakin titled his account of the relationship between Hitler and Mussolini *The Brutal Friendship* (Deakin, 1962) but that other relationship – between Stalin and Roosevelt – was equally central to the conduct of World War II and its many outcomes. There was, in actuality, in addition to the determination to destroy fascism, much common agreement between the two leaders. The British Prime Minister Winston Churchill, especially after 1943, become far less important to discussions of the post-war settlement. FDR was clear, whatever his personal admiration for the British Prime Minister, that there were significant differences between British and American visions for a post-war world. Roosevelt certainly did not want Stalin to believe that he and Churchill were 'ganging up' on the dictator (Harriman and Abel, 1976: 146). On the other hand it should be remembered that even if there were disagreements between Roosevelt and Churchill over the future of the British Empire, the British and the Americans remained close over cooperation on nuclear weapons. In Quebec in August 1943 a secret agreement was concluded by which the British and Americans agreed that they would never use the projected weapons against each other.

Not least, Roosevelt believed that there was a distinct gap between Britain and the other two members of the 'Big Three' on the question of empire and imperialism. This was an aspect of that ideological element in international politics that I have been emphasizing throughout, though for once the representative of Wilsonianism and the representative of Leninism were seen to be on the same side. For Roosevelt, war was not to be waged and American blood shed simply to preserve British colonialism. As he remarked to Churchill, 'you have four hundred years of acquisitive instinct in your blood and you just don't understand how a country might not want to acquire land somewhere else if they can get it'. Roosevelt was adamant that the war could not be fought for any plan that would further France's imperialistic ambitions or that would shore up the British in their empire (Ferguson, 2004: 67). At the meeting in Teheran, in conversation with 'Uncle Joe', Roosevelt revealed that he believed that India was perhaps ripe for revolution. Stalin, with far more experience of such issues, politely demurred: such issues were, after all, complicated (Montefiore, 2003: 472–80).

However, Roosevelt and Stalin seemed to agree that decolonization movements must be encouraged after the war. Both leaders also wanted control and occupation of both Germany and Japan. The American leader though was clear that he was a prisoner of his people and he was not sure what his Congress or people would permit in terms of a permanent US military occupation of Germany. He explained to Stalin that Americans would not accept the stationing of troops abroad in peacetime (Foreign Relations of the United States, 1961: 531). He explained instead that his country would seek to return to some form of normalcy but obviously with engagement in the new international organization he sought to create. As Melvin Small has argued the American President in 1943 'could not have imagined that within a few years hundreds of thousands of American soldiers ... would be on permanent guard in Europe and Asia' (Small, 1996: 80). But this is to look into the future. In the middle of the war, Roosevelt foresaw quite correctly that there would be a popular clamour for American troops to be returned to their families as soon as conflict was over.

In late 1943, Roosevelt was sympathetic to the idea of a settlement that would finally satisfy Soviet security concerns. It was on this issue that later problems were to emerge but there was certainly a degree of understanding among American diplomats for some form of Soviet geopolitical buffer zone in Central and Eastern Europe. Stalin was not hesitant in outlining his particular vision for future security arrangements. This is not to assert that there was a Soviet blueprint for the post-war settlement during the war years, for everything was fluid and changeable, but by November 1943, when the leaders first met, Stalin did indeed map out Soviet security requirements. His first requirement was to dismantle German power and strip that country of its material resources. The second was that Moscow sought control over the future politics of Poland. A third requirement was influence in the reshaping of Japan after its defeat. In fact the price of Soviet intervention in the war against Japan was the retaking of the former Tsarist possessions held by the Japanese; the north of Japan, namely the Kurile Islands, and the southern half of Sakhalin Island. These ambitions indicate, as was seen by the Americans, the desire by Stalin to occupy a foothold in Asia.

This perhaps brings us to one of the key ways in which the international politics of World War II increasingly – and even while the outcome of the war was still in doubt, although Allied victory became increasingly more likely after the Battle of Moscow and then Stalingrad – became mired in the question of the likely shape of the post-war world. And here, as many of the actors realized only too well, there were many pitfalls. The Soviet desire for security was understandable (and Churchill and Roosevelt certainly saw it as such) given the huge suffering of the Soviet people during the war, but then so was French desire for security after World War I and that, of course, had led to the 'Carthaginian peace' of Versailles which had created problems rather than solving them. (Some would argue it was not Carthaginian enough. Margaret MacMillan's recent book is much more favourable to the peacemakers (MacMillan, 2002).) And then there was the geopolitical question of a Soviet foothold in Asia coupled with the ideological problems such a foothold might bring (to India, to China and to European possessions in the Far East). Roosevelt might have been an anti-imperialist, but he also had to be sensitive to his British ally's concerns. It was these concerns that largely brought about the tendency of the Allies, at least in private, to start thinking in terms of 'spheres of influence', a move that was to have profound implications for the manner, as well as the matter, of the Cold War.

Spheres of Influence, Ideological and Political

'Spheres of influence' is a phrase that has a distinctly nineteenth-century ring to it. In formal terms it has become an offshoot of the so-called conference system that had emerged out of the Napoleonic wars. As Stevenson has argued, that system was not really a system in modern terms at all, 'It consisted rather of a habit of mind, a willingness by the European Great Powers to discuss matters of common concern in ad hoc conferences' (Stevenson, 1988: 4). The result of this 'habit of mind' was a tendency to set boundaries to the 'legitimate' interests of the powers, interests that other powers would refrain from challenging. These interests might sometimes include formal or informal 'spheres of influence'.

It is perhaps no accident that the one Cold War statesman to make most public use of the notion (and even he would often dress it up for public consumption) was Henry Kissinger, whose mind and style were steeped in the international politics of the nineteenth century and whose PhD thesis had been written on the creation of the concert system and its strengths and weaknesses (Kissinger, 1999). Indeed, much of the logic of Kissinger's policy of détente with the Russians was explicitly premised on the idea that the Soviet Union should be treated as a 'legitimate great power' which had, therefore, legitimate spheres of influence that other powers should respect (Eastern and Central Europe for example). While Kissinger was the most public advocate of the idea, and the philosophy that lay behind it, many other prominent Cold Warriors upheld some version of it (Dean Acheson, for example, as we will see in the next chapter). Yet, the fundamental rule of the concert system was reciprocity: I respected your spheres of influence because you respected mine. The problem was that the ideological elements of the equation, as well as the geopolitical uncertainty, made expectations of reciprocity increasingly problematic as the war came to a close.

What was troubling to Western statesmen, in the light of all this, was exactly what *degree* of control Stalin sought in Central and Eastern Europe and what *role* Communism would therefore play more generally in the politics of Europe. In view of the advances made in 1944 by the Red Army towards the Balkans, Churchill sought clarity on Soviet ambitions.

In the so-called Percentages Agreement of October 1944 the British Prime Minister suggested to Stalin a 'spheres of influence' deal on the future of Europe. Here we see at least the outlines of Soviet ambitions. The 'deal' was to divide up degrees of influence for East and West. So, in Hungary and Yugoslavia there would be a split of 50/50; in Romania a split of 90/10 in favour of the Soviet Union; in Bulgaria a split of 75/25 again in favour of Moscow; but in Greece a split of 90/10 in favour of the West.

Churchill himself came to believe that by and large the dictator held to this deal. Perhaps though the British Prime Minister was deluding himself in various ways. We know that Stalin attempted to strike deals with a number of European Communist parties but more importantly Stalin must have recognized clearly the limitations of any 'deal' that excluded the Americans. As the then US ambassador to Moscow Averell Harriman later remarked of the percentages agreement:

> I never took this thing seriously, and I don't think it was important as it did not affect the future ... This so-called agreement was one of those rather spectacular non-events that historians tend to pick up and make much of ... Roosevelt dissociated himself in advance from any understanding Churchill might reach with Stalin during their Moscow talks in 1944. (Harriman, 1982: 31–66)

The problem for Churchill was that, at least initially, the Americans and especially Roosevelt had little truck with spheres of influence agreements. The Americans wanted ideally to see fair elections throughout Eastern and Central Europe – hence the emphasis upon the 'Declaration on Liberated Europe'. But the Americans were and remained sceptical over whether 'broadly representative democratic elements' as enshrined in the declaration could possibly survive in areas of Soviet occupation. This for Churchill and indeed for some in American policy circles was unrealistic.

Roosevelt himself is often depicted as naïve compared to the hard-nosed realism of a Churchill or a canny Stalin. All diplomats who met with Stalin during the war years left his company impressed by his charm, his command of detail and his determination. As we noted , some like Eden found it incredible that the monster of the purges could appear so ordinary. No one though doubted Stalin's guile. Even to this day Roosevelt is seen as having allowed the dictator to take advantage. The American President is still accused of being duped by the dictator into agreeing to the 'betrayal' of Eastern and Central Europe at the Yalta Conference of January 1945. This is not quite accurate, not least because it privileges a perspective in which European affairs are placed wholly at the centre of Cold War politics (Beichman, 2003; Clemens, 1970; Mastny, 1979).

It is correct that Stalin remained intransigent on Poland, speaking in an impassioned way about Soviet security concerns; and it is also correct that the Americans and British did little to dent future Russian control of that country. But it is worth remembering that the American President had at Yalta a veritable host of issues to deal with: imperial concerns, economic interests, the reshaping of Asian affairs and his own great project for the post-war era – the United Nations. These all took their place alongside the concern over the fate of Central and Eastern Europe. On several issues Stalin in fact proved amenable and on Roosevelt's proposed international organ-ization made several concessions. He accepted the veto mechanism while also reducing the earlier demand that all of the Soviet republics be granted seats in the proposed General Assembly. The dictator settled for three seats instead, to be held by Russia, Belorussia and the Ukraine. Stalin too, despite his disdain for Paris and what he perceived as a lamentable military performance against the Germans, grudgingly accepted that France should be treated as a great power. Interestingly, Roosevelt at Yalta seemed to agree with the Soviet view of France. On one occasion he confided to Stalin that he agreed that De Gaulle had 'grandiose ambitions'. He was also critical – ironically – of the British insistence that France should be built up, since the US had mainly equipped the victorious French colonial armies of 1943–45 (see Harriman and Abel, 1976: 394). Roosevelt in the light of these concessions therefore saw the Yalta Conference as having succeeded, because it should as he saw it 'spell the end of the system of unilateral action, the exclusive alliances, the spheres of influence, the balances of power, and all the other expedients that have been tried for centuries and have always failed' (Graubard, 2004: 295).

Most importantly of all for Roosevelt at the conference in the Crimea, was his still having to ensure that the Red Army would, as Stalin had promised earlier, enter the war against the Japanese. In early 1945, it was not certain that the US atomic programme would yield imminent results. Therefore any cooperation over Eastern and Central Europe had to be balanced against the demands of an ongoing bloody conventional war in the Pacific. Looking at the casualty rates the Americans were suffering when taking islands such as Guadalcanal and Iwo Jima, it appeared that there would indeed be a huge toll on Allied forces taking Japan (http://hnn.US/articles/263.html). Russian intervention would help spread or share that burden. This specific concern over the costs of the war against Japan also helps explain why, despite Churchill's protestations, US troops did not in the spring of 1945 compete in a 'race' with the Russians to capture and hold the German capital, Berlin. From an American perspective, Churchill's demand that US troops be used to 'grab and hold' territory in the centre of Europe seemed rather pointless (Sharp, 1975).

As the Red Army advanced, though, there is little doubt that the dilemmas over the shape of Soviet occupation in Europe sharpened for the Americans. Somewhat inevitably those states regarded as 'hostile' by Stalin were regulated by Soviet/Communist control. The 'Red' advance to Berlin, when the Soviet commanders vied to take the German capital, brought in its wake an apparently endless catalogue of abuse, not just of the civilian population but the resources of the country (Beevor, 2002). By the time Soviet troops advanced into Berlin soldiers were full of hatred for the German people. Much of this may be explained by the barbarity of their own experiences on the Eastern Front, some by the propaganda they were subjected to by their own officers and political leaders, and some by the sight of the concentration camps. Nevertheless, Soviet troops were guilty of tremendous cruelty to those in the path of their advance. 'Totalitarian' man was not only armed but also represented a certain type of warfare. While feminist scholars of international relations have treated the issue of mass rape in war as originating with the Balkan wars of the 1990s, tens of thousands of German women were raped and abused as Berlin finally fell.

All of this alerted American diplomats – if they needed to be made aware of it – to the shape of future Soviet occupation. Yet there were inconsistencies in Soviet behaviour. Their troops were withdrawn from Denmark and Norway and perhaps more tellingly from Czechoslovakia. Finland too and Austria escaped the full wrath of a Soviet imposition of government and Stalinist-style Communism. There are reasons as to why a simple strategy of 'winner takes all' was not being pursued here. As Geoffrey Roberts has shown in his excellent studies, Stalin far from controlling Communism in Eastern and Central Europe had, at this point, only patchy control and influence (Roberts, 1994). Nowhere, as we will see in the next chapter, was this to be more obvious than in Yugoslavia.

Most crucially of all though, Stalin, despite victory in Europe, still sought some forms of cooperation with the United States and his Western counterparts. He saw that cooperation could produce benefits; not the least of these were joint control over Germany and eventually Japan (all of his suggestions for the future of Germany made during the wartime conferences had envisaged joint control) and of course he dearly needed Western cooperation to help reconstruct a devastated USSR. 'Going it alone' was not the preferred option. While scholars remain divided over the actual amount of control Stalin exerted over Communist parties in Western Europe, what influence he exerted in areas such as Greece was, as Churchill claimed, actually to discourage overt insurrection for fear of offending Western leaders (Sfikos, 2001). Although Stalin could not and did not compromise on the issue of Poland, his ambitions to control the Turkish straits and gain a foothold in Iran ran headfirst into American and British objections. As we will see below, in the light of these protests, the dictator withdrew from any prospect of confrontation.

Shocks and Turning Points

What was clear was that, in the immediate aftermath of the war, statist pragmatism took preference over ideological revolution in Stalin's mind. This was clear in 1945–46 in the attitude towards China and the emergence of Communism in that vast space. Stalin vacillated between support for Communism under Mao (who he appears to have personally disliked) and friendship with his fellow generalissimo, Chiang Kai-shek, the leader of nationalist forces and necessary to the subjugation of Japanese power in Asia. (Interestingly Stalin took the title of generalissimo above marshal on 26 June between the German and Japanese wars.)

Stalin's ambitions and hopes for cooperation with the West, but especially with the United States, were, however, dealt two significant blows in 1945 which began to change the situation. These were the death of Roosevelt on 12 April and the subsequent advent of American atomic power. Let us take the death of Roosevelt first. For those of us who have taught courses on Cold War politics, it is common to ask a question along the lines of: Did the death of FDR actually herald the end of cooperation with Stalin and the beginning of the Cold War? One angle already discussed above is that a special relationship of sorts did indeed exist between the dictator and the President. FDR was on record as believing in this closeness; Stalin too appears to have been upset by the death of the President.

Stalin, although somewhat wary of Roosevelt's successor, Harry Truman, was willing at least initially to see him as Roosevelt's heir. Again, as we saw earlier, while personal relationships may not always (possibly not even often) be that important in international politics, they do have an impact. It is also worth remembering that three months after the death of Roosevelt, despite Stalin's confident predictions of his victory, Winston Churchill lost the British general election. The pattern of personal politics among the three allies was transformed by these events.

Even more problematic for the dictator was the advent of American atomic power in the summer of 1945. It has been a source of considerable controversy among scholars of international relations as to whether the invention (and, let us not forget, the deploying and the use) of nuclear weapons in fact changed things as much as the first generation of nuclear strategists believed. The American strategist Bernard Brodie, as is well known, is reported to have said to his wife, after the report of the dropping of the atomic bomb, 'everything I have written is obsolete' (Kaplan, 1983) and went on to put flesh on the bones of that view in the book he wrote, and which became the first major statement of nuclear strategy: the title says it all: *The Absolute Weapon*. Latterly, however, some scholars have questioned this view suggesting in fact that nuclear weapons were in fact epiphenomenal and made little actual difference (see, for example, Mueller, 1989). What is perhaps certainly true is that in the context of 1945, the perceptions of the dawning of the nuclear age certainly did change everything.

At the Potsdam Conference in July 1945 Stalin first met Harry Truman and the new British leader, Clement Attlee. (Stalin's view of Truman was not helped by the fact that American Lend-Lease to the USSR had been cut off the day after military victory in Europe). It was at Potsdam that the dictator learnt officially of the successful American atomic test. Famously Stalin appeared to take the news well, even perhaps nonchalantly, remarking that such a weapon could be used on Japan. We now know that Stalin realized that the configuration of global politics had been irrevocably changed. Although Stalin had learnt from his spies that the American atomic programme was well under way, the actual test had come earlier than expected. There were at least three consequences of this to be considered. The first was that the nuclear monopoly bestowed a strategic advantage, one borne out only too cruelly in the two detonations over Japan in August and the subsequent surrender of Tokyo on 2 September. Even if the United States was friendly now – it surely needed to be less dependent on cooperation with Moscow.

From a Soviet perspective nowhere was this more evident than in the decision to cut the Soviet Union out of the occupation of Japan despite or perhaps because of the Red Army's 14-day annihilation of the million-strong Japanese Kwantung Army in Manchuria, and which began on the day that Nagasaki was bombed. Such 'unfriendly' gestures led to a second consequence that needed to be considered by the dictator. If cooperation should end then he needed, this time around, to be prepared. This made the occupation of the strategic periphery around the homeland crucial. It was not just the usual conventional land invasion that might threaten the homeland, it was a potential air attack. If attack should come, the USSR had to be prepared and not surprised as in 1941.

There was a third consequence of the atomic issue though. We might describe this as the social costs of the nuclear arms race. In 1945 after victory in war, rather than a relaxation of effort and a diversion of resources towards consumer products, the peoples of the USSR had to prepare for a new type of attack. Huge resources were utilized in a bid to catch up and overtake the American nuclear programme.

After Hiroshima, the Soviet nuclear research programme was given a special priority under the watchful eyes of the Deputy Prime Minister for Security, Lavrenti Beria. He reported directly to Stalin. Physicists assisted by German scientists captured during the war were established in secure laboratories deep in the interior of the country. A vast prison labour force was employed in the nuclear endeavour, including a large part of the construction of the buildings by prisoners of the NKVD (MVD since 1946). Amy Knight (1993) has pointed out that prisoners were used for atomic energy research in a manner described by Alexander Solzhenitsyn in *The First Circle*. This rather hidden history of the Cold War yields fascinating materials and stories.

It is, however, questionable as to whether Stalin did see the advent of atomic weaponry as decisive in strategic (as opposed to ideational) terms. After all, the US monopoly was small and there was no indication that Truman would attempt to use nuclear weapons again. But as we will see Stalin was correct to perceive the psychological impact of the atomic monopoly. The President and those around him did shortly come to believe that atomic power provided great leverage in negotiations and confrontations.

Truman, though, was all too aware of the multiple challenges facing him and his country after a global war. John Lewis Gaddis has perhaps done more than any other historian in highlighting the complexities of Cold War politics for American leaders (Gaddis, 1972). He has argued that the blame, if there must be blame for the Cold War, has to lie with the leader who had least choice in the post-war years. For Gaddis, this was Truman. In my previous work I have disagreed with such a view arguing rather that Stalin had the fewer choices (Kennedy-Pipe, 1998). But Gaddis is correct that there is a persuasive case to be made for the limitations which operated upon the American President as he and those around him struggled to come to terms with the shape of the post-war world. Specifically, if we compare Truman's position of 1945 to say that of Wilson in 1919, there are similarities – not least those embedded in the complex nature of US domestic politics. But there was a vast difference between 1919 and 1945. This time, Russia could not be relegated to the sidelines of international politics. Soviet power had been established over a vast geographic space in both Europe and in Asia. From an American perspective, this forward position, in addition to the ideology of Communism, made it impossible and indeed unwise to ignore the threats posed by the USSR.

For Truman though, in 1945 it was not clear that his Congress and the US public would wish to pay the price for continued engagement abroad. Not the least of these, as remarked upon earlier, was the overwhelming desire of many to see the demobilization of US troops. This, in fact, happened rapidly. In the spring of 1945, the United States had some 12.3 million people under arms. Twelve months later that figure had dropped to 1.5 million. This in turn raised fears that there simply was not enough manpower to fulfil all of the emerging obligations. As Truman himself wrote: 'Every momma and poppa had to have her boy home immediately, and every Congressman, of course, wanted to be re-elected' (Small, 1996: 83). It may be easy to forget that the American President facing multiple challenges in the international area also faced a rapid dwindling of his conventional military forces and a battle over preserving military strength. Perhaps, as Stalin remarked, a one-party system was preferable when it came to decision-making.

But if Truman had his challenges at home, challenges which we will return to in the next chapter, so too did Stalin. Indeed, far from the simple model of decision-making that we used to imagine the Soviet generalissimo operated in, we now know from some of the new histories that bureaucratic rivalries plagued the making of Soviet policy on the ground in Central and Eastern Europe. Competing bureaucratic interests in the Soviet zones of Germany for example rendered policy anything but coherent (Naimark, 1995). It is also true that there were in the Kremlin different voices offering competing views as how to pursue Soviet interests vis-à-vis Europe and in Asia. This was of course nothing like the robust and open debates we saw in Washington but one feature of decision-making within the Kremlin was the paranoid and competitive world in which Stalin operated. There is little doubt that in the post-war period he set his lieutenants against each other in the cut-throat world of Kremlin politics (Knight, 1993). This meant that pleasing the dictator came above truthful assessments of global politics.

The Decay of the Grand Alliance

Throughout late 1945 and 1946 Stalin and his officials continued to pursue cooperation with the United States while testing the limits of American tolerance. The Iran crisis of early 1946 saw a Soviet move to secure the oilfields of northern Iran in contravention, it is true, of an earlier agreement for the Great Powers to leave the country after the war. When Soviet troops were not removed the Kremlin received a robust response from Truman to 'give it to them with both barrels' (including, Truman later implied, a hint about American nuclear weapons), and which ensured a swift Soviet withdrawal. But many understandably on the British and American side had begun to measure Stalin not by his concessions or withdrawals but by the nature of Communist rule in Central and Eastern Europe, especially in Poland, Bulgaria and Romania, where, despite the earlier 'Declaration on Liberated Europe', Communist power had been irrevocably entrenched. American representatives on the Allied Control Commissions which operated in the East European states reported almost on a daily basis of the problems of trying to deal with Soviet officials. Here they were greatly influenced by the warnings of local anti-Communist parties to whom the future seemed obvious (Varsori, 2000: 283).

It was not as we noted earlier that American officials were surprised by the abuse of democratic politics in these regions. This had long been expected. It was, however, the fear that Communism might prove potent enough to perhaps spread into Western Europe and Asia. The political and economic chaos of states such as France and Italy, to the American mind, laid them open to the lure of Marxist–Leninist ideologies. Asia too had to be protected from Communism and this in part explains the decision not to permit Soviet occupation of Japan. To this end after the war the Americans occupied South Korea and Truman also sent military advisers to China to help the Nationalists against the Communist threat posed by Mao. By the middle of 1946, a catalogue of Soviet misdemeanours meant that many were adamant that, as a headline in *Life* magazine phrased it, 'Why kid around? There is no misunderstanding between Russia and the West. There is a conflict' (Varsori, 2000: 284).

American officials debated the nature of Soviet power and the agenda of the Soviets abroad throughout 1945 and 1946. It was left to George F. Kennan to actually flesh out a convincing view of what motivated the leaders of the Soviet Union and what the United States and its allies should do about it. He was clear that those in Moscow were inspired by a combination of Marxist–Leninist ideology and a degree of insecurity fed by the paranoid character of Russian history and the Russian polity. The Soviet leadership would expand as far as it could geographically, regardless of the norms of the international system, and thus 'normal' behaviour could not be expected from this totalitarian state. This threat in his view had to be contained. Composed in an almost deserted embassy, sometimes morose and depressed, Kennan sent his views from his station as chargé d'affaires in Moscow early in 1947 as a communiqué that is now known to history as the 'Long Telegram'.

Its effect on the debates within the administration was profound in part due to the advocacy of James Forrestal, the Secretary of the Navy and later Secretary of Defense, who was a convinced anti-Communist (he later committed suicide). It was as though Kennan had expressed the views of many who were feeling similar things but did not have the background knowledge of history or the first hand acquaintance with the Soviet system to properly voice.

It was this telegram, of course, that was later published under the assumed name 'X' as an article in *Foreign Affairs* in July 1947. Kennan's views and the advocacy of containment became the template for the conduct of American foreign policy towards the USSR, despite the irony that, as we saw in Chapter 1, it was the opposition to those views by Walter Lippmann that gave the gathering conflict its name.

Kennan's views, however, also chimed with those of Winston Churchill. In a March 1946 speech made at Fulton, Missouri, Churchill had argued that an 'Iron Curtain' had descended across Europe. Churchill had in fact tried out a similar phrase on Stalin at the Potsdam conference – to be met with the retort that he was talking fairy stories! (Montefiore, 2003). Even worse than the fate of those caught behind the Iron Curtain was the fact that Communism might yet destabilize Western society and civilization. With British power fading fast, Churchill called for an Anglo-American alliance to defeat Soviet ambition. Churchill was on record as saying that in his view the Soviet Union and Communism were 'like a troop of ferocious baboons', but in this speech he did also praise the Soviet Union as a leading nation (Young, 2001).

Perhaps more important than those of the former British Prime Minister, Kennan's views were representative of a number of those advising Truman. By the end of 1946 and early 1947 American officials clearly saw a new international architecture in which the Soviet Union was pitted against the United States. This perception continued to be reinforced by developments across Europe and Asia. As the Chinese Civil War became increasingly intense, throughout South-East Asia, the Dutch and the French struggled to restore their imperial positions against the forces of nationalism; the British too were irrevocably weakened and forced to plan for the withdrawal of their forces from Palestine. Yet, it was the perception of a growing crisis in Europe that really caught the attention of policy-makers. Communism appeared to be a potent political force in France and in Italy and within the Western occupation zones of Germany. Harsh winter conditions, a fuel crisis and shortages of food all conspired to undermine liberal political conditions.

It was the British financial plight that particularly worried American officials. The British position was a complex one. John Young has argued that Britain was the only major power to fight World War II from beginning to end and see victory. Except for the

United States, it was also the only Great Power to escape defeat in either world war. Survival itself was a huge achievement but economic decline after such exertions appeared inevitable. By early 1947, though, the position looked perilous. There was violence in Pakistan, calls for independence for India and renewed conflict in Greece. The British simply did not have the financial wherewithal to counter these problems. Attlee decided to withdraw most British forces from Greece and cease aid to Turkey. Attlee and Foreign Secretary Ernest Bevin had come to believe that the Americans could and should take over what had been traditional British responsibilities (Young, 1997; Ferguson, 2004).

There is a long scholarly debate about what motivated British officials at this point. Was the announcement of withdrawal in itself a ruse to alert the Americans to the necessity of a new Western alliance? Or was it that, as British power faded, bureaucrats were aware of a Soviet Union willing and able to take advantage. Americans were not, as some historians have argued, naïve but they were surprised by the speed of the British collapse. It was only in 1944 that William Fox had argued that there would be three super-powers, the US, the USSR and Britain (Fox, 1944).

From an American point of view the causes of British fragility was not the only or even the most important question. Their concern was that in the vacuum left by British withdrawal, whole regions might succumb to Communism. If this occurred, there would be consequences that would affect international trade, international stability and of course American patterns of trade. What revisionist historians have highlighted is the perception by US officials of an intimate connection between international economics, international stability and well-being (Williams, 1962). Truman himself feared in Europe the advent of nationalized industries, the closing of foreign markets to American trade and the increasing state centralization which left-wing politics in Europe would inevitably bring (Leffler, 1994). This would, to his mind, bring in its wake an adherence to socialist planning, a linkage to Moscow and increasing numbers of trade agreements between Moscow and particular West European governments – hence Communism would prevail: markets, allies and stability would be lost. This issue of allies is important. As Lundestad (1986) demonstrated some time ago, the creation of a Western alliance was not just an American invention alone: the Europeans themselves were pushing hard not just for American dollars but for American influence as a counterbalance to Stalin and Communism (Deighton, 1990).

'Bipolarity' and the Creation of the 'Cold War'

What is unquestionably true, however, is that with the decay of British global power, what had still been an effectively 'multipolar system' was increasingly becoming a 'bipolar' one. The notion of polarity has had a long history in international relations theory and, while it perhaps does not explain as much as some of its advocates have thought, it is not quite as empty as some of its opponents have supposed. Put simply, the argument has traditionally been about what makes for a stable international system. For classical realist accounts (those, for example, of Hans J. Morgenthau and Raymond Aron and, perhaps most especially, of Henry Kissinger) the 'balance of power' system typified by the nineteenth-century European system was the most stable, since it allowed the multiple powers in the system – traditionally the five Great Powers of the nineteenth century – to actively create a balance by always calling the others onto the scales. The relative uncertainty and constant fluidity of this 'multipolar' arrangement gave the best chance of avoiding conflict as risk-averse statesmen would be aware of prevailing instabilities and fluidities.

Neo-realists, like Kenneth Waltz, have contended, in contrast, that bipolarity – only two major powers in a system – because it minimizes the centres of decision and what political scientists like to call the number of possible conflict dyads in the system, is in fact much more stable than multipolarity. Many Cold War historians, most obviously perhaps John Lewis Gaddis, have shared this view using the period as their exemplar.

There is also a third view, to which we will return in Chapter 6, that argues that a unipolar world, that is a world where one major power is a hegemon, is the most stable system.

What, in fact, does the history of the Cold War suggest about this argument? In the first place, while it simplified the centres of decision (essentially Washington and Moscow) in terms of major threats to international peace, it also led to a heightening of perceptions about the risks of letting the 'other' side develop an advantage, military, geopolitical or straightforwardly political. Second, it sharpened the ideological elements that had been so prominent in the 1930s but which had to some extent been submerged in the common struggle against fascism during the war. The 'Free World' versus the 'Communist Bloc' added an edge to the 'bipolar' conflict that was absent in the largely (though certainly not entirely) non-ideological system of the nineteenth century. And third it raised in the minds of many, particularly in Western Europe, the question of threat.

The international relations theorist Stephen Walt has persuasively argued that states balance, not just against power but against power as married to perceptions of threat (Walt, 1986). Whether or not this is generally true it is a very good summary of the manner in which the emerging Cold War structures took their final shape. And this is suggestive, for it was after all Kissinger who emphasized in *A World Restored* the significance of polarity *plus legitimacy* as the key to stability. Bipolarity in his view was more dangerous because it encouraged a sense of certainty; if you married that to ideological certainty then you got a very unstable system indeed. It was in part to counteract both of these features that Kissinger in his own diplomacy of the 1960s and early 1970s sought to play, as he famously put it, the China card. By bringing China back into the fold, he both turned a bipolar system into a multipolar one, or so he thought, and diluted the 'ideological element' by bringing in a counter to 'Soviet Communism' in the form of Chinese Communism. Though, of course, in 1946/47, all this lay far in the future. Interestingly, both Waltz's argument and Kissinger's show that properly understood a concern for ideational, or at least perceptual, elements is not incompatible with realist insights.

In 1947, there seemed for some Americans a fundamental choice to be made. Tyranny could not be controlled once it had emerged outside the Soviet bloc and there was little doubt that once it spread the United States could be left isolated. By 1947 therefore two important ideologies were competing in the international arena. These visions were not just ideas but were linked to important geostrategic visions. As Truman remarked in his March 1947 appeal to Congress to permit aid to Greece and Turkey, the loss of Greece would be disastrous not just for the people of Greece but in global terms. It would also have a negative effect upon Turkey and would sow confusion and disorder across the Middle East. It would also discourage those in Western Europe from fighting to maintain freedom. The US therefore had to act and take over the leadership of the 'Free' world. This was the American mission. Truman's request to Congress for $400 million worth of aid to Greece and Turkey was deliberately designed to, in the words of Senator Vandenberg, 'scare hell out of the country' (Small, 1996: 84).

It succeeded and the idea of leadership and the defence of democracy became the staple fare of Cold War politics for American presidents. The US could not be left isolated so it had to act to prevent its allies falling to Communism. The Truman Doctrine, Containment and the Marshall Plan were the weapons chosen to wage and shape the emerging conflict, now increasingly known – thanks to Lippmann's response to Kennan – as the 'Cold War'. To these strategies, and their progeny, we now turn.

4

Far From Hegemony? Uncertainties and Constraints in the Early Cold War

The use of the word hegemony in relation to the United States has now become a commonplace of the analysis of international relations. Pundits, such as Charles Krauthammer, talk blithely of a 'unipolar moment'; politicians such as Madeleine Albright spoke of America as the 'indispensable nation'; myriad books outline how the US became a hegemon and might yet decline. The widespread use of the term hegemony – or even, in some contexts, its close cousin 'empire' – are in the public discourse over the place of the US in the international system. Much of this is traceable to the defeat of the Soviet Union and the implosion of the Soviet Empire. The US is generally perceived to have emerged from that particular conflict as the victor, its values victorious, its strategies and tactics seemingly vindicated (Buzan, 2004).

Yet, it was unclear in 1946–47 that the United States would emerge as such a dominant power. Although we now take the preponderance of American power for granted to those 'present at the creation' of the Western alliance – to use Dean Acheson's luminous phrase (1969) – American supremacy did not feel or look so certain. I have written elsewhere of the fragility of the Soviet position at the beginning of the Cold War and have argued that we must understand the military and economic fragility of the Soviet position at the dawn of the Cold War (Cox and Kennedy-Pipe, 2005), but in this chapter I want also to point to the uncertainties and anxieties of the US as it emerged onto a global stage (Gaddis, 1972). Understanding the sources of, and the character of, the anxieties and fears that concerned the United States in this period goes a long way to explain the policies Washington adopted in a crucial period of the Cold War (roughly 1946–53) and that in turn (I want to suggest later) can help us assess the strengths and weaknesses of the American position now.

This chapter, then, is concerned with the policies that the US pursued in this period to seek to buttress its position vis-à-vis the Soviet Union – and, of course, vice versa – in each case to cement the group of allies that had gradually been clustering around them.

The Marshall Plan

The first policy I want to address is the one that is most associated with the early days of the Cold War, the Marshall Plan. Announced on 5 June 1947, in the US Secretary of State General George C. Marshall's speech to the graduating class at Harvard University, the plan had been in preparation for some time. The appalling economic and social conditions of many countries in Europe after the war very quickly concerned many policy-makers in Washington, both on humanitarian grounds (William Clayton, in a report to the President before the plan was announced, pointed out that in Europe several million people were slowly starving to death) and geopolitical ones – to prevent European countries being swallowed up into a Communist alliance. Though named for Marshall, it was really the work of more junior officials, especially Clayton, George Kennan and Dean Acheson.

Before discussing the Marshall plan in any detail, however, it might be worth pausing for a moment to discuss some wider aspects of the global political economy that impacted on the emergent Cold War. The crisis of the 1930s that, as we have seen, had created the conditions for the outbreak of World War II was as much a crisis of the international economic order as it was of the political order that was congruent with it. And, as we shall see in a moment, Marshall Aid itself recognized the interdependence of the political and the economic. Of course the crisis of the interwar period was in part a reaction to the consequences of World War I. As Mark Mazower has pointed out four years of total war had completely destroyed the monetary foundations of nineteenth century bourgeois confidence and economic stability. 'The war had forced countries to suspend the convertibility of their currencies and to abandon those basic principles of Victorian capitalism: the gold standard and free trade. Governments had accumulated enormous debts to finance the war ... [which] had also boosted the power of organized labour and made it harder to keep down wages. It had destroyed old trading networks on the continent itself and it had encouraged new centres of industrial and agricultural production outside Europe'. (Mazower, 1998: 107).

The result was a highly unstable political economy immediately after the war, which led to various disasters such as the hyperinflation in Germany in the early 1920s and, eventually, to the great crash in 1929. The governments of Europe and, to a lesser extent the United States, tried various means to stabilize global markets: but there were serious problems whatever strategy was tried. To return to the pre-war norm – fixed exchange rates, a gold standard, free trade – seemed impossible, though various attempts were made including Britain's eventually ill-fated attempt to return to the gold standard in 1925. The world in which such a set of policies made sense had vanished in the mud of the fields of Flanders. Yet alternatives proved difficult. Attempts to institutionalize monetary cooperation – for example the Kellogg–Briand pact and the various manifestations of the League of Nations financial committee – were at best partial successes and stored up more often than not trouble for the future. There were also structural problems that had been established by the Versailles Peace Settlement, most problematic of all, the huge reparations bill that Germany had been saddled with.

Much of this had been foreseen, of course, in perhaps the most famous economic/political tract of that (or any other) age: Keynes's *Economic Consequences of the Peace*. This small book, as Keynes biographer has said, was written 'with the voice of an angel and with the knowledge of an expert' (Skidelsky, 1992: 3). Keynes asked the fundamental question which the economic dislocations of World War I raised and which were to echo throughout the 1920s and 1930s into the post- World War II world: were the economic assumptions and structures of the old, pre-war world adequate to the task of dealing with the changed circumstances of the twentieth century. Keynes's answer was a resounding negative, though it was

18 years before he produced his own version of how to organize a liberal capitalist economy in the General Theory. Yet elements of what came to be seen as the 'Keynesian synthesis' were apparent even before the publication of his great book, for example, in his influence on the 'New Dealers' around Roosevelt in the early 1930s. After the publication of the General Theory in 1937, Keynes's influence grew still further and it is worth noting that he was a central figure in the economic planning for the post-World War II settlement (he was the originator of, amongst other things, the International Monetary Fund and the World Bank) and was a friend of many of those engaged in the Marshall plan, especially Dean Acheson.

It is not part of the argument of this book to outline the specifics of Keynes's approach to the global economy but a few points are, perhaps, worth emphasizing. First, Keynes's approach was designed to save liberal capitalism both from itself and from the threat posed by a Soviet Communism that, in the 1920s and 1930s, seemed to many to be far more successful economically than its capitalist enemies. To do this, however, Keynes rejected many of the shibboleths of nineteenth-century economics and insisted on the positive role of regulation and government intervention. He was explicit, in other words, that politics and economics were intermingled. This was very much the approach that was also visible in the Marshall Plan. Second, Keynes's view emphasized that institutional cooperation and multilateral vehicles for such cooperation were likely to be central to any successful international monetary order. This was what the Bretton Woods conference (which Keynes attended as senior British representative) paved the way for and was how the US and its allies saw the emergent global monetary order after the war. Given the assumptions on which it rested, a power like the Soviet Union was inevitably going to be outside it, though this did not mean that, in some contexts, the Soviet Union could not be treated as a partner in the global economy and, indeed, it was so treated.

In other words, the overall impact of the financial aspects of the interwar crisis was to bring about the creation of what the IR scholar John Ruggie has called 'embedded liberalism' in the global order after 1945. It was this to which Marshall Aid helped to give strength and in doing so both helped the narrowly focussed aims of stabilizing the international economy and also effectively securing

Western Europe from any real chance of a Communist takeover from within.

In the months immediately after the Marshall Plan was announced, however, economic conditions did not rapidly improve throughout Europe. The British underwent a gold drain, production fell in Germany and, oddly from the standpoint of a now very prosperous Western Europe, there were real fears of a drought and food shortages. Once again it appeared that the Communist parties of Italy and France might take advantage and seize political power. Even so scholars are correct to point to the difficulties faced by Truman in turning his country to this task. Therefore, the advent of Marshall Aid and its deployment into Western Europe was not a forgone conclusion (Hogan, 1987; Truman, 1956: 176–80). President Truman struggled to convince the Republican majorities in the Senate and House to pass the requisite legislation allowing for Marshall Aid. In November 1947, Truman asked a special session of Congress to approve emergency legislation of some $600 million; the alternative he claimed was a Communist Europe.

While Congress deliberated, there were pressing issues for Truman and his officials as they surveyed the post-war world. Not the least of these was the political future of Greece, of Italy and of France. While hesitant even to think about committing US troops into these countries to shore up democracy, there was no doubt that the Communist parties posed a threat to the political stability of each state. It was for Truman imperative that the Communist appeal to those weary of war and poverty be countered by the activation of American loans and of course the opening of these markets for American goods. Here, the arguments made by revisionist historians over the nature of Marshall Aid are in large part correct – there were compelling reasons for Truman to see US prosperity as linked to the recovery of European and Asian economies. Key sectors of American industry and the economic base such as the car and steel industries and wheat depended upon the export of goods to these regions. The protection of West European states was therefore linked to American economic health. This argument was deployed to persuade corporate America, politicians and the public that Marshall Aid would help defeat Communism, but would also ensure prosperity at home (Small, 1996: 86–97).

Stalin surveyed the global scene with no more certainty than Truman. There is no doubt that the British, the French and any number of nations needed American dollars for post-war reconstruction – so too did the Russians. In addition to the general problems of economic reconstruction after the massive war effort the country was beset with woes. In 1946, for example, the Soviet Union suffered a drought causing a shortage in grain. The supplies of food under the arrangements of Lend-Lease, which had fed a third of the population, had been stopped abruptly in 1945 and there were few supplies from the United Nations Relief and Rehabilitation Administration (UNRRA). The Soviet authorities responded to the crisis by raising food prices, reducing the quality of bread and arresting those desperate enough to steal food (Zubkova, 1998). It is estimated that some two million people actually starved to death during the crisis.

None of this was unknown to the Americans. In a memorandum dated 27 March 1947, the State Department official John Hickerson compared the economic situation pertaining to the USSR as similar to the disastrous year of 1933. He argued that 'it seems clear that the Politburo desires to avoid major political developments that might lead to a showdown'. This, he concluded, 'was largely due to the weakness of the internal situation' (Foreign Relations of the United States, 1947, vol. 4 [1972]: 515–17, 535, 544). In addition to the agricultural and climate problems of 1946 the Soviet leadership also faced the challenge of the demobilization of quite literally millions of war veterans all of whom required employment, housing and food. It is not surprising therefore that the Soviet authorities should have exhibited some interest in US economic aid. When the Marshall Plan was initially announced it was at least in theory available to all the states of Europe (Deighton, 1990), although it is hard to see how a Congress sceptical of the scheme would ever have accepted legislation that provided for millions of American dollars to be given to Communist states. Yet the initiative was problematic for the Soviet elite. Despite the prevailing view, driven by a Marxist–Leninist critique, that inevitably capitalism would enter a period of crisis – in 1947 – the Americans were constructing a powerful economic bloc right on the edge of the Soviet Union. Stalin, as it turned out, could do little to prohibit such a development.

Yet this is the peculiar feature of Soviet politics in this period. Despite the increasing antagonisms between Washington and

Moscow over politics in Europe and Asia, the Red dictator still sought some compromise with the United States and did seek inclusion or at least negotiation over the Marshall Plan.

Initially Minister for Foreign Affairs Vyacheslav Molotov had advised the Central Committee that participation in the plan might be positive not just for the USSR but for the Czechs and Poles. It seems that the scheme was regarded in the same way as the Lend-Lease arrangements which had been beneficial during the years of war with Germany. The Soviet economist Eugene Varga, when asked to provide an analysis of the Marshall Plan, argued that it might be of benefit for the US to offer loans to the USSR as it would offer a way for the Americans to solve what he saw as their post-war problems of over-production. Varga warned therefore that the plan might simply facilitate a US dominance of Europe.

The Marshall Plan was clearly the subject of much debate within Soviet policy circles. Stalin anyway ordered Molotov to attend the conference on the Marshall Plan. As became evident at the meeting which was held in Paris at the beginning of July 1947, the terms (or strings from a Soviet view) on which Marshall Aid was to be granted were clearly unacceptable.

Most worrying of all was that the Russians learnt that the British and the Americans were quietly negotiating the terms on how to allow the Western zones of Germany into the plan and how to keep the Russians out of it. Stalin recalled his delegation from Paris and compelled the withdrawal of the Czechs from discussion. Perhaps what the Americans had planned all along came true – the Russians effectively ruled themselves right out of loans. Once Molotov had learnt the full details of the loans there was no option but to return to a form of self-sufficiency and isolationism (Zubok and Pleshakov, 1996: 104–8). Stalin himself had to find other strategies for countering the emergent Western bloc. For him the challenge was made more urgent by the fact that much of the planning for the Western bloc centred on a reinvigorated West German state under-written by American power.

The Soviet Response

Stalin's aim became one of securing an emergent Soviet bloc while still meddling with and attempting to restrain American ambitions.

Just as George Kennan had foreseen, the Soviet leader tried to ensure control in his own sphere (Kennan, 1947). In September 1947, the Comintern (Communist International) was re-established and renamed the Cominform. At its first meeting attended by representatives of the East European Communist Parties, Andrei Zhdanov (Stalin's chief of ideology) declared that there were two blocs operating in international relations – two hostile 'camps' – on the one hand the imperialists and on the other the anti-imperialists and anti-fascists.

Stalin hoped at least in part to establish discipline among and control over the Communist parties – most notably over Josip Broz Tito, the Yugoslav leader, and to ensure the adherence of the Czechs to Moscow's dictate. Some scholars have centred their analysis of this meeting on the attempts by the Kremlin to subdue Tito's ambitions and what were his tendencies towards unilateralist dogma (Roberts, 1994). Marshal Tito was of particular concern and had far greater room for manoeuvre than many of the other Communist leaders, as it had been his efforts and those of the partisans which had finally rid Yugoslavia of the Germans. The Red Army was not, as it had been throughout much of the rest of Eastern and Central Europe, the liberator of Yugoslavia; hence Tito did not depend on Soviet power for his position as leader. Tito's reluctance to bow to Soviet pressure marked out for Stalin a worrying trend towards independence and a distinct Yugoslav form of Communist endeavour. Stalin might have famously remarked that he could shake his little finger and there will be 'no more Tito', but with American aid the Yugoslav country remained free of Soviet dominance (Gaddis, 2005: 33).

It was really in this period that Europe was divided into the two competing blocs that became the staple image of the Cold War. In this sense at least the announcement and operation of Marshall Aid and the Soviet response did cement the division of the continent. One part of this story is the manner in which ordinary people suffered under Communist rule. For those who dared to oppose Communism within Eastern and Central Europe there were severe penalties. As Stalin exerted control, opposition leaders such as Nikola Petkov in Bulgaria were executed, while in Hungary the Democrats were forced out of national politics. Most dramatically of all, in Czechoslovakia, democracy in the form of liberal and centre parties was crushed by the Soviet-inspired coup of February 1948.

Two weeks after the coup had taken place the body of the much respected Foreign Minister Jan Masaryk was found in a courtyard in Prague after a fall from a balcony. Did he jump or was he pushed? This became a question that was almost impossible to answer at the time but his death symbolized the end of democracy for the Czech people. The coup caused outrage throughout the West, part of which was a feeling of guilt as Prague had been sacrificed to Hitler only ten years before at Munich (Armitage, 1982: 223–6).

These events signalled for many Americans and Europeans the futility of dealing with Stalin. More crucially, with a Soviet threat of multiple dimensions looming, the weaker states of Europe had to be bolstered not just politically but also militarily. For the Americans this meant a historic commitment to a permanent stationing of troops in Western Europe and a pledge to underwrite the military security of those states. Harry Truman, after the coup in Prague, asked for and received additional military spending from Congress. He was on this occasion supported by the Republicans. What Melvyn Leffler has called 'a Cold War consensus' emerged, uniting some rather strange bedfellows across the spectrum of the politics of the United States (Leffler, 1992, 1994).

For Stalin, Western moves in 1947 and 1948 meant that his postwar strategies had only half worked. There was, it was true, Soviet control of much of the periphery of Russia. Poland was subdued and Soviet power was recognized within its sphere. Yet the German question had not been resolved to his satisfaction and it appeared that the Western zones of that country would in fact be reorganized into an anti-Communist hub. He had also failed to secure the much needed economic assistance.

Stalin's response to the building of the American alliance was somewhat clumsy and as it turned out counter-productive. The Soviet leadership demanded discussion of the demilitarization and denazification of Germany, asked for participation in control of the Ruhr area and sought a unified German currency to avert the introduction of a separate currency in the Western zones. On 13 February 1948, a note to the Western powers stated that the Soviet government had learnt from the capitalist press (Stalin it seems took Western newspapers seriously (Montefiore, 2003)) of the intention to call a conference in London to consider key issues affecting the Western zones such as the control of the Ruhr area and reparations. According to Moscow these moves constituted a violation of the Potsdam agreements. Despite the objections, the conference went ahead in January. On the last day of March 1948 the Soviet commander in Berlin announced new rules for passage by road and river/canal routes into the city. Stalin attempted to exert pressure in Berlin as he tried to reopen discussion over the future of Germany (Narinskii, 1996).

Berlin – the First Crisis

At the end of World War II Berlin had been divided into four zones. Stalin controlled the land routes into the city and Western access into their zones. Many years ago, when studying the Berlin crisis for the first time, I was fairly confident that Stalin was motivated on this occasion by an attempt to retard the consolidation of the Western zones: that his actions were primarily defensive (Kennedy-Pipe, 1995). But given what we 'now know' about Stalin it is important to concede that he may also have wanted something more than to spoil Western plans. This was actually to force the Western Allies out of the occupation of Berlin, again consolidating Soviet control.

However, in a brilliant and unexpected move, rather than attempt to force a passage along the roads, the Americans opted for an airlift of supplies into the Western sectors of the city. President Truman facing election would not, indeed could not, countenance defeat on this issue. There were principles at stake, but also to back down would have handed Truman's opponents – and there were many – a political gift. Truman did win the battle of Berlin (Mann, 2002). (Truman's handling of these types of crises has made him a role model, in the eyes of some political commentators, for George W. Bush.) There were no attempts by Soviet personnel to interfere with the airlift (this had worried American commanders) and there was little hope of dissuading the Americans from their purpose which was to form a West German government. This goal was, after the blockade, one which found popularity with those in Berlin and the Western zones of Germany more broadly. It also signalled for those in Western Europe the determination of the Americans to act in the face of Communist aggression.

In sharp contrast to the gap between the diplomacy of what Donald Rumsfeld disdainfully termed the 'Old Europe' at the height of President George W. Bush's unilateralism in the 2000s, in

1948 Truman's actions and views were buoyed by the desire of many Western Europeans to share in a vision of a new world order based on US principles. It was the Western Europeans who demanded that the US accept an enduring military commitment to the continent and it was a British idea which envisaged the creation of the North Atlantic Treaty Organization (NATO). For the United States this was a historic commitment marking the first such enduring commitment since the alliance with France in 1778. By the time that Stalin finally saw that there was little virtue in continuing the blockade the arrangements had been made for the establishment of the North Atlantic Treaty Alliance. This treaty recognized a permanent military duty by Washington to act in protection of Western Europe and for the creation of the Federal Republic of Germany (Deighton, 1990; Harper, 1996; Kagan, 2003).

The Origins of the Cold War: Beyond Europe

Yet this story is not and should not just be about Europe (Dukes, 1998). The Cold War and the contest between Washington and Moscow had a much wider remit. Japan, like Germany, posed some very specific challenges. No one seriously believed that Stalin would attempt to interfere or instigate a coup in Japan but its future, after occupation, was a central issue. Like Germany, Japan had to be tied firmly into US alliance structures, thus ensuring a permanent political and economic ally for Washington in East Asia.

To American minds, despite their criticisms of European imperialism, there was no doubt that control of Asia was tied to the ability of the 'old' European powers to retain their influence in the region. Somewhat ironically, given the stated American preference for the abandonment of British, French and Dutch possessions, in the war with Stalin and the forces of Communism it was now imperative that London and Paris should not be rapidly ejected from their imperial domains. The end of World War II had seen a trend towards decolonization and the removal of the European powers from former colonial domains. Most worrying was Ho Chi Minh in Indo-China who had launched a nationalist assault on French imperial power within the region. The Americans supported the French not least because of the need to maintain French markets in Indo-China. The struggle of France, aided by the US, to defeat Vietnamese

Communist/nationalist forces would have long and dramatic consequences (Leffler, 1994: 88–90). In the late 1940s, however, American officials could not possibly foresee the tragedy that lay in wait.

It was not however just the French and their plight in South-East Asia that gave cause for concern. The British too were struggling in their colonies and would continue to do so over the coming decades. From Malaya, through Kenya, Aden and the Persian Gulf, British forces were deployed to counter insurgents. While it is true that the British did withdraw from empire there were many bloody campaigns along the way. It is hardly saying 'I told you so', to suggest that, in the context of the contemporary attempts to defeat an ongoing insurgency, these stories of counter-insurgency should be keenly studied by the Americans. But more of this in Chapter 7.

For Harry Truman, more ominously and urgently was the news that in August 1949 the Soviet Union had succeeded, following tests at Chelyabinsk-40 in Siberia, in detonating an atomic device in the deserts of Kazakhstan. Initially Truman could not believe that the news was true and that 'those Asiatics' had managed to build a device such as the atomic bomb (Herschberg and Conant, 1993, 2003; Offner, 1999). For many Americans this news, which was publicly announced by Truman (and not the Kremlin which merely confirmed the news), heralded a new age of vulnerability and a loss of the strategic advantage which had accrued hitherto to the only possessor of nuclear arms.

While perhaps never enunciated, there is little doubt that in the stand-offs over Iran in 1946 and in Berlin, the American nuclear arsenal worked to their favour albeit in the background. For the Americans there was the very real fear that the Russians might yet succeed in completing work on a hydrogen capability first. In 1947, scientists at the Soviet Institute of Chemical Physics did indeed accelerate the research into thermonuclear weapons. It was the Soviet creation of a hydrogen bomb in August 1953, one year after American success in this area, that really marked its arrival as a superpower at least in nuclear terms. It perhaps also cemented the Soviet habit of emphasizing resource investment into weaponry at the expense of the health of the people or indeed the environment (Holloway, 1994; Potter and Kearner, 1988). This legacy had long consequences for the country and was publicly exposed with the Chernobyl disaster of 1986.

Truman considered a range of options in response to developments on the Soviet side. The so-called arms race began with the decision to increase rapidly the production of atomic bombs (De Groot, 2004). In addition, the decision was taken to build a hydrogen bomb and increase conventional options. This latter course was actually the most controversial. Not least was the sheer cost of maintaining armies, navies and airpower at the levels required to meet a Soviet threat globally. Yet somehow Truman needed to be able to expand defence spending to meet the multiple threats from Communism.

Indeed, from the perspective of Washington, Soviet atomic success had emboldened it. Stalin had recognized Ho Chi Minh in Indo-China (but not until 30 January 1950, 12 days after Mao) and, worse, in 1949 Mao seized power in mainland China, created the People's Republic and defeated Chiang Kai-shek the nationalist leader. The nationalists were ousted and settled in Taiwan. Mao agreed with Moscow a treaty of mutual assistance. We now know of course the labyrinth of suspicion which would later bedevil Sino-Soviet relations but Mao, worryingly for Washington, was in this period a dedicated follower of Stalin and, unlike Tito, had little trouble in adhering to Moscow. Mao too did not forget that the Americans had favoured the nationalists during his long struggle and was convinced that Truman would sponsor some form of invasion to replace Communism with Chiang Kai-shek's national-ists. Mao's adherence to Moscow helped convince many in Washington that what they were witnessing was actually the growth of a monolithic form of ideology driven by Stalin. The subsequent treaty of the two, agreed while Mao visited Moscow in December 1949, pledged that they would aid each other in the face of an attack (Zhang, 2000).

The Enemies within

How then for the Americans to explain such a turn of events? While in Western Europe much had been accomplished with the creation of NATO, the Marshall Plan and the renegade actions of Tito, all of which pointed to a positive chain of events, the situation in Asia was bleaker. How could the Communists control the most populous state in the world? For some in the United States there had to be a darker theory of Communist successes. One explanation was not that the Communists had achieved all of this through their own energy and creativity but through cheating. Here we see the perpetual fear of spying and internal corruption which bedevilled American as well as totalitarian politics during the Cold War.

By 1947, Truman had instigated a system of loyalty checks on those employed within his own administration and Alger Hiss who had worked in the State Department was actually convicted of perjury in 1950 for having denied under oath that he had been in the pay of the Soviet Union. Also in 1950 the British government admitted that a German born scientist but British citizen – Klaus Fuchs – had confessed to having spied for the Soviet Union while working on the Manhattan project. This, surely, helped explain the rapid rise of Soviet geostrategic strength and its attainment of the atomic bomb in such a short space of time. These allegations of treason in high and low places were made most famously by Senator Joseph McCarthy, a Republican from Wisconsin. From his initial claims made in February 1950 he persistently argued that traitors, home grown traitors particularly in the State Department, were allowing the Communist movement to grow and he argued that Truman had done little to stop this development.

However inflated these claims might seem in hindsight, at the time they caused something of a sensation and allowed many to be accused of Communist sympathies. The degree of anti-Communist sentiment at this time is perhaps best brought out by looking at films of the early Cold War period such as *I Married a Communist* (1949), *The Whip Hand* (1951) and *My Son John* (1953). McCarthy (who had been voted the worst member of the Senate in a poll of Washington correspondents) assailed Dean Acheson for allowing Communists within the State Department to have abetted Mao in his victory in China. So bitter were these attacks that the columnist Walter Lippmann wrote that 'No American official who has represented his government abroad in great affairs, not even Wilson in 1918, has ever been so gravely injured at home' (Small, 1996: 93).

The suspicion of those regarded as unpatriotic and their denunciation within the United States was paralleled within the Soviet Union as fears grew that it too might be threatened by the ideology of the other side and that anti-Communist sentiment might spill back into the country. Citizens were banned from contact with foreigners, censorship was increased and travel abroad was restricted. Literature regarded as subversive was rubbished. *Pravda* newspaper, for example, attacked children's literature regarded as unhealthy and capable of poisoning 'our' youth. Music, too, had to be patriotic with jazz leaders arrested and saxophones confiscated as the symbols of a decadent society, such as that of the United States. Historians had to compromise the search for truth and upheld the Stalinist presentation of the regime. Certain figures were naturally revered – men such as Peter the Great – and, somewhat ironically given the monarchical nature of Peter, all such appreciations had to be overlaid with Marxism–Leninism. As John Keep has argued, the cult of the personality was mixed without criticism with the commitment to a Marxist–Leninist emphasis on the virtues of class struggle (Keep, 1996). It is rather an amusing feature of this dark period that for some in Russia the war experience had led to contact not just with jazz but with American films of the Hollywood variety: US films and records confiscated in Germany and taken back to Russia included those of John Wayne in his many action roles and Johnny Weissmuller as Tarzan (Evtuhov et al., 2004).

In a more sombre vein, many of those of the Jewish faith were singled out as 'un-Russian' as they were inclined to look outside Russia for a homeland and culture. Jews were replaced in employment by non-Jews and even though the Soviet authorities endorsed the founding of the State of Israel in 1948 (it was welcomed as weakening British and therefore Western power in the Middle East) when literally crowds of Jews greeted the new Israeli envoy Golda Meyerson in Moscow, their actions were seen as disloyal (Evtuhov et al., 2004: ch. 37; Vaksberg, 1994).

'Police Action' in Korea

The sense of crisis in the United States deepened with events in Asia. The onset of the Korean War in the spring of 1950 was testament to Communist boldness, at least for many Americans. Korea had, at the end of the war, been divided along the 38th parallel but with the expectation that a unified Korean government would be emplaced and that the occupation forces of both East and West would be withdrawn. The Soviet Army inhabited the north and American forces the south. While troops were withdrawn harmoniously enough from 1948 there was no consensus on what form of government should rule. The US though supported the Republic of

Korea after elections sanctioned by the newly formed United Nations while Moscow continued to sponsor the north in which no elections were held! Both sides staked the claim to legitimacy and threats were made to invade the other half of the peninsula. It does seem that the Truman administration had little real interest in the peninsula and rather was concentrating upon the defence of Japan, the Philippines and Okinawa. Indeed what officials feared was that the ambitions of the South Korean leader, Syngman Rhee, might actually lead them into a war with the north that they simply did not want.

It was not just in the south though that an ambitious leader sought the acquiescence of a great power to unite the country. Kim Il-sung in the north spent much time trying to persuade Stalin of the virtue of sponsoring an invasion of the south. In 1950, he finally succeeded in persuading the Soviet leader that this could be a mission without risk. After all the Americans had shown little interest in this peninsula with even Secretary of State Dean Acheson famously declaring that the 'defensive perimeter' did not extend to Korea. (To be strictly fair to Acheson he did also point out in the same speech that 'initial reliance must be on the people attacked to resist it and then upon the commitments of the entire civilized world under the charter of the United Nations'. He emphasized that his country did bear a responsibility for Korea in the same way as it did for Japan. This part of the speech though is normally not emphasized (Acheson, 1969; Chace, 1998: ch. 25).)

Kim, regardless of Acheson's view, was confident of a swift victory and Stalin was glad to seize an opportunity in Asia at what appeared to be little cost to himself. Mao could be counted on to provide support for Kim (Volkogonov, 1998: 151–66). Stalin had once again miscalculated American resolve. Just as over Berlin, he misjudged the way in which the invasion would be read by Washington and its allies. The dictator had hoped that the war would split Western opinion and provoke intra-bloc discord. With breathtaking naïvety, or perhaps hope, *Pravda* posed the question: 'Will not the war in Korea lead to the complete disintegration of the Atlantic Alliance?' (*Pravda*, 27 November 1950).

American officials, while not seeing Korea as central to their Asian strategy, read into the invasion some worrying features of Soviet behaviour. One was the disregard for the 38th parallel and the agreement reached over it under the auspices of the United

Nations. The other was the arrogance with which Stalin appeared to be staking a military claim on the peninsula. The response from Washington was rapid. US troops would be committed back onto the peninsula to save the south from Communism and the authority of the UN would be upheld.

Under the command of General Douglas MacArthur UN troops repelled the North Korean forces after a brilliantly executed landing at Inchon near Seoul in the autumn of 1950. MacArthur (despite orders) advanced into North Korea. Such was his success that Stalin began to contemplate defeat and withdrawal. The Communist endeavour was rescued by the actions of the Chinese. Mao had begun moving troops from China across the Yalu River and into North Korea. The Communists struck at MacArthur's armies in the north, which then were forced to retreat.

A question that is raised here is one that becomes a central aspect of the Cold War thereafter: why did the Americans not, even in the face of defeat, take the nuclear option. It would have been militarily possible to use these weapons to stem the Chinese advance – it would even perhaps have been possible to destroy Chinese cities if Mao failed to comply with American demands. The Americans did have nuclear superiority in nuclear arms – by the end of 1950 they had approximately 370 operational atomic bombs which could have been delivered into Korea or parts of China north of the Yalu river. Part of the problem was that of terrain (Gaddis, 2005: 48–9). There were few targets of an industrial, military or political nature to make a definitive strike against. And if China was bombed, the concern was that the war would not stay limited but would broaden out into a direct confrontation between Washington and the Chinese and, behind Mao, Stalin. For America's allies in Western Europe there was also the fear that Stalin could if he chose strike at their countries.

This was perhaps the origin of nuclear 'self-deterrence' for the United States, or what increasingly became seen as the 'nuclear taboo'. These new weapons used once in Asia very recently could no longer be used, not just for practical reasons but also perhaps for moral ones. Truman himself who claims not to have hesitated or lost a night's sleep over the use of such weapons on Japan certainly hesitated this time and refused to use them again. John Lewis Gaddis in his provocative account of the Korean War has argued that had a threat been directed at Western Europe, then nuclear weapons would have been used (Gaddis, 2005: 50–5). Perhaps; but both the Americans and the Russian leadership went to great lengths to try and limit the war after it had begun. Soviet fighter planes were deployed in the war, as were fighters with American pilots. We know now that there were in fact some engagements between the two sides, but neither formally admitted it.

Here, Geoffrey Roberts has made a very good if controversial point – it was not just the Americans who stepped back time and again from allowing the Cold War to escalate: Stalin and his successors too played a role in preserving the post-war peace and ensuring the non-use of nuclear weapons (Roberts, 2006). This is a theme to which I will return when we look at the Cuban Missile Crisis in the next chapter. It is perhaps correct that Stalin more than Truman acted provocatively in the early years of the Cold War, but the air clashes in Korea were perhaps salutary for the Soviet leader. It is even the case that Stalin was prepared to concede a defeat for Communism. Both sides were cautious in the extreme not to provoke the other – nuclear weapons therefore proved sobering for statesmen of whatever political complexion. This is a feature of the nuclear age we might note in our current vexation over dictators and the acquisition of nuclear power. I will return to this in Chapter 7.

Stalin's apparently cavalier green light to Kim had serious consequences for the ageing dictator and those who after his death in 1953 would succeed him. The Americans immediately saw the implications of the Communist attempt to take the peninsula. The National Security Council (NSC), a new body set up in 1947, produced a document – largely at the impetus of the new head of policy planning at the State Department, Paul Nitze. This document, known historically as 'NSC 68', was a confidential review of national security strategies and pointed out that what was needed were the type of capabilities that could respond to Communist aggression wheresoever it should take place. This expansion of capabilities was not the only lesson drawn from the onset of the Cold War. Leffler has pointed out that after the outbreak of the Korean War there was a determined effort in Washington to broaden and deepen alliance structures. Thus the Germans, so recently an enemy, were rehabilitated; the Europeans were rearmed; and Turkey was brought into the NATO alliance. A final peace treaty was negotiated with Japan and it too became important to the defence effort against Communism. Stalin's successors as we will see were quick to end the war in 1953 and seek stalemate not victory. As John Mueller (1995) has argued, for the Russians, the lessons of the Korean War must have enhanced those of the Second World War. Once again the United States was caught surprised and under armed, once again it rushed hastily into action, once again it soon applied itself in a forceful way to combat. If the Korean War was a limited probe of Western resolve, it seems that the Soviets drew the lessons the Truman administration intended. Unlike Germany, Japan and Italy in the 1930s, they were tempted to try no more such probes: there have been no Koreas since Korea (Mueller, 1995: 69).

The policy of containment appears to have worked, while Stalin's strategy of seeking Communist expansion and disrupting the new Western alliance had failed.

An Era of Perpetual Crisis

Truman's foreign policy ambitions brought immense domestic turmoil. Not the least of these was that the draft was put on a permanent basis and a programme for universal military training proposed. This would allow, argued its proponents, the country to establish a broad pool of trained men to be called upon if necessary. The advent of the Cold War demanded a ceaseless readiness to meet emergency after emergency in the international arena. In the discourse established over the new duties the United States should assume in the international arena, new concepts of citizenship and service were demanded – young men should serve and the expense of a permanent military establishment had to be met.

Yet these proposals and ideas were not uncontested. Universal military training did not sit well with some interpretations of the liberal state. Not least some critics of Truman saw the demands made upon the American people as more akin to that of authoritarian states or old world states. There were also concerns that the military establishment would grow into a political establishment that threatened the civilian leadership. This was something even George Washington had argued against in his Farewell Address (Gilbert, 1961). So, for some, Truman's efforts to meet the global obligations of anti-Communism undercut the tradition of the Republic. Worse still, foreign policy, it was argued, was leading domestic politics. Perhaps obligations to the UN, to NATO, to allies abroad should be curtailed (Hogan, 1998). Critics succeeded in modifying what they saw as the more radical proposal for universal military training.

More generally the power of the Presidency was buoyed by the continual crisis in foreign policy. Melvin Small has correctly pointed to the fact that foreign policy or foreign crises that seem to affect the national interest generally rallies the population around the President. Of course, the tragedy of 9/11 has shown us that phenomenon in contemporary times, but Truman could and did use the advent of the Cold War to great effect. In this era a host of new institutions were set up to aid the President, the most notable perhaps being the Central Intelligence Agency (CIA) and the National Security Council. The NSC specifically enhanced the ability and reach of the President to make foreign policy (Nelson, 1985). Truman for example bypassed Congress in his eagerness to engage in the Korean War (Herschberg and Conant, 1993: 737). He labelled it a 'police action' despite the huge cost in American lives and the fact that this 'police action' lasted some three years. As Melvin Small (1996: 93) has noted it was here that the way was paved for further presidential wars in South-East Asia and elsewhere. The centrality of the office of President to the making of foreign policy was a trend that Truman himself endorsed as preferable to decision-making over war laying with the military (Hogan, 1998: 251).

There was little question that Stalin would have agreed with this assessment. He had controlled and manipulated the making of foreign policy without the impediments of either a restless bureaucracy or a democratic system. He unlike Truman was free of accountability to a government or a people – although some scholars have pointed to the complexity of Kremlin politics and intrigue as promoting factional struggles over Soviet policy-making (D'Agostino, 1988).

As we have seen there is little doubt that in the early years of the Cold War the American President struggled to reconcile the competing visions of global politics in Washington. Truman succeeded in his foreign policy partly because of the fear of Communism posed by the Soviet vision but also partly because he was aided time and again by the misreading of international politics by Stalin. The Soviet dictator did seek cooperation with the United States after the war. From his desire for economic aid through the Marshall Plan and his backtracking in the Iranian crisis, he demonstrated a hope for a better relationship than the one which evolved through the years of crisis. Yet Stalin got the United States quite wrong. His view that he could promote Communism through the international Communist movement, through subordinates as unappealing as Palmiro Togliatti in Italy, through the encouragement of proxies such as Kim, and through the subjugation of Eastern and Central Europe, without penalty or opposition, was curious.

The US was initially 'fragile' in terms of its commitment to Western Europe and uncertain over what the broader post-war role should be in terms of alliance politics with that region (Adler, 1957). But Stalin's consolidation and expansion of his empire and his nuclear ambitions signalled to policy elites in Washington competition not collaboration. Ideology of the Communist kind and the threat to the ideas and ideals of the American Republic which it posed were taken seriously by Washington. We are now used to the idea that a radical version of Islam might undercut democracy; and we worry about the symbols of Islam and its attractiveness to our youth here in liberal societies. This is not new – Communism was perceived to pose a similar threat – at least in domestic terms. Here let me make the very obvious point, echoing what we have seen in earlier chapters: ideas matter; and just as Truman reconfigured US politics to meet that perception of threat so we can argue that George W. Bush has configured national security politics to meet the threat from radical Islam. The question, in both cases, was whether the configuration was, in fact, the correct one, or whether it made things worse, not better.

On 5 March 1953 Stalin, paralysed by a stroke, died aged 73. Perhaps his end was hastened by those around him. For both the Soviet Union and international relations generally this was quite literally a stunning event. Dictators do not arrange their succession because as Dmitri Volkogonov (1998) has written, they like to think that they will live for ever. There is little doubt though that the death of this particular dictator had profound consequences for the system over which he had presided for so long, beyond causing an immediate power struggle among his subordinates. There were, as news of his death broke, contradictory reactions: stories of rebellion in prisons, but also tales of genuine grief among ordinary people unable to envisage a country without Stalin. As Martin Amis (2002) has intimated, this seems somewhat extraordinary. Within the USSR, throughout the quarter-century of his rule, Stalin was an extremely popular leader. 'It is something of a humiliation to commit that sentence to paper, but there is no avoiding it.'

The process of easing the absolute conditions of the Soviet system, both at a national and international level, would begin in earnest under his successors. But American policy elites remained unconvinced that the Communist threat had receded in any way at all. Dictatorship did not, for Americans, die with perhaps the greatest dictator of them all. Cold War politics had become institutionalized, and to break down the structures would take more than the death of one man.

Reflections

In the case of the Cold War we can see, I think, the shadows of the earlier crises discussed in Chapters 2 and 3 mirrored in the events of the late 1940s and early 1950s. There is the same blend of ideological and geopolitical rivalry, the same perceptions of threat and attempts to secure against it. Yet in the 1940s and early 1950s two things changed which, I suggest, gave the Cold War the particular shape it had and was largely to retain until the late 1980s.

The first was the gradually emerging bipolar structure of the international system. As we saw in the last chapter, bipolarity heightened the perception of threat – and also the ideological conflict that was inherent in the Soviet commitment to revolution – but it perhaps might also be said, in the context of the analysis offered above of the emerging nuclear stand-off, that bipolarity with nuclear weapons placed a high premium on relatively cautious risk-averse behaviour, as was visible in the behaviour of both the United States and the Soviet Union during the Korean War (and as would be visible, as we shall see, at the moment of maximum crisis for the Cold War system, in the Cuban crisis of 1962). This curious mixture of heightened sense of threat with relatively cautious actual behaviour remained a hallmark of the system.

The second feature of the 1940s and the early 1950s was the global character of the confrontation. Again, there are echoes of those earlier conflicts – World War II was obviously a genuinely global war in a way that, for example, World War I was not – but also there is something very new, both for the United States and the Soviet Union as states and actors, and for the international system itself. Historians have remarked upon the fact that it is precisely in the period that the Cold War coalesced that the sense of the globe as 'one world' becomes a real presence in popular and elite opinion. One historian who has drawn attention to this, David Reynolds (2000), also points out that the 1940 US presidential candidate Wendell Willkie's *One World*, when it was published in 1943, was one of the biggest non-fiction sellers in publishing history. One could point to many other indications of a similar recognition of the 'global' character of political life during and after the war, for example the astonishing reputation achieved by Arnold Toynbee's massive *A Study of History* after the original publication of the last four volumes in the 1950s.

The significance of this was perhaps best pointed out by someone who was both a historian and an international relations theorist, Martin Wight. In the essays that make up one of his most enduring contributions to international relations, Wight (1977) distinguished between different kinds of systems, for example between states systems proper and what he termed 'suzerain' systems (such as China in the classical period) and also, and especially, between what he termed 'open' systems and 'closed' systems (open ones as 'pressured by' other, outside systems; closed ones as free of outside systemic pressures). But, he suggests, we only have one example of closed systems: the modern system roughly from 1941, when the only units that can be added to the system come from territory already in the system in one form or another.

The 'closed' character of the post-1945 system and its increasingly recognized global character gave to the Cold War a particular shape that in certain respects, as we shall see, survive its demise in the early 1990s. But the manner in which the Cold War habituated itself to these two conditions became a hallmark of the Cold War system, and thus of the world that was to grow out of it. The form it took in the period of the 'high Cold War' will be the subject of the next chapter.

5
The Shape of the Cold War

Certainly by the time of his death in March 1953, Stalin had left his successors a complex legacy. On the one hand, there were undoubted achievements: the extension of Soviet frontiers into East and Central Europe and the defeat and subjection of Germany. In addition to this, the victory of Mao in China gave at least a veneer to the idea of a legacy of Communist strength. Yet, the Stalinist legacy was not all that it seemed to be. Soviet successes, such as they were, had been achieved at costs which would return to haunt the men in the Kremlin. The occupation of the states of Eastern and Central Europe had resulted in a forcible and coherent American response and, as we will see within the bloc itself, occupation inspired unruly subjects to rebel.

In contrast, the Marshall Plan and the creation of NATO had signalled coherence in the West. Both initiatives had been roundly welcomed and in some respects actually driven by the peoples of Western Europe. Worse still from a Soviet perspective was that the division of Germany had been at the hub of the reinvigoration of the Western bloc and evidenced an obvious superiority of living standards and political legitimacy in the Western as opposed to the Eastern zones. The green light given to Kim Il-sung to invade South Korea had caused the West to redouble its rearmament efforts and had led to NSC 68. The actual conduct of the Korean War had meant that Mao and Chinese forces had had to 'dig' the Soviet Union out of the Korean quagmire. It was also the case that with the forcible Western response to that Communist 'probe' in Asia, ideological competition had spread out of the European arena into an Asian Cold War.

By the mid 1950s, then, the Cold War had begun to take the shape that future generations would see as its 'natural' form. This world-view took hold remarkably quickly and proved extremely hard to dislodge. Gaddis tells a story of how, even in the mid 1980s, he attended a seminar in Washington hosted by government officials at which he suggested that they might think about what to do if and when the Cold War ended. 'We don't expect it to end', was the reply, made a mere few years before it actually did (Gaddis, 1994).

In this chapter I want to illustrate in more detail the character of that shape and indicate also how some of the more important aspects of the international politics of the 1950s and early 1960s refined and in some cases solidified it. In particular I will focus on the ideational and geopolitical realties within Europe (both West and East), the implications of the decay of the Soviet-Chinese alliance, the role of nuclear weapons and, especially, the impact of the Cuban Missile Crisis. All of these are important, I think, if we want to grasp the shape, the 'inner logic', that the Cold War had developed and, as we shall see in Chapter 7, all of them are important for understanding the resonance of the early Cold War with our own times. First, however, I need to say something about the position both superpowers found themselves in during the mid 1950s.

Mirror Images?

At the same time as the Western defence effort was maturing the Soviet Union was faced with a series of challenges. Most notable was the challenge of providing increasing levels of economic prosperity. There was a shortage of consumer goods, something that Soviet citizens had learnt to live with since the War; but there was growing disquiet not just with the range of goods but also the quality of what could be purchased. A general attempt to 'release' the political and economic system from its Stalinist heritage was attempted but this too, as we will see, had consequences not just in Soviet Russia but throughout East and Central Europe. Soviet lead-ers continued to worry that political opposition in the Eastern bloc might result in a 'spill-over' effect back into the USSR itself. Stalin's Communist allies, whether in the Eastern bloc, China, or Western Europe, gave cause for doubt that the adherence to Stalin's Kremlin would remain without the dictator. Not least, it was unclear to those in the West after March 1953 with whom power actually resided. Individuals within the Soviet leadership jostled for position in a leadership competition that was not really resolved until 1956–57, when the former mineworker from Donbass, Nikita Khrushchev, emerged clearly as leader. That decision proved fateful in a number of ways. The extent to which an individual can impact upon the making of foreign policy is often debated, but certainly the story of Soviet foreign policy after 1955 is to a great extent that of Khrushchev's attempts to bring the USSR to an equivalent status with the United States, while at the same time struggling to control rebellious forces and his own 'clownish behaviour' (Gaddis, 2005).

Despite these shifts within the Communist world, as Melvyn Leffler has argued, the global strategy of the United States continued regardless. This is odd, as part of what drove the origins of the Cold War from an American point of view was the intransigence of Stalin, the struggle over the limits of Stalinist power abroad and, most importantly, a focus on the dictator himself. Remember John Lewis Gaddis's point that it was impossible to imagine the Cold War not emerging while Stalin was in charge. Therefore, it is perhaps somewhat puzzling that a change in leadership in Moscow, however hazy the details might have been to those in Washington and the attempts in Moscow to alter Russian foreign policy, did not bring about a transformation in US policy.

Why was this?

Partly it can be explained by the fact that President Eisenhower and those around him took Soviet talk of 'peace' or offers of negotiation as simply a desire to cause disruption between the Western powers and to ferment disquiet within the NATO alliance. It was, from an American point of view, important to avoid this type of trouble and to protect the core industrial/resource areas of Western Europe, Japan and the Middle East. These were areas which remained crucial to the health of the US economy. Eisenhower could see little evidence that there had been genuine change in Soviet behaviour and the struggle was, to his mind, to be maintained against yet further expansion of Soviet/Communist power. His strategy therefore remained fairly constant even after the death of the dictator. Military adventures such as that of Korea were to be avoided through the use of a nuclear threat if necessary and covert action taken to protect American interests in those areas weakened by the forces of decolonization. So, for example, in Iran in 1953, the Americans with the British worked to overthrow the nationalist leader Mohammed Mussadeq in so-called Operation Ajax. The rationale was that Mussadeq held dangerous socialist views and that his nationalization of the oil industry, which had previously been operated by the Anglo-Iranian Oil Company, threatened Western oil interests (Ansari, 2006). Operation Ajax was the first time that the CIA had been involved in a plot to overthrow a democratically elected government; and this was followed by similar action in Guatemala a year later.

Counterfactual history is fascinating and it is perhaps timely and rather fashionable to reflect on what shape global politics might have taken if a change on the Soviet side, say over a new European framework, had been taken seriously by the White House, as some have urged – for example Walter Lippmann in his 'Today and Tomorrow' columns (Steel, 1980). Is it possible to imagine NATO in the 1950s admitting a Communist power, in which Russian power was co-opted rather than isolated? (More controversially is it possible to imagine an American response to the Soviet intervention in Hungary as leading to a transformation in Kremlin politics and thus freeing the peoples of Hungary some thirty years earlier?) Well, we can try to imagine these things but there were very good reasons, as we will go on to see, why the Americans did not change Cold War tack. What this chapter aims to demonstrate is that by the mid 1950s the Cold War had taken on a clear and rather static framework. The Americans had already reached certain conclusions about the needs of the Western alliance and the nature of Communism. As we saw in the last chapter the US bureaucracy and economy had been reconfigured to fight a Cold War; and a Cold War mentality pervaded many levels of US politics and culture. Diplomacy and foreign policy was made more rigid by the nuclear element, which by the mid 1950s potentially rendered any error in 'reading' the other side quite literally catastrophic. So, Soviet diplomatic, military and nuclear moves (which were anyway sometimes poorly thought out and under Khrushchev usually accompanied by a lie, a bluff or a temper tantrum) were not likely to dent the resolve of the

Eisenhower Administration to continue and perhaps intensify Cold War mentalities.

As before, the intertwining of ideological beliefs and perceptions and the material interests of the central states in the system produced a system of mirror images, where each move made by the one was reflected in the moves made by the other. But the mirrors were perhaps distorting mirrors, rather like the convex and concave mirrors that used to be found in circuses or fairs: they did not produce a clear image but a distorted and often wildly exaggerated one. So it remained until the mid 1980s.

Europe in the High Cold War

But what, then, of the terrain on which this great contest was played? After the death of Stalin, the Soviet story is one of uncertainty and insecurity. Stalin's death removed the hope that a cult of personality could be used to overcome the very real difficulties faced by the USSR. As we noted earlier, the death of a dictator is always problematic because there are no clear mechanisms in a dictatorship through which to choose a new leader. Tensions had already arisen within the Kremlin as Stalin began to ail. Kremlin politics were marked by several dark episodes, including that of the so-called 'doctor's plot'. During this episode, some of the most prominent doctors in the USSR were accused of taking part in a plot to murder members of the Soviet elite. *Pravda* reported the episode as revealing 'vicious spies and killers'. These doctors were accordingly purged. This plot was later revealed as a total fabrication.

In the power struggle over the succession, three main contenders emerged. They were Georgi Malenkov, the Prime Minister; Lavrenti Beria, the Chief of Police and Minister of the Interior; and Nikita Khrushchev, the Party chief (*Pravda*, 7 March 1953). Initially they 'ruled' as a triumvirate and it appeared that the three were determined to follow a coherent line in foreign policy and seek a rapprochement of sorts with the Western bloc. At Stalin's funeral on 9 March, Malenkov called for the possibility of a lasting co-existence and a peaceful competition between the two different systems. The Soviet press became less anti-Western, and the leadership demonstrated a greater willingness to negotiate an end to the Korean War, and raised the issue of a great power conference to discuss once again the future of Germany and to begin to promote a peace campaign. All of this was watched by the Americans with trepidation.

The Americans had become used to Soviet initiatives designed to undercut the Western alliance. This apparent Soviet desire for an easing of tensions did not strike the Americans as particularly novel. Even before his death in March 1953, those around Stalin had moved to address what they saw as some of the more counter-productive aspects of the regime. In domestic politics, this took the form of trying to remedy the shortage of consumer goods and mitigate the excesses and arbitrary nature of the political system. In foreign policy terms this meant a reinvigoration of polices which might prohibit Western defence integration and specifically the continued development of a coherent Western bloc with the West German state at its core. In 1952, the Soviet leadership presented the Western allies with a note that envisaged a comprehensive peace treaty with Germany. Under this agreement, Moscow proposed that Germany be reunited, although it would have to cede all territories east of the Oder and the Neisse line. The note also contained the clause that all occupation forces be withdrawn a year after the conclusion of the treaty (Baier and Stebbins, 1953). Soviet notes were sent to the Western allies in May and August and they continued to urge them to take the proposal seriously.

The Soviet notes however were met with almost uniform cynicism in the West. The leadership of the Federal Republic under Konrad Adenauer was not willing during this period to risk what had been accomplished in West Germany for the price of an all-German solution. Indeed the West Germans were not prepared to countenance any form of arrangement in which a Soviet leadership might have influence. The American leadership, which had already in the wake of the outbreak of war in Korea moved towards a policy of military containment premised on a robust Western alliance and West German power, did not take notice of the Soviet initiative. Specifically, the Americans rejected any possibility of a Four-Power Conference on the German question (Loth, 1988: 267–73).

It was however in Germany that the new leadership in the Kremlin attempted to institute change. Soviet initiatives appear to have been taken at the instigation of Beria. This is interesting because, at least initially, it was Beria who appeared to be dominant in the policy-making process and specifically in Soviet–German policy. After the death of Stalin, it was he who was instrumental in ordering a relaxation of the regime operating in East Germany. Supported by Malenkov he attempted to prevent the German Democratic Republic (GDR) from blocking itself off from unification and he ordered the SED (Communist Party of East Germany) leadership to reduce the pace of the building of socialism. In part at least this was an attempt to deal with the considerable dissatisfaction of the East German population, which had resulted in an endless flow of refugees to the West that was unnerving the Soviet leadership. East German reform was the subject of debate within the Kremlin but was not endorsed by Khrushchev. (He later accused Beria of having been willing to give up East Germany in return for preventing Western defence integration (Knight, 1993a: 192).) The subsequent 'relaxation' of the regime in East Germany had profound consequences. 'Workers', those supposed to be happiest with the regime, staged large-scale disturbances and attacked Communist officials.

In Berlin, Halle and Leipzig, strikes affected industry and communications; prisoners were released and the resignation of the Communist leaders Walter Ulbricht and Otto Grotewohl was demanded. The Soviet regime had to respond to the collapse of the SED regime or it appeared that control in Eastern and Central Europe might itself be compromised.

On 17 June, the Soviet leadership decided to re-establish the power of the regime in East Germany. Soviet tanks were used to quell the uprising. Beria, who was removed from his posts at the Party plenum, was accused of compliance with the imperialists and was eventually executed on 24 December (Knight, 1993b). Meanwhile, on 22 August, Moscow agreed a deal with the SED leadership which included the cancellation of all reparation payments and post-war debts, as well as a clause agreeing that Moscow would supply goods and credits to the value of 465 million rubles. Ulbricht became indispensable to Soviet control in Germany. The impact of the rebellion of 1953 reverberated over the coming decade leading an already nervous Kremlin to eventually acquiesce in the building of that terrible symbol of repression – the Berlin Wall – in August 1961. The coercion and imprisonment of many thousands of people behind the wire, concrete and security guards of the wall did at least temporarily stabilize the situation but was, in Khrushchev's own words, 'hateful' (Gaddis, 2005).

Throughout the crisis of 1953, though, the Soviet leadership did not forgo the notion that it would be able to manipulate the differences amongst West European states on defence integration. The Kremlin hoped in particular to retard the growth of a European Defence Community (EDC). The Soviet leadership instead tried to renew notions of neutralization and reunification. The idea of a reunified Germany was revived to prohibit what the Soviet leadership believed would turn out to be a new coherent Western alliance centred on West Germany – in the shape of the EDC. Soviet commentators claimed that Germany would dominate any such defence alliance. In early 1954, at the Berlin conference the Soviet delegation proposed that Germany should be both united and neutralized. The idea was mooted that troops would be withdrawn and Germany would then be prohibited from joining any defence alliance. In addition, Molotov called for the abandonment of NATO and the creation of a pan-European organization without American participation. John Foster Dulles after the meeting claimed that when this proposal was made it was regarded as so preposterous that laughter rippled around the Western sides of the table, much to the dismay of the Communist delegation (Gaddis, 1997). The Western delegation countered with a suggestion that the future of Germany should be decided through free German elections. The Soviet regime obviously could not, after the 1953 rebellions, accept any plans for reunification, which were based on the free choice of the German people. In March, a Soviet note finally conceded the point that Western defence structures would include the West Germans and a permanent American contingent in Europe.

The Soviet leadership did though draw some comfort from the collapse of the EDC. The French resisted pressure to be drawn into the European military alliance and refused to ratify the EDC treaty. Soviet attempts to undermine the proposed alliance centred around exerting pressure on the French. Here two tactics were apparent. One was to raise the spectre of German revanchism. In particular, the USSR tried to depict the EDC as an instrument through which the Germans would again dominate the continent. Second, the Kremlin sought to play upon tensions between Paris and Washington over the French involvement in Indo-China. At this stage, the Americans had refused to support the French effort in Asia, and Moscow offered to use its influence in Indo-China if Paris rejected the EDC. Soviet triumph at the failure of the EDC did not last long. Moscow was almost immediately confronted with the British idea of a West European Union (WEU). The British revived the idea of a Brussels Pact, which had been raised in 1948, and which would include both Italy and the Federal Republic of Germany. French fears over possible German revanchism were met through the suggestion that all key decisions would be taken by NATO and that the US would make a permanent military commitment to Europe. These ideas were formalized in the Paris Treaties of October 1954. What this meant in practice was that Germany was formally divided. This proposal provoked from Moscow another determined attempt to mitigate any prospect of a formal military alliance with the Federal Republic at its heart. The SPD organized a series of strikes and Moscow mobilized a campaign, which again aimed at promoting the idea of a neutral and unified Germany. In the early part of 1954, Moscow actually offered to join NATO and proposed a new collective security arrangement for the continent.

By early 1955 though Moscow had to settle for the division of Germany, consolidation of the Eastern bloc and renewed attempts to harness the technological power of the Western bloc. On 25 January, Moscow ended its state of war with Germany and announced an intensification of its links with the GDR. It had threatened in November 1954, immediately after the signing of the Paris Treaties, that if the West went ahead they would create a defensive organization in the East. The Paris Treaties were ratified on 26 March 1955 and the Warsaw Treaty Organization (WTO) was formally established on 14 May 1955. This new organization included the USSR, Poland, Czechoslovakia, Hungary, Romania, Bulgaria, Albania and the GDR. Article 5 of the WTO founding documents was the establishment of a Political Consultative Committee to coordinate foreign polices. Soviet sources claimed at the time that the creation of the Pact arose out of the refusal of the Western powers to include the USSR in the Western security alliance, although the official *raison d'état* of the Pact was the threat from German revanchism (Maltsev, 1986).

Indeed, with the Paris Treaties and the creation of the Warsaw Pact, both sides had secured spheres of influence and had at least tacitly signalled that there would be no large-scale intervention in the affairs of the other half of the bloc. Khrushchev continued to attempt to manipulate what he perceived as tensions within the Western alliance, following the Geneva conference. Although, improved relations with the West permitted a short period of détente or what became known as the 'Spirit of Geneva'.

The agreement over Austria in May was one important example of a Soviet willingness to negotiate on some of the outstanding issues of World War II, although it should be noted that the Soviet withdrawal of its troops from Austria made precious little difference as there was small chance of Communism developing there. Indeed, the population within Austria had been noticeably anti-Communist and it was unlikely that Soviet-style ideals would have gained ground. The example of Austria was however held up by the Soviet leadership to other states, particularly the West Germans, but also to some third-world states as demonstrating the advantages of what could be achieved by a state which with remained neutral.

A seeming desire for rapprochement with the West was demonstrated at the Great Power meeting, which was held in Geneva in July 1955, leading to the so-called Geneva spirit mentioned above. Khrushchev travelled to Switzerland to meet the American President, Dwight D. Eisenhower; the British Prime Minister, Anthony Eden; and the French Prime Minister, Edgar Faure. In terms of concrete achievement, the Geneva meeting was noticeable for the great power collaboration over the war in Indo-China and the establishment of an International Control Commission for the country chaired by the British and the Soviet Union. Whilst little else of substance was actually achieved, the delegates did discuss a number of questions, most notably West Germany and the issues of reunification and disarmament. Nuclear power and disarmament were also issues high on the agenda and the Soviet delegation had the idea of transferring control of nuclear production to a UN organization. The American counter-proposal to have a so-called 'open skies' verification regime for nuclear arms not surprisingly met with little enthusiasm on the Soviet side (Khrushchev, 1970). The Soviet account of the meeting at Geneva is illuminating. There appears on the part of the Soviet leadership to have been a genuine desire to lower Cold War tensions; there was also an obvious feeling of inferiority vis-à-vis the American delegation. In his memoirs, Khrushchev revealed the awe with which the Soviet delegation greeted the Americans and in particular their chagrin over the inferior Soviet aircraft. Soviet officials had arrived in a two-engine plane in contrast to the more modern aeroplanes that transported its Western counterparts.

This was a clear understanding of the rather inferior nature of Soviet 'superpower' status. Soviet insecurity manifested itself in two obvious ways. One was what we might call 'the management problem' of Eastern Europe, laid bare in 1953; and the other was the question of how to rival US nuclear power. By 1955–56, both had become urgent for the Soviet regime. Let us look at each in turn.

Resistance and Repression

Khrushchev had, during 1955, invoked a programme of destalinization through which some of the worst excesses of the Soviet regime had been eradicated. He also sought to reform the command economy to produce greater benefits for citizens. The uprisings in East Germany during 1953 had provided a dire example of what could happen in a regime that failed to meet, even at a basic level, the expectations of the people. At the Twentieth Congress of the CPSU in February 1956, Khrushchev took the opportunity to make two dramatic statements. In a public report to the Congress on behalf of the Central Committee he highlighted aspects of shifts in foreign affairs. The Soviet leader asserted that the main feature of international relations in the contemporary era was the evolution and strength of the socialist camp and the pursuit of peaceful co-existence with the West. Khrushchev reinforced the notion that a temporary alliance against the imperialist enemy was possible, although he noted that in the longer term Socialism would triumph through peaceful competition: war, he asserted, was not inevitable. Thus far he was paving the way for a period of peace with the West. (He also noted, wrongly as it turned out, that despite the recent show of Western unity over Germany the fierce struggle within the capitalist camp would continue and intensify.) Khrushchev argued that Soviet foreign policy should follow and pursue peaceful co-existence as its primary goal with the West, and should strengthen its relationship both with Yugoslavia and 'so-called' fraternal allies in the third world.

In his second set of declarations in what has become known as the 'Secret Speech', the Soviet leader criticized Stalin for his lack of military preparation in 1941 and for his unrealistic assessment of the risks involved in the Korean War (Cohen, 1985). Khrushchev denounced the crimes of the Stalin era and admitted for the first time that mass repression, purges and excesses had taken place. This constituted a major questioning of the Stalinist regime and the laying of blame for past Communist crimes solely on Stalin. As Roberts has argued part of the Khrushchev agenda was to develop his own cult of personality, albeit a more minor one than Stalin had (Roberts, 2006: 4).

Nevertheless a shift had occurred within the politics of the Kremlin. This proved the old adage that reform or the perception of reform can lead to revolution. Beria had learnt this to his great cost in East Germany, but, during 1956, Khrushchev confronted a similar situation in Poland. The crisis there was provoked by the death of the Communist Party leader, Bolesaw Bierut. This had led to the release of some political prisoners and the removal of some of the old hard-liners. Part of this can be attributed to the publication of the Secret Speech. Such was its impact that strikes and riots ensued in Poznan. By October, the situation had deteriorated and the Polish Communist Party wished to install Wladislaw Gomulka as leader. This was a worry for Moscow as he had actually been purged by Stalin. Khrushchev believed that Gomulka might move Poland into an anti-Russian position and leave the USSR facing a hostile power. On 19 October, Khrushchev flew to Poland to persuade the Polish Communists not to elect Gomulka, but he was refused permission to enter the plenum at which the matter was to be discussed, despite throwing a temper tantrum! Gomulka was duly elected and warned that if the Russians attempted to intervene the Poles would resist (Kramer, 1996/97). Thus was a crisis defused; but Hungary was the next 'domino' to fall into crisis.

Pressure, too, had been building in Hungary since the spring of 1955. The reformist Prime Minister, Imre Nagy, had been dislodged by an old Stalinist Party leader, Mathias Rakosi, who had himself earlier been forced by Moscow to cede the post to Nagy. When Khrushchev managed to out manoeuvre Malenkov for the Soviet leadership in early 1955, he decided to reinforce the leading role of the Communist parties throughout Eastern Europe. In the case of Hungary, the Soviet leader was worried that Nagy's attempts at reform might go too far. Nagy had proven himself to be something of a reformer. Specifically the idea floated by Nagy that Hungary might withdraw from the recently founded Warsaw Treaty Organization concerned the Kremlin. But Rakosi's rule sparked popular protests and the Russians had to authorize his removal in

July. However, this proved to be a temporary expedient and popular unrest continued to mount. The surge of discontent culminated in October when a huge demonstration was organized in Budapest by students inspired by the Polish example. The Hungarian security forces were unable to contain the crisis.

Until recently little was known about what actually occurred in the Kremlin when the protests were mounted in Hungary throughout the spring and summer of 1956. It appears that the Soviet leader ordered that the Presidium discuss the crisis but failed to reach an immediate decision on whether Soviet troops should be sent into Hungary. Despite a lack of unanimity, Khrushchev sent an order through the Soviet defence minister, Zhukov, to 'redeploy' Soviet units already in Hungary into Budapest to assist the Hungarian security forces. They were joined by two divisions stationed in Romania and two more from the Ukraine. Yet the arrival of Soviet troops proved to be largely counter-productive.

Khrushchev had ordered the Soviet Army into Budapest to restore order. But it had failed. The Hungarians resisted. It even appeared that some of the internal security forces might join the anti-Soviet forces. This provoked a crisis in the Kremlin. Nagy insisted on the withdrawal of Soviet troops and on 28 October joined with the rebels. He then caused further consternation in Moscow by announcing that Hungary would indeed leave the Warsaw Pact and might become a neutral state. Khrushchev believed that this declaration could hasten a wholesale crisis igniting dissident groups throughout the bloc and within the USSR. On 31 October, Khrushchev secured the approval of the Supreme Presidium for an 'all out' intervention in Hungary. He also managed to rally the Polish and other East European leaders behind this move. On 4 November, the Red Army intervened and three days of fierce fighting ensued. Some 20,000 Hungarians were killed, along with 3,000 Soviet troops. Hungary was saved for Communism, for the moment, but at a high cost in human lives. Nagy himself was executed in 1958 (Gati, 2006).

Throughout the crisis, Khrushchev had had to take into account the possible response of the West. After all the Americans had during the early 1950s attempted to use a variety of tactics to undermine Communism in parts of East and Central Europe, most notably in Albania. The Americans too had for a number of years spoken of a process of so-called 'rollback'. This term was used to denote attempts by the Western powers to literally roll back Communism by military means if necessary throughout Central and Eastern Europe. Actually, as we will go on to see, rollback in the 1950s was predominantly not a military strategy but a political one. Ironically, the Soviet leader had a degree of luck in that the Americans, the British, and the French had actually been focussed on confrontation in the Middle East – over the Suez crisis.

On 26 July 1956 the new Egyptian leader, President Gamal Abdul Nasser announced that he was nationalizing the Suez Canal Company. The British, the French, and the Americans, throughout the summer, made a determined effort to persuade him to revoke his plans, but failed. In late October, Israeli forces, backed secretly by the British and French, moved into the Sinai peninsula and launched air raids. The British and French issued an ultimatum calling for the removal of both Israeli and Egyptian troops to a distance of ten miles of the canal. The Egyptians refused at which point the British and French sent troops to ensure the free navigation of shipping though the canal. As is now well known this had in fact been arranged in secret collusion with the Israelis. Washington condemned the Anglo-French-Israeli alliance, and exerted pressure for withdrawal. The upcoming presidential election meant that Eisenhower was in no position to ignore the conflict. He could not really condemn aggression in Hungary and yet condone his allies for their actions in Egypt. Indeed, Eisenhower was upset by British actions. Eden's expectations that Eisenhower would 'lie doggo' while the British reclaimed the canal were misplaced in a spectacular fashion. Eden, already highly agitated by the crisis, apparently dissolved into tears during a phone conversation when rebuked by the US leader (Graubard, 2004: 385).

Despite or perhaps because of the crisis in Hungary, Khrushchev attempted to make political capital out of Anglo-American differences in the Middle East. The Soviet regime backed Egypt and Suez was a disaster for the imperialists. Khrushchev himself made a series of crude threats including one with an obvious nuclear intent that 'we are fully resolved to use force to crush the aggressors and to restore peace in the East'. On 5 November, the Soviet Foreign Minister sent notes to the three 'aggressors' and to Washington. The note to the United States proposed the joint use of Soviet–American naval forces to bring a halt to the aggression in Egypt (Kramer, 1996/97). Not surprisingly, this was rejected by a

United States appalled not just by British actions but also by Khrushchev.

Khrushchev, though, drew two immediate lessons from the Suez crisis. He held it up as an example of protracted and counter-productive action by great powers. This was an example not to emulate in Hungary. He argued therefore that the Russians must act decisively against the rebellion. He also deduced a belief that the Western powers would not/could not put together a coherent response to Soviet intervention. This was not the critical decision in the debate, which took place amongst Soviet leaders over whether to intervene, but it certainly helped strengthen the position of those who advocated a military solution. Not to intervene, Khrushchev argued, might provide the imperialists with evidence of Soviet weakness (Kramer, 1995, 1996/97).

Yet, the determining factor in ordering the intervention in Hungary appears to be the belief that, unless the revolution was quelled, there would be a spillover into the USSR itself. This anxiety was heightened by a series of intelligence reports from both Romania and Czechoslovakia. Soviet sources transmitted evidence that in the border areas there had been contacts between Hungarian rebels and Czechs and Romanians. Both countries contained lively student demonstrations. Quite apart from the worries over the satellite countries, there was evidence that the Secret Speech had resulted in a series of protests within the USSR, most notably in Tibilisi and other Georgian cities.

Eisenhower, looking at reports from the CIA on Hungary, was told of some 250,000 people on the streets, calling for free elections and the withdrawal of Soviet troops. Intelligence findings initially reported some 5,000 Hungarians killed by Soviet soldiers. The American President denounced the aggression and spoke of the intense desire for freedom of the Hungarians. As the crisis unfolded, however, Eisenhower became increasingly worried by a situation that might lead to a general war, especially as the crowds on the streets appealed for American help. Perhaps they had been misled by the rhetoric of so-called 'rollback' and the inherent promise that the Americans would actively as opposed to covertly aid resistance to Communism. Indeed it would be left to a later Republican President, Ronald Reagan, to resurrect the idea of rollback in the 1980s.

Yet what could the Americans actually do in the 1950s about Soviet power and repression? American nuclear superiority there might be but it certainly did not translate into the raw power to intervene in a crisis within the Soviet bloc.

Eisenhower had not expected the Soviet intervention, describing it as a 'bitter pill' to swallow and worried that actually Khrushchev, like Hitler (note the parallel to the infamous dictator), might yet be emboldened by his success.

In fact, as Adam Ulam (1971: 244) has, to my mind, correctly argued, by 1956 there was a problem with American foreign policy:

> American foreign policy was stymied and incapable of major initiatives or probes for a new approach ... foreign policy was well suited to counteract Soviet misbehaviour, to isolate and contain a Russia of the Stalinist model. But it was ill prepared to deal with intermittent Soviet behaviour combined with appeals for friendship. (Graubard, 2004: 384)

In short, containment meant precisely that – to isolate and contain the Soviet Union but not to engage or intervene. Graubard, who has been immensely critical of Eisenhower, alleges that he failed to understand the world abroad, as it had changed since he commanded troops on D-Day. This assessment should not hide though that what Eisenhower did foresee was that the Soviet leaders might be tempted to embark upon a wild adventure – a theme to which we will return shortly. It is also worth noting that in 1957 the US President did formulate what became known as the Eisenhower Doctrine which stated that the United States would support states that opposed Communism. In a special message to Congress, Eisenhower avowed that the US would respond to aggression.

Because of the events of 1956, Khrushchev's position as General Secretary came under threat. At the December CPSU Central Committee meeting, it was noticeable that Khrushchev did not make a speech. On 5 May 1957, there was an attempted political coup against him within the Presidium, which demanded his resignation as First Secretary. Khrushchev refused to resign and instead rallied the support of important figures such as Marshal Zhukov (Miller and Feher, 1984). Khrushchev summoned the Central Committee and managed to gain a reversal of the Presidium's decision. (Ironically he accused Zhukov of 'Bonapartism' and removed him from high office.) In the course of the debates of June–July 1957, Khrushchev accused his rivals of not supporting his foreign-policy initiatives and during the course of the debates managed to oust his most serious rival, Malenkov. Yet even as he secured his domestic position (after the 1957 showdown, he was a dictator, enjoying considerable power) the foreign-policy agenda became yet more complicated. The difficulties, as in 1956, centred on the issue of alliance solidarity within the Communist world, specifically the issue of relations with Mao's China and the return of the problem of control in Germany.

China: the Personal and the Political

If Khrushchev's pronouncements had unleashed a wave of unrest throughout the Soviet bloc, they had also fundamentally altered the relationship with China. Khrushchev did not inform Mao of what would occur at the Twentieth Party Congress, although this may have been because he himself had not really decided on whether he would actually go ahead with his denunciation or not. The Chinese, unlike other delegations, decided to protest over the content of the speech. They objected to the criticisms of Stalin. As Mao pointed out in the aftermath of the Party Congress, Stalin had been leader of the Communist Party and to criticize him and to criticize his achievements, yet still wish Moscow to continue to head a global Communist movement, was somewhat contradictory (Goldstein, 1994). Behind Mao's criticisms also lay a deep personal dislike of Khrushchev.

At first, Khrushchev's relations with Mao had appeared positive. In 1954, during a visit to Beijing, he offered to return the Port Arthur naval base and substantial credits were agreed. There was at this stage a degree of personal antipathy between Khrushchev and Mao, but it did not really surface until 1956 and the Secret Speech. Mao decided, not unreasonably given what we now know of him, that Khrushchev was 'unreliable'. According to one source the Chinese leader barely concealed his irritation and dislike for Khrushchev during a visit to Moscow in November 1957 (Cold War International History Project Bulletin, 1996/97).

Mao had profound concerns over the unmasking of Stalin within the Communist movement, for he remained an important symbol of the stages through which China had to progress to achieve Communism. Chinese experiences did differ significantly from that of the USSR but Mao believed that the Soviet example was critical. Mao initially supported the Soviet handling of the uprisings in

Eastern Europe in 1956 but he was quite clear that Khrushchev was wrong in his political reforms at home. He worried that the Soviet example would encourage those around him to warn against autocratic tendencies within the Chinese Communist Party. His attitude towards Moscow hardened during 1958 as he launched the reform of the Chinese economic system – the 'Great Leap Forward'. Part of the reform was intended to reduce Chinese economic dependency upon Moscow. At the same time, Khrushchev asked for a radio station on Chinese territory to communicate with its new nuclear-powered submarines. Mao demanded that Khrushchev visit Beijing to discuss the matter properly; but when he did so he found his welcome less than warm. The Soviet suggestion of reciprocal rights in using naval bases to develop a 'common fleet' to counter the American Seventh Fleet met with open derision on the Chinese side (Gaddis, 2005; Westad, 2000). Mao's attempts to prove that China remained independent of the USSR continued shortly after the visit when the Chinese shelled the two islands of Quemoy and Matsu (offshore islands of Taiwan) without prior consultation with Moscow. Part of this appeared to be Mao's desire to show that Khrushchev could not control Chinese actions but it was also to demonstrate his displeasure at what he perceived to be attempts by the Soviet leader to 'please' the Americans. The growing rift in Sino-Soviet relations was confirmed in 1959 when Khrushchev made a third trip to China and was rebuffed on a number of issues, not least the Soviet request that Mao release two American prisoners of war who had been shot down over China during the Korean War. By 1960, Khrushchev was attacking Mao by name and the Chinese were openly ridiculing 'Khrushchevism' and its many failures. In July 1960 the Soviet leader decided to withdraw all advisors from China immediately and tore up over 300 contracts which had been signed with Beijing.

Part of the problem was that of nuclear weapons. Mao could not understand Khrushchev's attitude towards capitalism given what he had been led to believe was the advanced state of the Soviet missile programme. The problem for Khrushchev was that he knew that Soviet nuclear forces were vastly inferior to that of the US, but he was determined not to allow Soviet weaknesses to be made public. Sadly for Khrushchev, his nuclear strategy would eventually be exposed for exactly what it was. As John Lewis Gaddis (2005) has so aptly argued, Eisenhower's nuclear strategy was about covering up the gap in his conventional forces, Khrushchev's strategy was about hiding the gap in his nuclear armaments.

Khrushchev and Nuclear Weapons

It is worth bearing in mind the long, if not especially noble, history of dissimulation, of bluffing, perhaps lying, and certainly of exaggerating the issue of nuclear threats. Just as Khrushchev deliberately lied about the Soviet nuclear capability to impress local and regional allies, such as the Chinese, but also to try and outwit the Americans, it is at least a reasonable assumption to suppose that, more recently, Saddam Hussein refused to simply admit that his weapons programme had effectively ended after the first Gulf War, partly to impress his enemies, both foreign and domestic.

By the mid 1950s, the full implications of the nuclear revolution were beginning to be felt but on both sides of the Iron Curtain differences were emerging about what they actually were. In the United States, the implications of the bomb had been hotly debated for some time, both by the military but also by a growing cadre of 'civilian' experts, many of whom occupied office in the newly founded air force think tank known as the RAND corporation (Freedman, 2005; Kaplan, 1983). Out of these debates came the new theology of the nuclear age: deterrence theory. All of the concepts that made up the arcane logic of deterrence had their origin in these debates: first strike, second strike, escalation dominance, Mutually Assured Destruction (MAD), flexible response and so on. The official policy of the United States in the 1950s and early 1960s was MAD, thus assuming that no one could 'win' a nuclear war. But amongst civilian specialists a fearsomely complex debate was being waged over whether in fact that was true. For some, including the doyen of the civilian strategists, Bernard Brodie, MAD was the inescapable logic of the nuclear age, but for others, most especially Brodie's chief critic within RAND, Albert Wohlstetter, this was not necessarily the case. Perhaps the ultimate logic of the criticism of Brodie's position could be found in the unlikely shape of Herman Kahn, whose massive book *Thinking about the Unthinkable* proposed a 44-stage 'ladder of escalation' which suggested that the carefully calibrated use of nuclear weapons would be possible. Scholars such as Henry Kissinger would later refine this thesis, as did another RAND intellectual (and recent Nobel Prize winner in economics), Thomas Schelling (1980). These developments led to a change of Western policy in the 1960s towards what was called 'flexible response'.

There were also debates about this issue on the Soviet side following the death of Stalin. One of the major areas of disagreement between Khrushchev and Malenkov had been on the impact of atomic power on foreign and military affairs. After the Soviet Union had achieved an explosion of the hydrogen bomb in August 1953, Malenkov had developed new ideas about international relations. Specifically he argued that given recent Soviet achievements in fusion, a state of deterrence existed between the two blocs; war would now be disastrous for either side and therefore peace was necessary and possible. This represented a radical break with the standard Stalinist line in thinking about nuclear weapons. Stalin had held that war was inevitable between the two camps and that nuclear weapons made no difference to this state of affairs. Under Stalin, military affairs had been paralysed by the notion of the 'permanently operating factors'. Even the Soviet achievement of a fission bomb in 1949 had made little impact upon this idea (Holloway, 1983). Stalinist 'military science' held that factors such as surprise attack could make little decisive difference to the outcome of war. There were obvious reasons why Stalin had held to this type of thinking. Not only did it excuse the blunders of 1941 when surprise had almost proved decisive but it justified the Soviet position in the period from 1945–49 when the US had held a monopoly on atomic power. Immediately after the death of Stalin, however, military theorists changed the mission of the armed forces to take account of nuclear weapons. It was admitted that a surprise attack could prove paralysing and decisive in war.

Throughout 1954, Malenkov continued to claim that a form of deterrence existed between East and West. (Malenkov also argued that, because of this, the USSR could now afford to divert some of its spending away from the defence sector.) After the successful test of the hydrogen bomb, Malenkov had argued to the Supreme Soviet that: 'Now we can and consequently we must accelerate the development of light industry in every way in the interests of securing a faster rise in the living standards ... of the people' (*Pravda*, 13 March 1954).

Khrushchev and the Soviet military did not endorse this position and shortly after he had first aired his views, Malenkov was forced to retract them. By April 1954, he claimed that a nuclear war could actually only bring about the downfall of the capitalists. The Soviet service chiefs were adamant that Malenkov was wrong in seeing nuclear weapons simply as a deterrent. Rather they argued nuclear weapons should be incorporated into conventional force structures. What this debate pointed to was recognition that nuclear weapons had certainly changed international relations and that some accommodation with the US had to be sought.

This view influenced Khrushchev's attempts during the mid 1950s to find a peaceful co-existence with the West and to achieve a 'breathing space'. The strategic balance was actually still weighted in favour of the US at this point. The USSR could not and had not matched the extensive strategic modernization programme that the US had carried out in the 1950s. The US Strategic Air Command had by this stage 1,300 aircraft capable of nuclear strike missions against the USSR. It had B-47s and B-52s capable of carrying bombs from the United States to the USSR and then returning (*Pravda*, 9 August 1953). The Soviet strategic bomber force only had medium-range planes centred on Europe. Despite this weakness, or more probably because of it, the USSR felt compelled to conceal its weakness and bluff about its strength. On Aviation Day in July 1955, the Soviet Union made an ostentatious display of Bear and Bison bombers, although in fact the same squadron of bombers flew over Red Square repeatedly. This actually set off a brief if heated debate within the United States as to whether in fact a 'bomber gap' existed or not. The launching of Sputnik, the Soviet satellite, in 1957 seemed to make Khrushchev even more intent on creating the impression of strength. He cultivated this impression as to the advanced nature of the Soviet ICBM force for the West. These exaggerations masked the fact that in reality the USSR had only four of them. The Americans did not know this at the time and, as John Lewis Gaddis has put it, Khrushchev's 'rhetorical rockets' made an enormous impression upon both the US public and government. Despite what we now know about the relative strengths of the two systems – many Americans were understandably shocked and a great deal of hand-wringing went on as to how the Soviet Union could have achieved such a development (Gaddis, 2005).

Contemporary students of international relations tend not to appreciate the impact which the idea of nuclear weapons had on ordinary people during the period of the Cold War, but Sputnik was, in its own time, and in many ways, a visible reminder of the potential vulnerability of the American homeland. Some observers blamed the American education system for what appeared to be a lamentable shortcoming in American science. Melvin Small (1996) points out that such was the critical impact of Sputnik that far higher spending was agreed on for education, including the one billion dollar National Defense Education Act.

One of the consequences of the arms race then was to try to improve scientific schooling. Another was the establishment of National Aeronautics and Space Administration in 1958. The President, though, was the subject of much criticism from the Democrats for allowing the US to 'fall behind' the Communists in nuclear capabilities. Yet, this was not accurate. What Eisenhower knew, but would not reveal at this point, was that secret U-2 flights had actually revealed the full extent of Soviet nuclear weakness (Graubard, 2004: 385–97).

On 1 May, the Soviet leader was informed that an American U-2 plane had penetrated Soviet airspace. He ordered that it be shot down. It was, and the pilot, Gary Powers, was captured. Khrushchev attempted to embarrass President Eisenhower, and only gradually revealed that he knew the full story. He allowed the Americans to release a cover story and then demonstrated its falseness. Eisenhower at this point decided to take full and public responsibility for the U-2 flights. The problem for Khrushchev was that U-2 flights had revealed that the 'rhetorical rockets' were just that. His bluff was exposed. Khrushchev's nuclear strategy, if we can use that phrase, was a shambles (Gaddis, 2005).

At the mid May summit in Paris in 1960, Khrushchev demanded an apology from Eisenhower for the U-2 incident. This was not forthcoming and the summit broke down. By 1960, Soviet foreign policy appeared in complete disarray. Khrushchev would not negotiate whilst Eisenhower was still in the White House; the Chinese continued a barrage of criticism against Khrushchev; and finally, at the United Nations in September, the Soviet leader quarrelled with the Secretary – General Dag Hammarskjöld – over his handling of the UN operation in the Congo, and banged his shoe on the top of the table. This incident was caught on television.

It is difficult to know what Khrushchev hoped to achieve with his bluffing, apart from perhaps an enhancement of Soviet status, particularly valuable with China, or so he hoped, and in the Third World. Perhaps he also sought to negotiate from a position of strength. He was however to be disappointed. The Eisenhower regime accelerated its military programmes and in particular, to reassure the West European allies, produced a NATO nuclear stockpile and offered to station Thor and Jupiter intermediate-range missiles at bases in Europe. These were actually of little military or strategic significance in the longer term, for while they might counteract Soviet intermediate-range missiles until the American strategic rocket force was fully in place, in the medium term they could only provide 'cover' for NATO allies facing Soviet IRBMs. They had, though, for the Kremlin leadership a disastrous portent – these Western missiles could reach Soviet soil from their European bases. This initiative, to Soviet minds, confirmed the fears long prevalent that the West Germans were in fact to be given nuclear weapons.

During the period 1960–61, despite the bleak general outlook, Khrushchev still found Soviet nuclear weaponry useful, not least in helping him push forward conventional arms cuts as part of a cost-cutting exercise in the Soviet armed forces. On 12 January 1960, for instance, he suggested a radical reduction in Soviet troop levels. He proposed that the army be reduced by one third. This he argued would be possible because the Soviet strategic rocket force was the backbone of the armed forces. This was despite the fact that the USSR still had only four R-7s on a launching pad near Plesetsk in Northern Russia. Khrushchev claimed that he had thought through all the implications of such a massive proposal and had recognized the fact that such a massive demobilization would have ramifications for those involved. Indeed throughout January 1960, continual assurances were given by both the political and military leaderships that those demobbed would be looked after. *Izvestia* even carried the headline for those awaiting demobilization that 'You are being awaited everywhere Dear Friends' (26 January 1960). The government promised a package of economic benefits which included the promise of jobs primarily at industrial enterprises and construction projects in transport and in agriculture. Loans were promised worth 700 rubles to soldiers engaged in home construction. The evidence though shows that 250,000 Soviet officers were forced into premature retirement without actually receiving adequate compensation or housing. The Soviet military had not been consulted; indeed Marshal Malinovsky warned on 20 January that the cuts might mean that the military would find itself in a position similar to that of 1941 (*Krasnaya Zvezda*, 20 January 1960). Khrushchev had, as part of the reform process, hoped that the living standards of ordinary people could be raised. Yet in June 1962, the Soviet Army had had to fire upon strikers in Novochevkassk who were protesting about food prices. This sat uncomfortably with the tone of the Twenty Second Party Congress in October 1961, at which Khrushchev had again launched a public assault on the 'monstrous crimes' of the past.

The Nuclear issue remained – and was to remain for the rest of the Cold War – one of the central aspects of the conflict, but while there were temptations to abandon the policies of restraint, on which both superpowers had acted up till now, the temptations were always overcome. Brodie's assumption about the central logic of deterrence frayed but remained largely intact. Except perhaps for 13 days in 1962.

The Tipping Point? The Cuban Missile Crisis

Perhaps the most important event for the overall shape of the Cold War in the later 1960s through to the 1980s, was the Cuban missile crisis. As we shall see, while it came close to destroying what Albert Wohlsetter had famously called the 'delicate balance of terror' it didn't. And as a result it helped stabilize the superpower relationship in ways that created a more stable nuclear order and helped mitigate some of the later major crises between the Cold War adversaries (such as that in the Middle East in 1973). But, in looking at the unfolding of the crisis, the very instability of the Cold War system is evident.

Khrushchev was aware of the sustained efforts of the newly elected administration under the Democrat John F. Kennedy to eliminate Fidel Castro who had taken power in Cuba. Whilst the Bay of Pigs episode, in which a group of Cuban émigrés were equipped and supported to overthrow Castro, was perhaps the most infamous incident of American attempts to overthrow the regime, it was followed by others. Various parts of the US government were determined to overthrow the Marxist-inspired dictator who occupied islands so close to the US mainland. During the spring and summer of 1962 a series of US military manoeuvres took place in the Caribbean area, and it was clear that at some point the Americans would invade. From the Soviet point of view, the portents did not look good. John Kennedy himself had said, after the Bay of Pigs debacle, that the Americans could not stomach having Castro's Cuba next door. There was genuine concern within the Kremlin over what the Americans might attempt in Cuba, but it remains unclear as to whether Khrushchev expected a direct military intervention. The interesting question in 1962 was why Khrushchev concluded that the deployment of nuclear missiles on Cuba might be the best way to defend the Communist revolution. According to his memoirs, Khrushchev (1970) argued that he developed the idea during a visit to Bulgaria in May:

> I had the idea of installing missiles with nuclear warheads in Cuba without letting the US find out that they were there until it was too late to do anything about them ... I thought ... my thinking went like this; if we installed the missiles secretly and then if the US discovered the missiles were there after they were already poised and ready to strike, the Americans would think twice ... In addition to protecting Cuba, our missiles would have equalised what the West likes to call the balance of power. The Americans had surrounded our country with military bases and threatened us.

If this account is to be believed there are several factors that Khrushchev identifies as central to his decision. The first was the desire to protect Cuba for the sake of Communism. The 'loss' of Cuba, had the Americans succeeded in overthrowing Castro, would have hurt the USSR both in Latin America and in the Third World. A successful placement of missiles could have served as a symbolic but also real display of Soviet power. A second factor identified by Khrushchev was equally important. This was that the Americans had placed Jupiter missiles in Turkey and which were operational under American command in 1962. Khrushchev had objected to the deployment of these missiles in Turkey and more broadly to American influence in the region (*Pravda*, 31 October 1959). Khrushchev also had in mind the overall Soviet strategic position. The public exposure of his nuclear 'bluffing' had damaged the Soviet leader domestically.

In September, the Soviet leadership assured the American President that there would not be trouble in either Berlin or Cuba before he had to face congressional elections in November. Even so, Khrushchev was planning the deployment for Cuba, and on 14 October a U-2 overflight showed that missile installations were under construction. On 18 October, President Kennedy held what had been a pre-planned meeting with Gromyko who lied to the President about the nature of shipments to Cuba, claiming that they consisted of 'defensive armaments' (Graubard, 2004: 424–43). The President was calm. He commented that he took on trust Soviet statements. On 22 October 1962, Kennedy in a TV address to the world informed the US people that the Soviet leadership was engaging in missile construction on Cuba. He warned that he would consider any attack from Cuba as the equivalent of an attack from the USSR. He also announced a naval blockade (or quarantine, as it became known) to prohibit further shipments of missiles to Cuba – a high-risk strategy as there were several Soviet vessels already on their way there (Savranskaya, 2005; Graubard, 2004: 424–31).

Some Soviet officials suggested that Khrushchev stage a 'diversion' in Berlin as a response to Kennedy. The Ambassador in Washington, Anatoly Dobrynin, cabled an analysis to the Kremlin, which recommended a rebuff to Kennedy that might include a hint that the Western powers in Berlin might suffer. There were also suggestions that Khrushchev might respond with a troop build-up around that city. This 'linkage' between Soviet actions in Berlin and on Cuba had been suggested at an earlier point in the crisis, when parts of the Soviet leadership had thought that 'pressure' on Berlin could distract attention away from the deployment on Cuba. Berlin though, at this point, was not the primary focus of the attention of either superpower, which remained firmly fixed on the drama in the Caribbean.

Kennedy had placed the initiative for any resolution of the crisis firmly upon Khrushchev. On 26 October, Khrushchev sent Kennedy a long letter that appeared to contain a 'solution' to the crisis. In part the letter justified the presence of the missiles as 'defensive'. Khrushchev proposed that if the US declared that it had no intention of invading Cuba, future shipments there would not carry any kind of armaments. The next day a second letter arrived from the Soviet leader, which demanded as a quid pro quo the removal of US missiles in Turkey. On 28 October, the Kennedy Administration chose to ignore the second letter and accept the terms of the first, believing that the second letter had arisen out of factional wrangling within the Kremlin.

While a nuclear clash was averted and Khrushchev could claim to have saved the peace, the crisis had irrevocably damaged the Soviet leader in several respects. The first was in the relationship with Castro. Soviet–Cuban relations had become strained because of disagreement over the conduct of the crisis. The Kremlin had grown concerned by Castro's apparent desire to rattle nuclear sabres and his advocacy of the use of nuclear weapons if necessary. Like Mao, Castro found Khrushchev's caution in this respect mystifying. Castro was also infuriated by the resolution of the crisis, which had taken place without consultation with Havana. The lesson drawn by the Cuban leadership was that it had been entirely mistaken to have believed that Khrushchev would have protected Havana at the expense of Moscow. Castro later declared that had he been aware of the 'real' state of the Soviet strategic arsenal, he would have 'counselled prudence'.

The second consequence of the crisis in the Caribbean was that Khrushchev was ousted. It is difficult to judge how far the debacle in the Caribbean was directly responsible as by this stage domestic reform was failing and as we saw earlier Khrushchev had antagonized the Soviet military. Officially, he was released from his duties in 1964 because of advanced age and deterioration in the state of his health (*Pravda*, 16 October 1964). It is testament to how much the Soviet Union had changed since Stalin's time that the dictator was allowed to end his days peacefully. With his passing, the Cold War entered a period where the internal logic remained largely static until the domestic pressures on the Soviet Union became irresistible.

Cold War Frameworks

By 1962, after the crisis in Cuba, the Cold War had reached a static shape. By the time that Khrushchev was removed from office, the international system had changed dramatically since the Stalinist era. Two blocs had developed which confronted each other directly in Europe and Asia and maintained a form of stability through nuclear deterrence. The Khrushchev era had seen a high degree of mirror imaging between the blocs particularly with the creation of two military alliances in Europe and in the arms race. On the vexed question of Germany, and particularly the status of Berlin, a modus vivendi had been reached in Europe and Asia with a grudging recognition that 'spheres of influence' existed and that, as the building of the Berlin Wall signalled, there would be no direct intervention by the United States.

Stability there may have been at the international level but stability at a domestic level was, as we now know, a chimera for Communism. The rifts that had developed between Khrushchev and Mao proved fatal to Communist solidarity and, by the 1960s, global politics developed into a triangular contest, with Moscow facing competition from both Beijing and Washington. The schism with China was particularly dangerous to the Soviet regime, as it openly questioned its leadership of the Communist world at a time when the peoples in Eastern Europe had proved unreliable. The tale of Soviet decline from this point onwards is, however, another story – as is the tragedy of the American engagement in Vietnam. In the next chapter I will suggest what we might learn about current global politics from a consideration of the origins and evolution of the Cold War. Before that, however, let me just close this chapter with some concluding remarks.

The first is that the United States, despite unsteady beginnings, proved resolute in protecting the Western world from the threat of Communism. The second is that the United States did, despite isolationist tendencies, commit itself, at some cost politically and economically, to the peoples and economies of Western Europe throughout the 1940s and 1950s. Of course, Washington benefited from an expansion of markets and the creation of a global network of allies but we should not ignore what was a very real desire on the part of the West European powers to construct and share in the US bounty and it nuclear expertise.

A third point is that the United States in this period 'over rated' the enemy and saw dictatorships as more robust in their internal structures than they actually were. This is puzzling to a younger audience who know the fate of the Soviet Union and fascist Germany, but it is probably less perplexing to the generations who remembered and perhaps had lived through the 1930s. Dictators were strange creatures who did not play by the rules of the international game. Here Khrushchev's erratic behaviour seemed to fit the mould of an autocrat. What may be equally odd to students of contemporary international affairs familiar with the exercise of US military might in places such as Iraq, Kosovo and Afghanistan is why the greatest power on earth did not in the 1950s do more to intervene to save 'others' (or, as we would now term them, 'strangers') enslaved by Communism in places such as Berlin, Hungary, Poland or China. Here we need to think perhaps of the restraints of US domestic politics and the hard-fought debates over how best to meet the Communist threat and, at the same time, avoid war, especially nuclear war. This question would rear its head throughout the decade after the crisis in Cuba as American politicians sought to make sense of the entanglement in Indo-China. It was a war which resulted from the American attempt to shore up its imperial French ally against a Communist and nationalist uprising. That tragic episode is not part of this story but let us note that the later Vietnam War, like the Cold War itself, casts long shadows into contemporary world politics. As we shall see in the final chapter.

6
Reflections on the Origins of the Cold War

The preceding chapters have outlined in some detail the general trajectory that led to the Cold War. The two remaining chapters provide respectively a summary and assessment of the story of the origins of the Cold War as I have recounted it and, in Chapter 7, some more general conclusions about the implications for international politics more generally.

Shapes

If we were to caricature the two main accounts about the origins of the Cold War we would find diametrically opposed interpretations of Soviet and American behaviour. The first, which we could enlarge from the traditionalist version, has Stalin master-minding the subjugation of Europe and Asia, prevented only by robust American actions. The second has at its centre a desire on behalf of Washington to rule the world, create and sustain its own economic prosperity while ruthlessly casting adrift its wartime ally, the USSR. This is not to mention thrusting the states of Eastern and Central Europe into the darkness of a Communist Empire. Since the end of the Cold War, 'we know now', to once again paraphrase John Lewis Gaddis, that neither of these are accurate accounts of either American or Soviet foreign policy in the period after 1945. At the end of the World War II, the Soviet leadership under Stalin pursued a mix of ambitions. One agenda was indeed as we have seen obviously expansionist and therefore potentially threatening to liberal states. Soviet planning necessitated the control of some but not all of Eastern and Central Europe, and there was as we have seen an attempt by Stalin to finally fulfil historic ambitions to secure the western approaches to Russia, bring about a permanent resolution of the German issue and ensure the position of Moscow as a power in Asia. A second and as it turned out contradictory agenda was to continue the alliance with the West and to gain from the United States the economic and technological wherewithal for the future reconstruction of the USSR. Behind this lay a complex set of calculations by a Stalin who remained convinced that the United States too had an interest in prolonged peace, mutual trading relations and the emasculation of Germany and Japan.

This was not a mistaken view. American leaders certainly saw during the war years and the years of alliance with the USSR the benefits of co-opting the Russians into a post-war settlement based on democracy, free international trade and the construction of new gobal institutions. The Americans, like the Russians, sought the destruction of fascism and also at least in theory shared a common dislike of old-style European imperialism. But the Americans too were motivated by a number of complex factors. One was as we have seen the desire of the American people to return to a form of normalcy after the strains of another war. It was not clear that they would wish to, or would tolerate, the burdens of global leadership. This factor played out in the ardent desire of many ordinary Americans to see troop numbers abroad reduced and for conscripts to be returned home. This meant that where Stalin had some form of certainty in his agenda for the shape of international politics, the American one was actually more contested, publicly at least. (However, as we have seen, Soviet politics was never quite as simple as seeing Stalin as the sole agent through which Russian foreign policy was made.) There was therefore nothing preordained about the American confrontation with Russia. Yet, lurking between the two partners were a series of issues which would and eventually did lead to conflict. First, there were ideological differences. These emerged not just over the future of Europe but also over the shape of politics in Asia. Would Communism rather than democracy prevail and would this battle affect American interests? And, as we have seen, democrats came to be deeply mistrustful of a Soviet agenda which refused to allow truly free elections or to countenance the establishment of representative government.

A problem of trust therefore underlay the newly bipolar world: a world which pitted Moscow's ambitions directly against Washington in a variety of regions. This was especially the case as British and French power faltered. Increasingly American diplomats came to read Soviet foreign policy not as defensive, but as offensive, and actually by 1946–47 as potentially fatal to American interests – both political and economic. This was a breakdown in alliance politics which nobody sought but it arose as we have seen out of geostrategic rivalries underpinned by ideology and the growing conviction on the American side that the international structure demanded a confrontation albeit a 'cold' type of confontation with Communism.

As we saw during the closing stages of World War II, the issue of Soviet ambition in Europe had became one of the major issues superseded only for the Americans by the necessity of military victory. The Soviet leadership was determined to fend off any demands by the Allies for a mitigation of its influence; yet it too did not engineer the breakdown in relations. The negotiations which took place over post-war issues were on the whole right up until the summer of 1945 and were marked by pretty amicable discussions with, it has to be said, the Americans certainly displaying a rather remarkable appreciation of future Soviet security requirements. This was clear for example during the Stalin–Hopkins talks in the spring of 1945. On 26 May, Harry Hopkins, a close friend of Roosevelt, was sent to the Kremlin. The primary purpose of the meeting was to secure a date for Soviet entry into the war against Japan, but inevitably the shape of the post-war settlement was also discussed. Hopkins, like many Americans who had trodden the path to Stalin's door, in fact reassured him that Washington did not object to Soviet interests in Eastern Europe but it was the shape of how those interests might play out in political terms which gave cause for concern. For example, the United States, he explained, understood the need for a Poland which was 'friendly' to Moscow, but it would be preferable if the Polish government was more representative. In response, Stalin advocated a scheme whereby the present Warsaw Government would form the basis of any future administration but that representatives from other Polish groups, friendly both to the West and to the USSR, would occupy a proportion of ministerial posts. Hopkins accepted this idea although he must have known that, in reality, it did not and would not fundamentally alter the political situation in Poland. The meeting with Hopkins was typical of the wartime discussions between the allies. It revealed a determination on behalf of the Soviet leadership over the security of borders and a disregard over the sovereignty of free nations such as Czechoslovakia and Poland. This mix began to prove infuriating to the Americans.

However, on the Soviet side there was also frustration with the Americans especially over the issue of future German power and potential. Given the size of Soviet wartime losses and the devastating destruction of the Soviet economy and people there was no doubt that Germany should in the Soviet mind be not just punished but become the crucible for Soviet regeneration. Hence, the demand for enormous reparations. At the Potsdam Conference, for example, Molotov demanded that for the purposes of economic planning Germany should be treated as a whole and he pressed for the creation of central German 'agencies'. In particular, the Soviet Foreign Minister suggested that the Ruhr area (which had enormous economic potential) be internationalized under the control of the Great Powers, thus ensuring Soviet access to its resources. Secretary of State James Byrnes, who was present at the conference, wrote that Moscow's primary concern throughout the discussions was that of economic compensation. Indeed, the Soviet delegation demanded that Germany should pay directly to the USSR at least $18 million in reparations. However, the Americans had no intention of allowing Germany to be stripped of all its economic potential and, as in the vitriolic years after World War I, to be allowed to sink into poverty and financial depression. Here the historical memory of the mistakes made at Versailles was important. The Americans therefore countered the Soviet suggestion with the idea that reparations would be payable from within each individual zone of occupation. This was not acceptable to the Russians as it would have denied them access to the Western zones. The failure of the Western allies to come to some form of satisfactory agreement with the Russians on this issue had immediate consequences. In July 1946, a paper written by the Soviet Foreign Affairs Ministry stated that the $10 billion figure was the 'minimum' sum that should be accepted in compensation for the losses suffered by the USSR during the war with Germany. After the failure to get what they wanted at the Potsdam Conference, the Russians immediately intensified the procurement of reparations from their own zone. This included the wholesale stripping of industrial plants, agricultural goods and precious minerals. Here, as we have noted throughout this book, was a core demand by the Russians – to punish the Germans of course – but also to ensure that the costs of war were not to be borne in a disproportionate manner by Moscow.

The Cold War Crystallizes

Part of the shape of the post-war era was moulded at the last conference of the war years. The Potsdam Conference was in so many ways a decisive one in terms of the emergence of the Cold War. Roosevelt had died suddenly and his successor, the Vice President, Harry S. Truman, was regarded with a degree of suspicion by those in the Kremlin. Potsdam was the first meeting between Truman and Stalin. Although willing to cooperate and continue the legacy of Roosevelt the new American President made a very poor impression on the Russians. There were any number of unflattering assessments made by Soviet sources of Truman, including that of Molotov, who famously had been rebuked by Truman for his attitude and demeanour. Matters were not helped when Churchill lost the British General Election which had taken place during the conference and was replaced by the Labour leader Clement Attlee, who was for the Soviet delegation an unknown quantity. We have debated in this book the issue of personality and its impact upon politics and alliance politics and although we cannot 'know' for sure what may have happened had Roosevelt lived a little longer, at this critical juncture the substitution of Truman for Roosevelt did not help resolve the emerging problems of trust in international politics. The challenges of adjustment to new personalities were further compounded by the fact that it was during the Potsdam Conference that Stalin was informed that the US now possessed an atomic capability. Contemporary accounts record that Stalin displayed little emotion at this news and to Western observers did not seem to fully understand its implications. They were simply wrong. Stalin already knew through Soviet espionage networks that the Americans had the Bomb and the explosions over Hiroshima and Nagasaki in August 1945 did make a particular impression on the Soviet leader. The explosions underlined US technological superiority. Stalin ordered that the Soviet nuclear programme be accelerated to provide Moscow with atomic weapons in 'the shortest possible time'. The dictator noted that Hiroshima had shaken the whole world; that the equilibrium had been destroyed (*ravnovesie navrushilos*) (Holloway, 1993). In September 1945, although Molotov joked about the US nuclear capability, remarking that 'we must pay attention to the US, they are the only ones who have the atomic bomb', this did in fact mean that the Americans were less dependent upon a continuation of the Grand Alliance.

In practical terms for the Soviet leadership the patent evidence of American power was significant, not least because the sudden and brutal nuclear termination of the war in Japan denied Moscow a major combat role in the Pacific region and effectively ruled out any hope of influence in the post-war settlement in Japan. Stalin as we saw had to find other ways of exerting influence in Asia. In this he was significantly aided by the emergence of Communism in China after the victory of Mao in 1949. This again, as we have seen, changed the shape of the Cold War. China's emergence as a Communist state certainly added to fears in Washington that this type of ideology posed a global threat. Hence the American occupation of Japan became a necessary counter-balance to Soviet ambition in Asia. The US could occupy a strategic redoubt and contain perhaps the emerging Sino-Soviet alliance.

And yet even as the shape of the Cold War emerged in Asia, and as Truman proved more incendiary in his speeches than Roosevelt, none of this was actually an impediment to the Soviet belief that cooperation with the West remained important, maybe even crucial, to the USSR. Indeed, a complex picture emerges on the Soviet side. Whilst there was awe at the US atomic achievement and a patent desire to benefit from American technology, this aim co-existed with a second belief which was that the White House itself sought and indeed needed economic cooperation with Moscow. Soviet experts argued that during the war the economy in the United States had been producing at full capacity, which had had several beneficial effects – not least that of high employment. The end of the war, however, meant that demand would decrease and, as a consequence, Soviet economists argued that Washington would be compelled to find new overseas markets in order to continue to produce at full capacity. This search for markets, it was presumed, would lead the Truman Administration away from its traditional isolationism and necessitate trade with the Soviet Union. Here again ideological perception of a crisis of capitalism, rather like that of the crisis of 1929, coloured the views of the dictator and indeed those around him. And in one sense the Russians were correct in this view. The Americans did fear a fall in production and did seek overseas markets. Unfortunately for the Kremlin the Americans read the international system rather differently and saw economic buoyancy as dependent not on cooperation with the USSR but on the con-struction of a vibrant system of alliances with democratic states in Western Europe and in Asia. The United States determined after the provocations of Russian behaviour to simply close down the option of cooperation with them. Here too the Americans were under-standably heartened but not made reckless by their nuclear supremacy.

What was curious in this period was that Stalin, the much admired diplomat of the war years, made error after error about what the Western allies would tolerate. Here we see that actions do indeed have consequences. In early 1946, Stalin provoked the first crisis of the Cold War when he refused to withdraw Soviet troops from Northern Iran. American attitudes hardened. Reports in the spring of new and heavy Soviet troop movements in Azerbaijan confirmed the view that action was needed. As we have seen the Americans took a forceful line. When informed of Soviet troop movements towards Teheran, Byrnes stated that this constituted 'military invasion' and meant that the United States could 'give it to them with both barrels'. A telegram was sent to Stalin asking for an explanation of the manoeuvres but the message was ignored. Soviet pressure continued on the Iranian Prime Minister, Ahmad Qawan to grant oil concessions, whilst Moscow remained adamant that its troops would remain in Iran. A combination of US diplomatic pressure, an Iranian appeal to the Security Council of the newly established United Nations, plus perhaps the nuclear element, appears to have persuaded Stalin to change his mind. In April, Moscow reached an agreement with Teheran that Soviet forces would indeed withdraw. President Truman recorded that 'the Soviet Union persisted in its occupation until I personally saw to it that Stalin was informed that I had given orders to our military chiefs to prepare for the movement of our ground, sea and air forces. Stalin then did what I knew he would do. He moved his troops out.' For scholars of the contemporary period, oil and access to oil, so familiar to us now as a determining factor in US politics, were from the beginning of the Cold War an issue that literally dictated the shape of Washington's reactions to Russian probes. At this point the reader may wish to dwell upon the choice made in the early Cold War years to protect Iran but not gallant and democratic Czechoslovakia and, as we will see in the final chapter, the American interest in Iran from 1946 onwards casts a long shadow over its engagements in the Middle East.

The crisis in the Middle East therefore was a turning point in shaping Cold War politics. The Soviet failure to withdraw from Iran indicated to some in the West that Moscow had territorial ambitions which overrode agreed limits. Analysts, including George Kennan, made certain deductions from the Iranian crisis, most notably that Soviet conduct was untrustworthy in more general terms. Famously it was Kennan who provided the rationale for a new approach to the USSR. For many months prior to the Iranian crisis, Kennan had as we know been sending dispatches from Moscow analysing Soviet behaviour in deeply pessimistic terms and stressing the futility of policies which sought cooperation with Moscow. He predicted that expansionist tendencies, such as those displayed over Iran, would dominate Moscow's foreign strategies. His analysis which interpreted Soviet foreign policy as an outgrowth of an ideologically pre-determined set of expectations and ambitions, provided the intellectual basis for a new strategy towards the Soviet Union. The idea of such a strategy had actually been given their first public expression by Winston Churchill in his so-called 'Iron Curtain' speech. Although the British input into the origins of the Cold War has been the subject of much study, certainly within the United Kingdom, it would be wrong to place too much emphasis on a British lead in shaping it. Truman himself had grown determined to confront Stalin. In this respect the convictions of both Kennan and Truman himself began to sharpen the politics of confrontation, a process that was enhanced by the decline of the British and French empires and the apparent inability of the European powers to afford vigorous foreign and defence policies. Simply put, economic and imperial decline in Europe brought the Americans into direct confrontation with the Russians. Nowhere was this more evident than in the arguments over the future of Germany.

In September 1946, Byrnes outlined Western policy in Germany. During a speech in Stuttgart, he stated that Washington was committed to the unification of the Western zones and to the economic, social and political recovery of Germany with or without Soviet cooperation. For the Kremlin, this was distinctly alarming. It signalled that the Western powers intended to rebuild and rehabilitate their zones of Germany. This had two implications for Soviet leaders. The first was that while the presence of US troops in Germany could act as a safeguard against a resurgance of German militarism, they also had the potential to form the basis of an anti-Soviet alliance in Europe. A second and more important implication of unification for the Eastern zones was that Soviet leaders feared that economic and political rehabilitation in Western zones might threaten Communist control in the economically precarious Eastern zones. This fear of a loss of control was also apparent in the negotiations over the timescale for the withdrawal of both Allied and Soviet troops from wartime positions.

In 1946, both Truman (for electoral reasons) and the British were keen to reduce the number of Soviet occupation forces throughout Eastern Europe. In May 1946, an American estimate placed the number of Soviet troops at 700,000 in Romania, 65,000 in Hungary and 280,000 in Bulgaria (Barker, 1983). The British War Office estimated that there was a rough total of 905,000 troops in southeast Europe. Yet there was as we know significant impediments as to how to persuade the Kremlin to withdraw its forces from Eastern Europe. The Western Allies suggested that Soviet troops in Romania and Hungary should be measured against Western forces in Italy. This idea was vehemently rejected by Molotov. He argued that Soviet troops in Romania were necessary to protect Red Army lines of communication with Austria. Eventually, Molotov appears to have carried this point. Byrnes and Bevin accepted the idea that troop levels in Bulgaria and Italy should be measured against each other, but also conceded that Soviet troops should remain in Hungary and Romania. This 'troop trading' has a degree of significance. Molotov did not concede that Soviet troops should be withdrawn. The Soviet outlook remained subject to the need to avoid any substantial weakening of its grip on Eastern Europe.

This was particularly pertinent from Moscow's point of view as it perceived there was a growing US military presence in Europe and specifically in Germany. Soviet protests over the presence of American troops in Europe had grown stronger. Exception was taken to the establishment of American bases throughout the continent. Soviet objections in the first instance centred around the case of Italy. The USSR perceived that the West was intent on turning Italy into a base for air and naval bases, which they claimed formed part of a wider plan to establish a military network throughout Europe, stretching from Iceland right around to Italy. From May 1946, the Soviet press began to comment unfavourably on the influence of Washington in both Reykjavik and Rome (*Krasneya Izvestia*, 1946). Once it became apparent that the consolidation was beginning of US air and military power in Europe, the Kremlin began to advocate schemes for demilitarization and neutrality on the European continent. These notions, they suggested, should be applied to Italy in the first instance, but later could be a solution to the so-called German 'problem'. Even if an 'Iron Curtain' had descended throughout Europe, it was a permeable one. Both the Americans and the Russians were concerned to influence and manipulate the nature of the political–military arrangments on the other side of the curtain.

The Kremlin's strategies of occupation in Eastern Europe, its intransigence over Iran, and its mode of negotiating in general, confirmed for many in the West the view of the Soviet Union as an inherently aggressive and expansionist power. Although no extra pressure was exerted by Moscow upon Iran in 1946 and 1947, Washington remained concerned by what it perceived as aggressive and subversive Soviet actions throughout Europe. The United States was particularly anxious about what they perceived as a covert Soviet involvement in the civil war in Greece, which had broken out again in the winter of 1946. A report by the State Department concluded that the Greek Communist Party was being used, by Moscow, to undermine British influence in the region. There was concern over the levels of aid being given to the Greek Communists. In Washington, it was assumed that Moscow was both coordinating and directing Tito's activities in Greece. As we saw earlier Stalin actually found Tito's activities there, to say the least, irksome. The Soviet dictator had already long conceded that Greece fell outside a so-called Soviet sphere of influence. By February 1946, the State Department was informed by the British that the situation in Greece was so serious that the government might collapse at any moment.

While Greece was not a central strategic concern for Washington, the Truman Administration perceived the civil war and the role of the Communists as part of a Soviet plan to dominate Europe. Again, it was George Kennan who noted that a Communist victory in Greece would be followed shortly afterwards by Communist control of Italy. Once Italy had fallen, nothing would prevent the takeover of the Communists in France, Germany and Britain. The dominoes would fall. Here we see the American view that poverty, disarray and a lack of leadership by the British and French would merely fuel the inclinations of ordinary people to subscribe to Communism. In short the Americans understood that ideas/ideologies mattered.

Communism was regarded as a particularly potent force during the winter of 1946–47 because of the growing economic crisis in Europe. The winter was severe and by March 1947 the British Cabinet warned the American Ambassador in London that the country was heading for a financial crisis and that funds for British forces abroad would have to be reduced. During May 1947, the French Coalition Government did in fact fall, and Washington feared that the Communists might take power. During the spring of 1947, American officials considered that the situation in Europe was so serious that Moscow was being encouraged to take a harder line over negotiations. Not least it was believed that Soviet intransigence over Germany was strengthened by the belief that Europe would succumb to Communism.

The American reaction to the threat to the stability of Western Europe took the form of the Truman Doctrine. This was followed by the announcement of Marshall Aid on 5 June 1947, by the Secretary of State, George Marshall. The purpose of both the Truman Doctrine and Marshall Aid was to strengthen the structures, economies and institutions of West European states to withstand the threat from Communism. The theoretical basis of these initiatives was wholly ideological – that democratic structures based firmly on liberal ideals would not be subverted by Communism.

The Soviet decision to reject participation in the Marshall plan was a pivotal moment in the development of the Cold War. This is because involvement in the Marshall Plan was in tune with Soviet objectives of cooperation with the United States in trade and the rehabilitation of the Soviet and East European economies. It appears odd that Stalin eschewed this opportunity to acquire aid. Why then did the Soviet leadership reject Marshall Aid? In short, the answer is that it promised to subvert Soviet control in East and Central Europe and perhaps within the USSR itself. Stalin might have wished for aid but not with the potential for damaging Soviet interests.

Marshall Aid raised the real possibility that in return for US aid, a central organization would intervene in the economies of the Communist bloc. It also now transpires that the Soviet leadership had received information which told them of the central role that West Germany would take in any reconstruction plan for Europe. On 2 July, after consultation with Stalin, who had remained in Moscow, Molotov publicly rejected the offer of Marshall Aid. So ended any hope on the Soviet side that it would be possible to receive economic aid without political strings. As we have seen this marked the beginning of a new stage of ideological conformity on the Soviet side and a determined attempt to consolidate Soviet control.

1948 may accurately be termed a year of crisis. During the early months, the Soviet leadership used a range of instruments to try to maintain control in the East and to ensure the cohesion of a communist bloc. While making treaties of friendship and cooperation was one method, a less subtle means was tried in Prague when the Communist coup was engineered. Communist actions were triggered by the fear of losing power within the coalition. Elections were actually set to take place in the spring of 1948 and there were indications that the Communists faced substantial losses. By mid January, the Czech Communist Party was entering a period of crisis. Moscow had, in the summer of 1947, intervened to prevent the Czech Government accepting Marshall Aid. Moscow had been prepared to allow socialism to develop at its own pace in Czechoslovakia, but once this possibility began to disappear, Stalin could not afford to allow Prague to turn Westwards. Western statesmen, many of whom remembered the betrayal of the Munich Agreement, were horrified that once again Czechoslovakia had been sacrificed to an authoritarian leader. But as we noted there was little that the Americans believed that they could do to save Prague. Rather the Americans turned to the reinforcement of a Western bloc. Here they were ably supported by a British Government determined to ensure that the special relationship between Washington and London could be maintained into the post-1945 era.

By the spring of 1948, the Western powers had succeeded not only in merging their zones of occupation in Germany, but also in laying the foundations for military-political integration into a Western coalition. Soviet actions in the blockade of Berlin in 1948 were closely linked to Western measures aimed at German military and political integration. The Berlin crisis as we know resulted in a triumph for American resolve and a humiliation for Stalin had achieved.

As William Taubman has pithily commented: 'Stalin always made the worst of a bad job' (Taubman, 1996). The Soviet provocations over Berlin merely hardened Western actions. The Soviet leadership were surprised by the determination with which the Americans operated the airlifting of supplies into the city and were careful not to interfere with their actions. An estimate has been made that, of the 162,275 flights that took place into Berlin between June 1948 and June 1949, less than 1 per cent were interfered with (Rodrigo, 1960). There is little doubt that Stalin underestimated the lengths to which the Western powers would go to ensure the success of the airlift, especially through the winter of 1948–49. This was understandable since many throughout Europe had doubted the ability of the Americans to sustain the airlift. Second, Stalin recognized that any interference with air access could push the conflict into an area where the margins for error and accident might be reduced and result in war. Following the single incident in which Western and Soviet aircraft collided over Berlin, Western officials formed the impression that the USSR was defensive and concerned over possible repercussions.

As the success of the airlift became ever more apparent, Stalin moderated his political demands in an attempt to salvage something from the stand-off. By January 1949, he no longer made for example the withdrawal of Western currency reforms a *sine qua non* for lifting the blockade. Here again the nuclear element provided the US with leverage. A non-nuclear Soviet Union obviously had an interest in playing down the significance and potential of nuclear weapons, but public pronouncements on the non-importance of nuclear weapons are belied by the fact that in the 1940s the USSR was striving to create its own nuclear force. Soviet concentration on the production of nuclear weapons in the 1940s signalled clearly the recognition of the strategic power of such weapons. The Soviet fear of a strategic air attack in the late 1940s is also indicated by the emphasis upon the forward integration of East European countries into Soviet air defences. The fact was that Soviet conventional military power in Europe in the late 1940s was not what it was assumed to be at the time. So Kremlin appreciation of the US nuclear potential was acute. The Berlin crisis therefore was a localized confrontation (but one with much wider possibilities and dangers) in which Moscow eventually had to accept defeat. Stalin had hoped to force the West to negotiate on larger issues through the application of pressure on a small isolated enclave in Germany. Ironically, he succeeded only in providing the rationale for Western rearmament.

On 8 April 1949, it was announced that the United States, Britain and France had agreed 'on all questions relating to the establishment and control of a West German Federal Republic'. As soon as the Republic was established it was agreed that foreign troops would remain for security reasons under a new occupation statute. In April 1949, the defence ministers of the five Brussels Treaty powers, with American and Canadian participation, announced their agreement on a sweeping plan for the defence of Western Europe. On 12 April, the United States and Britain reached agreement on establishing facilities in Britain to provide for the stationing of nuclear bombers. Thus began a generation of debate within the United Kingdom on the legitimacy of the stationing of American nuclear bases on that country's soil.

There is little doubt over the relief that the Soviet leaders felt in September 1949 when they succeeded in exploding an atom bomb. Commentators openly stated that the United States could no longer blackmail the USSR. Indeed, in a speech in November 1949, Malenkov included the possession of the atomic secret as a contributory factor to the strength of the Soviet position. He proclaimed that the global balance was now tilted in favour of socialism and the Soviet state. He listed factors which had contributed to this favourable trend, in particular the Communist success in China, the success of the peace movement and the state of the Soviet economy. However, the emergence of Mao as victor in the Chinese Civil War had ramifications for Soviet foreign policy conduct, not least because Stalin feared that the Chinese leader would and could challenge him for leadership of the Communist movement. It is against this backdrop that the Soviet actions on the Korean peninsula have to be judged.

It is odd looking back at the origins of the Cold War how certain regions or states preoccupy us even now. Looking at the Korean War we see how Korea was divided and how one part of the country remains the hermit kingdom we see today. Stalin 'we now know' approved the plan, provided the arms and equipment to make the attack possible and sent military advisors to assist. Moscow had been excluded from influence in the settlement of the Japanese question despite its protests, and if the North Korean invasion of the South could have been accomplished quickly, without American opposition, Stalin would have recouped control of the whole of Korea under the influence of Communist powers at little cost to Moscow.

The American military reaction to the North Korean aggression was rapid and from a Soviet perspective unexpected. On 27 June, the Security Council of the UN, from which the Soviet delegation had absented itself, condemned the invasion of South Korea, and called upon the North Koreans to withdraw. Within three days, US ground units, under the auspices of the UN, were ordered into action. The Americans developed a double pronged response to the conflict, a military response in the East and a building up of defences in Europe. There was recognition within the US that the European allies believed that this was an attempt by the Kremlin to probe American resolve globally. This was an assessment that Truman shared and decided to act on. It was Stalin who blinked again in this crisis as he had over Berlin. One thought here is that perhaps dictators are not so bold in the international arena as we might expect. So, as I argued in Chapter 5, after American troops had crossed the 38th parallel, Stalin ordered Kim Il-sung to abandon the defence of North Korea and pull out the remnants of military forces into north-east China. Almost immediately the dictator changed his mind over withdrawal, not least because Mao was determined to fight on. This reveals the limits of Stalin's commitment to Third World allies and the influence that Mao himself exercised over the conduct of the war.

The End of the Beginning

By the time Stalin died in March 1953, the Cold War had taken on several characteristics. The first and most obvious one was the division of Europe betweeen a Soviet controlled East and an American dominated West. It has to be said that for the Soviet leadership this was in many ways a satisfactory outcome to their historic security concerns, not least the control of the heart of Europe. Yet this had been achieved at high cost. The control of Eastern Europe and the Soviet refusal, after 1947, to mitigate political conditions within the bloc ended any realistic hope of positive trade and aid packages from Western states. This effectively consigned the Soviet leadership to a long-term management problem in the East – how to reinvigorate poor economies, control restive peoples and establish the legitimacy of the Communist model. It was made more difficult by the visible economic 'success' of the capitalist model in the other half of the continent. Yet even though we now take the vibrancy of the capitalist model for granted, Truman took many risks politically to ensure the extension of aid into Western Europe and Asia. It is also the case that even as Soviet power and diplomacy faltered, US politics was dogged by critical debates over the shape of the Cold War and the construction of new institutions to counter the growing Soviet threat. There was confidence in Washington but no certainty that American values would prevail; hence the degree of paranoia over the internal threat from Communism. Hegemony was not a foregone conclusion and American global leadership was contested, at least in the early years. There is no doubt that while American values shaped the Cold War, its own values were transformed by the conflict with the USSR. Not the least of this was the enhancement of the powers of the President and the requirement for a panoply of new instruments including that of the CIA.

A third feature of our story is the considerations that led the Cold War to stay 'cold', that is not to escalate into a 'hot' war as many informed oberservers expected after the late 1940s. Perhaps the most obvious reason – and one we looked at earlier – is that the origins of the Cold War lay not as the traditionalists asserted in ambition but rather in fear – Soviet fear of Western encirclement and Western fear of Soviet expansionism. We have seen that both sides did not initially want to end the Grand Alliance, and that both sides, as it became obvious that the alliance was proving impossible to maintain, wanted to ensure that differences and difficulties did not escalate and become a 'hot' war. The whole idea of 'containment', however it was misinterpreted and misunderstood, and to whatever extent George Kennan later disowned its military dimension, was designed on the premise that by 'containing' the USSR you could prevent the US/Soviet conflict spilling out into a major conflict of the sort the allies had just been through.

A second reason is perhaps made clearest if we look at the two most obvious historical parallels to the Cold War, often invoked for their formal similarity. These are the analogies that have been drawn with the alliance system which operated in Europe prior to World War I (perhaps an obvious comparison to draw) and more intriguingly with the Peloponnesian war in Ancient Greece (between Athens and Sparta).

If we turn to the years before World War I, we see an international system that was bound to break down into war for a number of reasons. The pre-World War I alliance system was cumbersome because it was composed of two separate alliance structures, each of which were comprised of states roughly equal in power. For that reason both alliances were difficult to manage as states jostled for power and the balance of power between the two sides was unwieldy as states defected from one alliance to another. That system, coupled with the exigencies of military technology at the time, was what made state military mobilization when it came very hard to stop. State leaders had to prepare for war just in case. We saw this clearly earlier in the book when we looked at the nature of the inter-war system and the struggle by Russia to find allies and avoid a war with Germany. In the Cold War, however, the alliance systems operated by the two great powers were both hugely unequal as both the US and the USSR, as the dominant states, were able to restrain, constrain or persuade their allies to comply with great power preferences. Hence, a war arising from a breakdown in the balance of power became less likely than in the inter-war years.

The example drawn from the ancient world is even clearer in providing some neat understandings of the Cold War (Kagan, 2003). It draws on the Peloponnesian War. This refers to the great war between Athens and Sparta, the two leading Greek city states of their day, in the fifth century BC. As with the United States and the USSR, Athens and Sparta had been allies, leaders of the Greek Alliance against the Persians. But after victory, the alliance had soured.

Sparta had been the leading Greek power of the day – literally the Greek 'hegemon' or leader ('hegemon' is an Ancient Greek term). But after the Persian Wars, Athenian power grew very rapidly, partly due to the position of Athens on the shores of the Aegean and partly because of its naval forces which were the finest in the Greek world. Rapidly (rather like the United States after World War II), Athens created an 'empire' of allies and colonies across Greece and Asia Minor along what is now the Turkish Coast. There was in this period ideological rivalry. Sparta was a military oligarchy ruled by a monarchy and its power was buttressed and supported through the brutal suppression of a whole underclass in the Peloponnese where Sparta was located – these were the Healots. Athens in the years after the Persian Wars had become the world's first democracy and the cultural and artistic centre of the Greek world. Under these conditions, as the great historian of the conflict, Thucydides, relates, conflict was inevitable (Thucydides, 1972).

We must however also note another feature of this ancient conflict. In both Athens and Sparta, to a much greater extent that in the United States and the USSR, there were very strong war parties pushing for a root and branch conflict. The US often saw itself as Athens in the Cold War period but there was no comparable desire for war in the years of Cold War.

My point is that for both of the 'superpowers' after 1945 there were powerful incentives to restrain and moderate competition, prevent it getting out of hand and thus keep the 'Cold War' cold. This has to be one of the major 'lessons' of the origins of the Cold War: that it is possible to manage even the most profound conflict – and, as we have seen, the conflict was, on many levels, very profound indeed – if sufficient desire is present to do so. In that respect my version of the Cold War offers a lesson that qualifies standard assumptions of international relations theory about the 'causes of war'. These often assume that war will usually 'find a way' since it is the structurally determined nature of the system that determines the occurrence of conflict. The Cold War, for all its iconic status as an overarching and powerful type of 'structure', also reminds us of the importance of intention and agency in international politics. This is a point to which we will return.

The above considerations, taken together, also perhaps account for the rather static nature of the Cold War after 1953. This could be attributed to bipolarity but it also had to do with the acceptance that the logic of the Cold War was divison and confrontation and that this was really quite natural. Hence we see during the years of Eisenhower a reluctance to engage in war or direct intervention. Despite the plight and then rebellions within the Soviet bloc the Americans preferred rhetoric to action. This may be explained by fear of a nuclear exchange but, as we saw, by the mid 1950s the Cold War had its own inner logic. Here we might consider that this inner logic was at least in some ways beneficial to the Western bloc, happy with its civil liberties, economic prosperity and growing sense of unity enhanced by NATO and the emerging European Union. The logic was in the main to leave the Soviet bloc alone, and to contest politics outside that arena and then usually through covert rather than military means. This satisfaction with the Cold War was stronger on the US side than on that of other side. It was the Russians who suggested new ways of configuring politics in Europe. But their suggestions were rebutted on every occasion. Indeed, changes on the Soviet side in domestic terms under Khrushchev were by and large ignored. Tyranny remained tyranny. In this respect of course the new Soviet leader did not help himself. Actions over Berlin and more especially in Cuba did little to help the image of the Soviet Union as a more reasonable and indeed a more normal power. The sheer brutality of the Soviet intervention in Hungary in 1956 revealed not a modernizer in the Kremlin but a typical Soviet style bully. Khrushchev's nuclear adventures did threaten to bring the world to crisis and it took a monumental effort by the White House to avert the world's first nuclear exchange. Here we might note the importance of personality in the making of the high Cold War. Khrushchev was certainly responsible for an American perception that the Russians could not be dealt with through ordinary diplomacy. After 1962 therefore the shape of the Cold War, its inner logic, became ever more pronounced.

7
The Cold War Then and Now: Landscapes and Shadows

This book has sought to offer an account of the origins of the Cold War that does two things. First, to provide a relatively straightforward account of the Cold War and its origins; one that is not simply a narrative but which emphasizes certain key themes. Second, to highlight the importance of the history of the early years of the Cold War for understanding the pattern of international relations after 1945.

In this final chapter the focus shifts to the resonances of the origins and eventual shape of the Cold War for international politics more broadly. My central aim here is to illuminate the shadows those events cast over the world today and contemporary conflicts – not merely the current 'war on terror' (though certainly also that) but the ideational and geopolitical challenges that the twenty-first century seems likely to throw up in general. However, before I do this, I need to clarify what can and cannot be expected from such parallels and in particular to draw out my understanding of what international history and international relations from the past might tell us about our present. Here I want to develop that idea. In the first place though it is obvious that anyone with the kind of historical sensibility will and should be suspicious of easy attempts to see the 'past in the present' but let us try.

The Importance of History

I want to begin with a phrase from someone I have already quoted many times in this book, John Lewis Gaddis. But not Gaddis the magisterial historian of the Cold War (which he is, even when disagreements over details and interpretations about the nature of the early years might be had with him); nor the Gaddis who himself reflects upon the historical resonance of contemporary events (though I will come on to him in due course); but the Gaddis who wrote, in 2002, a marvellous reflection on the 'craft' of history itself. It is the title of that book that I want to highlight. Gaddis called it *The Landscape of History*. The significance of this is clear from the following. He tells us:

> If you think of the past as a landscape then history is the way we represent it, and it's that act of representation that lifts us above the familiar to let us experience vicariously what we can't experience directly: a wider view. (Gaddis, 2002: 5)

It is that wider view that is central to historical reflection in international relations, both in interpreting the particular – the origins of the early Cold War, in this instance – and in finding something of importance to say about the general – both the character of the early Cold War and the resonance of the early Cold War for the present. It is the overall sense of the landscape of the past that can help us do that, to move constantly, as Gaddis goes on to show, between particularization and generalization and therefore to have a sense of how the particular then affects the general today.

As he says, in his own words:

> Studying the past is no sure guide to predicting the future. What it does do though is to prepare you for the future, by expanding experience so you can increase your skills, your stamina and, if all goes well, your wisdom. For while it may be true, as Machiavelli estimated, that fortune is the arbiter of half our actions, it's also the case that she leaves the other half for us to govern. (Gaddis, 2002: 11)

Essentially this provides a flavour of what I want to do in this chapter. The accounts I have given of the early Cold War cannot feed directly into accounts of the origins or course of (say) the 'war on terror'. But by seeing the past as a landscape, one might be able to suggest certain features or shapes of that particular landscape, which were prominent then and are also apparent now. We might then be able to reflect upon whether the consequences of those features might be similar. In other words, we will be engaged in reflecting upon the 'wider view' that Gaddis suggested we might achieve and see how it might help us as we prepare ourselves for the task of thinking about international relations today.

To begin with, then, I want to see what kind of a 'landscape' my discussion of the origins of the Cold War has created, what are the 'shapes and shadows' that appear from my story. Following this, I will offer some thoughts on particular aspects of that landscape that, I suggest, were both central to the Cold War itself and that have most resonance for the contemporary period. I will finish with a meditation on the specific resonances of the Cold War that are specific to the present. Let me say something about each of these in turn.

There are three aspects of the origins of the Cold War that are especially significant, and that I want to stress here. The first is the crucial way in which ideological and ideational concerns blended with more traditional material and geopolitical concerns to create what I have called the 'shape' of the Cold War. This trajectory was manifested from the beginning of the Soviet–American relationship, that is, from the Russian Revolution itself and the Bolshevik declaration of the correctness of Marxist–Leninist thought in opposition to the ideologies of the other great powers both in Europe and beyond. This competition had 'hardened' by the 1950s into a confrontation of ideas that lasted right up until the unexpected and largely unpredicted collapse of Soviet Communist power in 1989. Here, as we noted in Chapter 5, there was an acceptance of the general rightness of a strategy of containment on the part of statesmen in the United States in dealing with the Soviet threat. This meant for many an acceptance of the shape of the Cold War.

The second aspect lies in the structural questions that we saw were central to the emergence of the Cold War itself in the 1940s and early 1950s and how those might be seen in the light of contemporary structural concerns. Many have argued that since the end of the Cold War we have entered a new or distinct era of geopolitical rivalry, where multiple powers (multipolarity) or a sole power (unipolarity) dominate – unlike, it is said, the 'bipolar' structure of the Cold War. Looking more closely at the actual history of the Cold War, however, suggests – I want to argue – a rather more complex story, not least that outside of Europe the shape of global politics was less tidy than bipolarity might suggest, and this because of the emergence of China as a competitor.

This second aspect also looks at the extent to which 'agency' – the actions of particular actors, whether states, groups or individuals – is bound up with structure, in both the early Cold War and in the contemporary period. That is to say, the particular way in which decisions of actors shape the manner in which states interact and therefore the 'structure' that their interactions actually create. As we have seen many stories of the origins of the Cold War stress the role that personality played in the maintenance and then the breakdown of the Grand Alliance. Stalin's personality and reputation, as we have seen, casts a gigantic shadow over any tale of the Cold War, but here I want to stress a different feature of that story. This is to emphasize the skills of those statesmen operating in the uncharted territory of the nuclear and bipolar world by highlighting the fact that the Cold War, during the early years, was ensured to be – precisely because of their efforts – Cold.

I will sum up the argument of this chapter with regard to the third aspect of the Cold War, that of the modern resonances of its origins, and I will offer some thoughts on the overall implications that the story in this book tells for international politics more generally.

Ideology

One of the determining features of the Cold War, it must be remembered, was that of ideological confrontation. Some analyses (most notably the so-called revisionist accounts) of the Cold War have tended to down play the idea of ideology in favour of emphasizing the material factors that created the rivalry (and we will turn to those in a moment). Some interpretations have actually over emphasized the ideational aspects of the conflict portraying it as a long war of 'good' against 'evil'. To separate these themes is misleading. One of the most interesting aspects of the story of the Cold War is the manner in which these two themes intertwined and combined.

In this context, reflecting upon the experience of the origins of the Cold War should, I think, suggest a number of things to us. We have seen how Western perceptions of the radical character of the Russian Revolution isolated the Soviet Union both in the 1920s even when Lenin and then Stalin – reluctantly – came to the view that accommodation with the West and the international system was necessary. This was also true after World War II when Stalin sought to continue cooperation with the West (without, to be sure, surrendering any idea of an intense ideological competition). We have seen how ideological hostility and fear, certainly on the American side, foreclosed the possibilities of cooperation after 1946, even when it would have been in the broader interests of both sides to pursue it. Stalin certainly saw that the best interests of the USSR would be served by a period of peace, of economic cooperation and of a great power entente over Germany. But we also saw how ideological competition fed material and later geopolitical insecurities. Stalin feared US intervention and influence in the USSR, hence the closing down of cooperation in the wake of the Marshall Plan. Truman feared Communist subversion throughout Western Europe and he too foreclosed any chance of Soviet inclusion in the economic rebuilding of the continent.

This is not to assert that Western perceptions of the Russian Revolution between 1917 and 1923 were wholly false, and that Western fears of the Soviet Union were not wholly misplaced. The point is that a more nuanced reading of the actions and dynamics of the other side might have kept aspects of the successful war-time alliance in being after 1945. This then might have softened the edges of the harsher versions of the conflicts that came to dominate international politics in both periods. Yet, fear of the other in international relations led to an exaggeration of the threat actually posed by both the Soviet Union and its version of Communism.

As then, similarly now the tendency today is to see 'fundamentalist Islam' as monolithic (as Western critics saw Communism even, for example, when China and the Soviet Union were drifting apart in the 1950s and when it was obvious that Mao was not prepared to follow Khrushchev's international agenda). This pushes the West to adopt a stance of outright hostility to all versions of it, when it might well be possible to come to an accommodation with an ideological other. There are doubtless some versions of Islam to which the West could not – and should not – seek to accommodate itself to, but this may not be anything like as universal a phenomenon as many seem currently to suppose. Surely the histories of the Cold War that I have offered here offer a stark warning of the dangers of overestimating the monolithic tendencies of our ideological opponents or assuming that they are at one with themselves, any more, often, than we are.

But here we need to exercise a degree of caution. At a historical distance from the origins of the Cold War it seems inevitable that American leaders would choose to wage ideological battles on all fronts after 1945. Yet, the United States as a global power was itself a new creation of World War II and, in the shape in which understandings of the new configuration of global politics took root in the American policy community, was itself a creation of the reaction to perceptions of the Soviet threat from 1946 onwards, as we saw in Chapters 3–5. But there was no clear consensus that the United States should assume the responsibility for global confrontation. There has always been a sizeable group within the United States who we might characterize as isolationists, who did not see or want to see the United State assume the mantle of an energetic global power. It was, though, the experience of the early Cold War years that largely marginalized those 'doubters' in the context of American politics. The differences between the undoubted power of the isolationist voice in the 1930s and its virtual absence after the 1950s (until really very recently) is testimony to that fact. As we have seen, a kind of consensus did emerge within the United States about taking on the burdens of global leadership through, for example, the Marshall Plan and the creation of NATO. Although as we also saw earlier there were fierce battles over the Marshall Aid programme, there was a longer-term commitment of US troops into Europe and the expansion of domestic institutions to meet the Communist threat.

The reaction to the threat posed by Communism in America in the late 1940s and early 1950s was every bit as profound as that caused by 9/11 and the emergence of radical Islam. Indeed one might say that the Soviet threat had an even deeper impact since there had not been an overt Communist attack on the American homeland. The changes in the structure of the US bureaucracy – the creation of the CIA, the National Security Council, NSC 68, and of what many have termed the National Security state in the 1940s (Hogan, 1998) – all bear a distinct resemblance to the founding of the department of Homeland Security, the rearrangement of other institutions of the domestic scene under its influence, as well as the creation of a new overall coordinator of government intelligence.

What was associated with these developments in the Cold War period ought at the very least to give us some pause in the contemporary context. These changes made during the early years of the Cold War did, after all, usher in the atmosphere of so-called McCarthyism that made even some of the most important statesmen of the day hostages to forces they disapproved of and disagreed with. It may well be the case that McCarthy's pursuit of spies, real or imagined, in the State Department, constrained Dean Acheson's policies – especially in certain areas, such as towards China or some policies of partial accommodation that Acheson had actually favoured – to a much greater extent than he would have liked. There were, as we saw in Chapters 4 and 5, also the domestic consequences of McCarthyism, the blacklists, the vendettas and, most pernicious of all perhaps, the compromising of certain civil liberties. The point here is merely to rehearse what may look obvious. The choices made by agents in international politics are not made in a vacuum and are often made without a full set of the relevant information. But the experience of the Cold War suggests that great caution is required when embarking on the kinds of constitutional tinkering that occurred both then and, even more so, now.

In perhaps no sphere of Western policy have the choices that Western governments taken in the light of their reading of the 'new threats' created by 9/11 and its aftermath been so controversial – and so radical – as what we might term the relation between traditional assumptions about civil liberties and the allegedly changed character of the threat, and therefore of the security measures necessary to meet that threat. In both the United States and within the United Kingdom wholly new legislative and executive powers have been deemed to be warranted – for example the creation of the whole apparatus of homeland security in the US and the new anti-terror laws and new potential crimes such as are suggested in the Government's new draft anti-hate speech legislation in the UK (Bamford, 2004).

But let us not forget another feature of Cold War politics. US leadership was sought by many people in many places. There is little doubt that American hegemony, US dollars and American nuclear power were welcomed. But there is another story too which is that the very creation of the structures of the Cold War and the creation of an American led bloc also led to the exclusion of huge numbers of people from the prosperity and protection of this superpower. In short the provision of American power while privileging many including the populations of Western Europe excluded many others. Here we can see the origins of a very long shadow that reaches into our own age and especially the rise of opposition to US hegemony.

So, for example, much of Osama bin Laden's apparent appeal to Muslims worldwide lies in his skilful use of the very real grievances and humiliations many of his audience have or feel they have with American power during the Cold War. Just as Communism genuinely appealed to many who were, or felt themselves to be, at odds with or excluded by a rich and perhaps decadent West, so too does Islam now. Hence, as we saw, Communism did appeal to any number of Western writers, poets and philosophers – all of whom were beguiled by the apparent appeal of an authoritarian system and an ideology that promised, even if did not deliver, some notion of social and economic equality.

Bernard Henri Levy wrote shortly after 9/11 that there has been a tendency in the West to ignore the voices throughout the developing world antagonized by a succession of American policies over a considerable period:

> There are other kamikazes ready to say to the nations of the world, You ignored us while we were alive: now we are dead: you didn't want to know about our deaths as long as they happened in our own countries; now we throw them at your feet, into the same fire that is consuming you. (Levy, quoted in Chan, 2005: 50)

Perhaps we might add that there have always been the powerless or the disenchanted in local, regional and global politics that have in various guises launched individual actions against the bastions of local or regional power. 9/11 surely can be seen as part and parcel of longer-term patterns of resistance to established power, but my point is here that the statesmen of the early Cold War understood the quagmire which poverty and hardship might produce, even in democratic states – which is why they realized very quickly in fact how imperative large-scale economic reconstruction for a post-1945 Western Europe was. The Marshall Plan was designed explicitly to counter the negative effects of poverty and hardship and a slide into radical and, in that era, left-wing politics. Here we might be critical of the denial of American aid through the Marshall Plan into

Czechoslovakia or even to the USSR itself. The logic of Marshall Aid was surely that prosperity subverts radical ideologies. Is it too far fetched to suggest that this was an opportunity lost and that the extension of aid into Eastern and Central Europe, perhaps even the USSR itself, might have altered the terms under which ordinary people existed? Is it also possible that the early years of the Cold War set in train a pattern of politics in which the concentration of American wealth and talent in the battle with Communism rather misled that superpower as to the nature of politics on the ground in say the Middle East or more famously in Vietnam?

There is perhaps another point we can make here about the relationship of the contemporary period to the origins of the Cold War. Much of the context for the exercise of agency now in our world remains deeply affected by the origins and development of the Cold War and by the choices made by earlier generations of 'agents'. The rise of militant Islam itself, for example, can be traced to the emergence of groups like the Muslim Brotherhood in Egypt, groups who were profoundly affected by the revolutionary changes of the inter-war period and by the emergence of the Cold War. We have already had occasion to comment earlier on the US/British-backed coup against the Iranian Leader Mossadeq in 1953. Events, as the old saying has it, have consequences. The Iranian Revolution of 1979 was in many respects independent of the Cold War, but the revolutionary methods of the Bolsheviks had been studied to great effect by some of the Iranians and the passions released and the events that followed it (such as the Iraq–Iran war and the growth of groups like Hamas and Hizbollah) were all framed by the overarching structures of the Cold War and the decisions taken in the 1940s by those in Washington to contest the ideological battles with Moscow on every front, including those of the Middle East.

This is most obvious of all in the case of al-Qaeda itself, and the leadership of Osama bin Laden in particular. All accounts agree that this radical grouping was forged in the reaction to the Soviet invasion of Afghanistan in 1979 and the passions that subsequently inflamed much of the Muslim world. Yet that invasion itself was an offshoot of the Cold War obsession with spheres of influence set out quite clearly in the 1940s (Keppel, 2005; Rashid, 2001). Soviet concerns over its southern periphery and fear of encroachment onto Soviet soil in large part inspired the leadership in the Kremlin to actually overstep its borders and venture into a risky and as it turned out ill-fated war. The mujahideen in Afghanistan – including Osama bin Laden and al-Qaeda – were supported by the Pakistani Intelligence Service (ISI) for largely Islamic reasons, but they were also supported by the United States and the CIA for geopolitical ones. They were a thorn in the side of the Soviet military thus proving another instance of the relationship between the ideational and the material. The logic of the Cold War had, in some respects then, more than a hand in the creation of al-Qaeda, an irony of history best summed up in Chalmers Johnson's now infamous term for it: 'blowback' (2002).

Structures and Agents

The impact of ideologies and the stress that I have placed upon ideology in the Cold War quite properly can and I am sure will be contested. Realist accounts of international politics – most especially neo-realist accounts – have always emphasized the flimsiness of ideational concerns next to structural ones (Waltz, 1979). In this book I have sought to criticize that view, but I have also pointed out above that there certainly were structural aspects in the origins of the Cold War and that structure remains important today. How do therefore the structural concerns of the Cold War period map on to the structural circumstances that we find ourselves in today?

One of the most obvious areas to examine in this context is the relationships between the major players in world politics. From a period of relative stability in relations between the major powers – one that is usually traced to the manner in which the Cold War ended in the early 1990s (Clark, 2001; Ikenberry, 2000) – we appear to have moved to one of a high degree of geopolitical fluctuation. Very quickly, after 9/11, both out of genuine shock and horror and perhaps also out of a recognition of the likely ferocity of the US response, states that had been rivals or even – in the case of Russia – adversaries for much of the previous century stood, and announced that they stood, shoulder to shoulder with the United States. It was a French newspaper that bore the famous and in retrospect highly ironic headline 'We Are all Americans Now'. But this was a sentiment that was shared in many parts of the globe, notwithstanding the celebrations which broke out in parts of the developing world to gloat over the 'humbling' of the United States.

But again, we have been here before. As we saw in Chapter 3, the destruction of Germany and Japan, and their occupation, made for a new shape in global politics. Their demise – followed shortly afterwards by that of the United Kingdom (and France) as global powers – created a political and economic vacuum in both Europe and Asia. The surviving great powers sought to fill the spaces.

The result was the shift – in structure – from a multipolar to a bipolar structure which, according to the neo-realists, created a much more stable structure than the multipolar structure of the 1930s. Indeed it is now quite common for analysts and politicians to lament the loss of the simple old bipolar structure of the Cold War years. In retrospect the idea of a two-bloc world had an elegant and stable simplicity. To policy-makers at the time, however, there was nothing certain or stable about the world between 1945 and certainly the mid 1950s. As we have seen, a host of questions played out against the backdrop of the war-time conferences and the post-war meetings. What to do with Germany and Japan? How to confront a China that had after 1949 succumbed to Communism? How to deal with the decline of British and French power (and remember that few took the rapid collapse of these empires for granted)? How to confront the reality of nuclear weapons? For the Americans by no means the least of these questions was how to preserve the economic well-being of the US and its allies. Added to this list was, after the death of the great dictator Stalin in 1953, the question of what shape Soviet leadership and politics might or could take. As I indicated earlier, dictators were and remain immensely problematic for Western policy-makers, inclined as they are to view them as always unreasonable, irrational and monstrous. Tony Blair for example even now is on record as describing Saddam as a monster. In Blair's words you would not wish for a monster to possess nuclear weapons (Blair, 2003). Think how American leaders must have felt after 1949, faced with a Stalin and a nuclear threat.

Most crucially of all there was the question of Soviet potential. It is easy now that the USSR is a historical memory to downplay the fears which dominated decision-making in Washington and indeed in London. After 1946, and certainly after the attempted foray to stay and extend Soviet influence in Iran, how could/should Soviet power and Soviet ideology be contained? How could the Republic be protected from Communist penetration and how could US ideals and markets flourish in a world dominated to some extent by not just the Soviet Union but, after 1949, Mao's China?

As we also saw in earlier chapters, the emergence of bipolarity and the nuclear question was central to the emerging shape of the Cold War. It is held by some scholars that in fact the early Cold War years demonstrated something quite important about the world of international politics – that bipolarity plus the nuclear age meant a so-called 'long peace'. The emergence of nuclear weapons generated an enormous amount of reflection upon the consequences of 'the nuclear revolution' for international politics. We saw clearly, under President Truman, the relish over what US nuclear strength might bring in diplomatic terms. But this relish was accompanied by a real fear over what the actual use of nuclear weaponry entailed especially in a world with authoritarian states. We saw clearly a developing assumption within the United States that dictatorships did not/could not appreciate entirely the logic of nuclear deterrence. Hence, the fear during the Cuban Missile Crisis or indeed any of the crises of the late 1950s, in Berlin or the Suez Crisis, that a Soviet dictator might just prove irrational or ambitious enough to unleash this power. Dictators after all have little regard for the human costs of politics and would it was claimed not balk at the annihilation of others. But actually a study of the Cold War demonstrates that even dictators as bad as Stalin or as allegedly 'maverick' as Khrushchev understood the catastrophic consequences of such weapons.

Let us point to another feature of early (not late) Cold War politics. This was that the Americans and their allies systematically over-estimated the nuclear strength of its opponents. This was actually quite striking. Western diplomats believed the lies told about the state of the Soviet arsenal. Surely this was very odd, because the assumption was also ingrained that dictators or authoritarian leadership were habitually deceptive. Khrushchev's fabrications were allowed to stand for many years until he was revealed to a global audience as an emperor without clothes.

The management of nuclear deterrence – as an aspect of the structure of the international system – is therefore part of the experience and legacy of the early Cold War and can only be understood in the light of what was learnt during the period 1945–62 (Walker, 2004). The claim that is often made now is that rapid technological change – including the deployment and actual or possible use of WMD – are changing the context in which force is used. It is however worth pointing out that as far as the structural dynamics of nuclear weapons are concerned – and in this respect at least their conflation with chemical and biological weapons – does not to my mind affect the argument. It is hard to see how the dynamics analysed so well during the early Cold War have changed. The logical and structural changes associated with WMD have been acknowledged and discussed extensively since at least the late 1940s and such discussions have formed part of the panoply of strategic discussion that became deterrence theory (Freedman, 2004). The basic proposition is that nuclear weapons are simply not usable.

Indeed, the issue of military restraint is one that emerges clearly from a study of the early Cold War years. Western statesmen did not see the military instrument in those years as necessarily the sharpest or most effective instrument with which to engage ideological foes. Certainly when faced with the prospect of any form of direct confrontation leaders of all political complexions demurred. In that sense nuclear weaponry and the consequences of its use provided for caution and the search for other tools short of war. The Berlin crisis of 1948 provided a classic case of provocation by the Russians, countered by an ingenious and careful use of airpower. Equally the Cuban crisis of 1962 demonstrated the ability of statesmen to avoid nuclear and military confrontation. Of course we can debate whether subversion, intelligence and proxy wars were 'better or more moral' instruments than outright intervention, but looking back at US restraint in say the politics of Eastern and Central Europe provides an interesting case study. The US chose not to support the rebellions in those countries against Soviet rule, not out of callousness but because of a keen understanding of where intervention might lead. Here I make the point that such restraint certainly on the part of the United States over the use of war is not a feature of contemporary international relations. The United States followed up 9/11 not only with the invasion of Afghanistan but also (in 2002) with its new National Security Strategy which made it perfectly clear that the United States now saw pre-emptive war as a legitimate form of defence and also expanded and redefined the general assumptions on which defences of pre-emption had rested in the past. These shifts are hardly limited to the United States. The 'war on terror', the Iraqi insurgency, the ongoing Palestinian intifada, the Russian wars in Chechnya, all give substance to the claim that world politics at the opening of the twenty-first century may be even more violent and disposed to violence than the latter part of the twentieth century and raise the spectre that this century could even be as bloody – or even bloodier – than its predecessor. For nearly all agents in international politics, on this reading, force is once again, it would seem, the weapon of choice.

Modern Resonances

All of the above lessons or themes taken from the early Cold War years have a real resonance with contemporary international politics. The ideological dimensions of the present struggle with radical Islam are supposed to express something very important about the real nature of the geopolitical conflicts that face us today: to wit, that they are fundamentally civilizational, or cultural (and religious) in character. Among the most widely cited (semi-) academic books of the last ten years that sought to emphasize this was Samuel Huntington's controversial *The Clash of Civilizations: And the Remaking of World Order* (1996). Huntington's thesis is now well known. It is perhaps worth pointing out just how widely taken up his ideas are. It is not now unusual to speak of the inevitable 'clash' of civilizations as a motor of conflict in twenty-first-century world politics, and there are echoes of this language in both academic, journalistic and political commentary of, for example, the collapse and bloody wars of the former Yugoslavia, or the possible emergence of a Chinese 'threat' to American primacy.

Yet as some of the language that has already been used clearly indicates, past parallels readily come to mind. The term of preference for the 'Islamic fundamentalism' of Osama bin Laden and his peers, for example, seems increasingly to be 'Islamofascism', a deliberate harking back to an earlier period of ideological struggle. References to the struggle against Communism are also frequently made, especially in the United States.

Some have therefore seen in the undeniable ideological rigidities and certainties that have characterized world politics after 9/11 a trend that is new and distinct. One aspect of this that has perhaps been most commented on – and for some years now – is the apparent resurgence of religious sentiment in world and in domestic politics (Rengger, 2003; Thomas, 2005). But here, we suggest, it is not really that religion has suddenly been resurgent, but rather that Western scholars, policy-makers and journalists have begun to take more note of it. Religious debates have been central to many aspects of world politics in the twentieth century and one can even see the Cold War, for example, as – in part at least – a religious conflict or at least a conflict informed by a certain kind of religious sensibility (Gleason, 1995). Michael Burleigh has recently emphasized the centrality of the religious dimensions of politics in his magisterial volume and has highlighted the extent to which the struggles of the Cold War should be seen as akin to contemporary struggles (2006).

So, the struggles of the early Cold War years should help us to understand and to place the contemporary ideological and ideational conflicts in perspective. But much the same is true of the structural and the agent-centred aspects of international politics which was outlined above. A similar, if not identical debate, to the one that preoccupied Cold War strategists in the mid to late 1940s is already under way today. The world then looked every bit as disorienting and confusing to the victorious allies of 1945 as to those seeking to come to terms with the threat posed by so-called new terrorism.

How to characterize the contemporary structure is, of course, open to a good deal of debate. In a recent book Barry Buzan (2004) has provided perhaps the best general assessment of the possible candidates for the structural shape of early twenty-first-century world politics. But suffice to say it seems unlikely that the structure could be accurately described as unipolar. The significance of this is simply to say that in this situation of uncertainty we would do well remember the missteps, blunders and, yes, the great achievements and lasting accomplishments that characterized that earlier period when the structural fault lines of world politics were also shifting.

Reflecting on the impact of the structures of the origins of the Cold War may well tell us a good deal about how to think about the impact that structures might have today; and that, surely, is important.

Reflections about personality and leadership bear repeating in the contemporary context. We have seen how Roosevelt came to believe that he could charm the dictator Stalin and we have seen how Stalin himself dominated the Soviet system. In this respect the impact of Osama bin Laden on contemporary international politics springs to mind. If Lawrence Wright's (2006) darkly impressive account of the origin of al-Qaeda is to be believed, bin Laden's personal idiosyncrasies, experiences and obsessions were what drove the 9/11 plot; al-Qaeda, or something resembling it, might well have emerged anyhow, but it was bin Laden's distinct personality that seemed to shape the form it actually took.

There are, however, many other ways in which the Cold War became central to the experience of, certainly, the West (and to some extent the East as well) over the period from the late 1940s to the late 1980s and which have retained a capacity to shape our current experiences of international politics. One might look, for example, at the way in which the Cold War was represented in popular culture. The genre of spy fiction predates the Cold War (distinguished examples of it can be found as early as Erskine Childers celebrated *The Riddle of the Sands* in 1912) but it was in the Cold War that it really came of age. And, of course, this was also true of cinematic versions of it. If one thinks of films as subtle and powerful as *The Spy Who Came in from the Cold*, or *The Third Man* (both of which were made very soon after the beginning of the Cold War), one can see the way in which the images that dominate these films become increasingly images that shape perceptions of the Cold War in general. In part it might be that these two films both had the mark of great writers on them (John le Carre and Graham Greene respectively) but it is also, I think too, that the sediment of the Cold War settled very quickly.

Perhaps more important still is the extent to which one might see the Cold War itself as the logical centre of the experience of the twentieth century, at least in political terms. It was Eric Hobsbawm, of course, who called the twentieth century a 'short' century and dated it as having run from 1917 to 1991 with the collapse of the Soviet Union (Hobsbawm, 1994). On this telling, the Cold War becomes the fulcrum on which the whole century pivots; the moment at which all of the contrasting trajectories of the century, ideological, technological, geopolitical, come into opposition. The Cold War becomes the moment at which the two great continental empires that had grown slowly throughout the nineteenth century finally dwarf the European continent that had, in different ways, created them both, as some Europeans like Tocqueville had predicted would happen. But it is also the moment at which the great ideological fissure of the century was finally made clear.

In part this was simply because, as this book has tried to point out, the shadows that created the shapes of the Cold War were long in the making and, by the time they were truly visible, had become relatively familiar and seemingly 'set'. Some of the trajectories inherent in that earlier confrontation have now become more marked even than they were then. The globality of the Cold War conflict, the cultural dissonances within it, the multiple complexities of differing ideologies and interests, were all present in the Cold War, as we have seen, but now all have been, so to say magnified, by technology and by the very diffuseness of the conflict and the fact that so many of the reference points of the earlier conflict have been removed.

The Cold War was, after all, a global conflict, a global conflict within the ideological universe of Western thought and practice. While the struggle with al-Qaeda clearly is not, it is also worth remembering the argument of John Gray (2003) and others that al-Qaeda, while not Western, is most certainly 'modern': in that respect at least, it resembles the struggle against Communism and fascism.

The origins of the Cold War, in short, have much to teach us about today, simply by teaching about yesterday. It speaks to some of the permanent questions that characterize the study of world politics – the blending of interest, power and value, the centrality of military force, the ubiquitous character of perception (and misperception), the role and character of alliances, the inevitability of error in human life and conduct. At the same time, it has some distinctive features. The role – and gathering pace – of technology, the peculiar character of modern ideologies and indeed mass ideologies, the enlarging of the canvas of state, struggle genuinely to a global level.

To understand these, in their historical setting in the context of the early Cold War, is, I suggest, to start at least to begin to understand them in their modern setting as well. This is not to imply simplistically that a study of the origins of the Cold War can tell us 'what to do' about al-Qaeda. That would clearly be ridiculous. But it is to say that understanding the character of that earlier conflict might help us to understand the character of this newer one.

A Wider View?

This point suggests, perhaps, one final 'lesson' of the Cold War with which we might close. Towards the end of *The Landscape of History*, Gaddis (following the example of the historian Geoffery Elton) argues that historical consciousness helps to establish human identity: that it is part of what it means to grow up (2002: 147). And it does this, he further suggests, by allowing us to achieve an optimal balance between what he terms oppression and liberation both within ourselves and within our societies. His concern is that in the twentieth century, as he puts it, 'disruptions in the balance became far greater than ever before'. Without implicating Gaddis in the use to which I want to put his metaphor, I suggest that he is correct in his overall view and correct also to see the disruptions of the twentieth century as of a different order than what had gone before. One of the central 'disruptions', was, of course, the Cold War.

Meditating on that earlier 'disruption' and the extent to which it did not allow us to achieve a good equilibrium between liberation and oppression could perhaps be the best preparation for trying to achieve a better fit this time around, notwithstanding all the differences and not gainsaying all the resonances. The 'wider view' that Gaddis thinks that history can give us if we see the past as a landscape naturally throws up certain patterns of light and shadow when it is trained on any aspect of history – as it has, in this case, been trained on the Cold War. And there are in our current predicament, I have sought to argue in this chapter, echoes of that earlier landscape and so some reason for supposing that the patterns of light and shadow we see there are relevant to our own times as well. That wider view is not a simple (or simplistic) reduction of history to a 'repeating decimal'; it does not assume there is a simple translation from past to present or future; rather it is, as with notions of authenticity in art history or literary interpretation, a question of judgement, of attribution.

Understanding the origins of the Cold War gives us, I suggest, just this wider view and thus enables us to better attempt the questions of judgements of attribution in our own time. This book has been primarily concerned with the task of explicating and accounting for the early Cold War. Its main task is simply to offer an interpretation of that series of events that is coherent, plausible and suggestive of reasons why events unfolded the way they did. But if, in the process, this book helps its readers to understand the way in which historical processes in general can work and how we can all too easily misread them and in that context help readers to reflect more systematically not just on their history, but on their present, then its intentions will have been amply fulfilled.

Guide to Further Reading

Chapter 1   Cold Wars

For general background reading see Hobsbawm (1994). See also for an account of the impact of World War 1, MacMillan (2002). On American foreign policy and its trends and themes the book written by former diplomat Henry Kissinger (1954, 1994) remain amongst the best. On the nature of the Soviet system, see the compelling story told in Merridale (2000) and the account of Soviet concentration camps in Applebaum (2003). For an understanding of the international system and its workings, consult the now classic text by Waltz (1979). For a version of twentieth-century history and American perspectives, see Robert Kagan (2003).

Chapter 2   Casting Long Shadows

For an excellent account of the long history of Russia's relationship with the United States, see John Lewis Gaddis (1990) and (1997). The origins of the ideological and political divisions between the two states is also covered by the excellent Melvyn P. Leffler (1994). On Stalinism see Volkogonov (1991), and for an older but compelling account reprinted in the 1990s see Deutscher (1996). Perhaps the classic account remains that of Tucker (1990). One account of the nature of the Soviet system, which perhaps has not had the attention it deserves, is that of Lane (1981). On Stalin the man and his times the most colourful and lively account is that by Montefiore (2003).

Chapter 3   Wars and Empire

On the build-up to war see Roberts (2006) and Overy (1997). For a good general account of the evolution of Soviet politics in this period see Service (1997). On the American road to war see Gaddis (1972). For the end of the war in Europe, Beevor (2002) provides a clear account, and on the beginning of the nuclear age and its impact see Holloway (1994). A more detailed story of the impact of nuclear weapons and the arms race is to be found in Freedman (1989). Outstanding accounts of the impact that domestic politics had on the making of US foreign policy are provided in Small (1996) and Hogan (1998). Hogan in particular explores the dynamics of the construction of a new type of American bureaucracy to deal with the demands of Cold War. On empire see Doyle (1986) and Ferguson (2004).

Chapter 4   Far from Hegemony?

For a first-hand account of the early years of the Cold War, see Acheson (1969). On the emergence of China and its impact on Cold War politics the most illuminating source is that of Westad (2003). For those interested in a novelist's account of Stalin, the man, his end and his legacies, see Amis (2002). On the Korean War and its various dimensions, read Stueck (2002) and Wethersby (2003). For a general and very readable assessment of these Cold War years see Gaddis (2005). Perhaps the very best critique of the emergence of Cold War is that of Walter Lippmann (1947). For an appreciation of the presidency of Harry S. Truman see Graubard (2004), and for his own memoirs see Truman (1956). For a view of how the great powers might emerge see Fox (1944).

Chapter 5   The Shape of the Cold War

For a compelling and very detailed account of the years of confrontation the best source remains Garthoff (1994). On Khrushchev see his own account (1970), and perhaps a more reliable account is that of Allison (1971). For a more detailed account of the Cuban Missile Crisis and its meaning read Blight *et al.* (1993). On Soviet policy in and around the bloc, see Nation (1992). On the general Soviet failure to impose itself on the politics of the Middle East, see Heikal (1978). On the impact of the Suez crisis a readable account is provided in Kyle (1991). For those readers wishing to learn more about the nature of Chinese Communism, see Zhisui (1994) and Becker (1996). On John F. Kennedy the outstanding book is that written by Sir Lawrence Freedman (2000). See also Wohlforth (1993) for an account of power politics during the Cold War.

Chapter 6   Reflections on the Origins of the Cold War

For more detailed readings about the origins of the Cold War, see Westad (2006). He provides an excellent account of the development of the super-power competition throughout the developing world. On the nature of politics within Central and Eastern Europe one of the most distinctive voices is that of Garton Ash (1989) and (1997). It is also worth revisiting the work of the American architect of containment, George F. Kennan (1947) and his book *American Diplomacy* (1951). For the best overview of the development of US society and politics see Sherry (1997).

Chapter 7   The Cold War Then and Now: Landscapes and Shadows

For additional reading and information on how the past shapes our present and especially in terms of past American actions see Johnson (2002) and Kagan (2003). For the best account of the legacy of the US engagement in Iran, see Sick (1985). On the impact of 9/11 see Gaddis (2004), and on the war on terror see Croft (2006) and Chan (2005). For an accessible account of contemporary US foreign policy see Jackson and Towle (2006). For a left-wing reading of US foreign policy, see Noam Chomsky (2003). For speeches made by President Bush comparing and contrasting the current long war on terror to the war against Communism, go to http://www.whitehouse.gov/news/releases. For reflections on the nature of US strategy and foreign policy see Dershowitz (2006).

Documentary Collections

Foreign Relations of the United States (FRUS) Diplomatic Papers

Bohlen Minutes of the Roosevelt–Stalin Meeting, 29 November 1943. Read *The Foreign Relations of the United States: The Conferences at Cairo and Tehran, 1943*, p. 531.
The Conferences at Malta and Yalta, 1945 (Washington DC: US Government Printing Office, 1955).
Joint Chiefs of Staff Files, Combined Chiefs of Staff Minutes, *Foreign Relations of the United States, The Conferences at Cairo and Tehran, 1943* (Washington DC, 1961), pp. 501–5.
FRUS 1944, Vol. IV *Europe* (Washington, DC: US Government Printing Office, 1966).
FRUS 1945, Vol. III *European Advisory Commission: Austria: Germany* (Washington, DC: US Government Printing Office, 1968).
FRUS 1945, Vol. IV *Europe* (Washington, DC: US Government Printing Office, 1968).
FRUS 1946, Vol. II *Conference of Foreign Ministers* (Washington, DC: US Government Printing Office, 1970).
FRUS 1946, Vol. IV (Washington, DC: US Government Printing Office, 1972).

Conference at Berlin Potsdam, 1945, Vol. I, Department of State (Washington, DC: US Government Printing Office, 1960).

Conference at Berlin Potsdam, 1945, Vol. II, Department of State (Washington DC: US Government Printing Office, 1960).

The Near East and Africa, 1946, Vol. VII, Department of State (Washington, DC: US Government Printing Office, 1970).

Paris Peace Conference Proceedings, 1946, Vol. III, Department of State (Washington, DC: US Government Printing Office, 1970).

Other Diplomatic and Government Papers

'Draft of Soviet Government of Peace Treaty with Germany', *Diplomatic Correspondence Relating to Germany: Soviet Note to the United States, the United Kingdom and France*, 10 March 1952, in C. W. Baier and R. P. Stebbins (eds), *Council on Foreign Relations, Documents on American Foreign Relations* (New York: Harper and Brothers, 1953).

Molotov, V. M. (1949), *Problems of Foreign Policy, Speeches and Statements, April 1945–November 1948* (Moscow: Foreign Languages Publishing House).

Special Message to Congress on Greece and Turkey; The Truman Doctrine 12 March 1947, *Public Papers of the Presidents of the United States: Harry S. Truman, 1947* (Washington, DC: US Government Printing Office, 1963).

United Kingdom Government, Racial and Religious Hatred Act 2005 <www.publications.parliament.uk/pa/cm200506/cmbills/011/2006011.pdf>

United States Government, Executive Order establishing the Department for Homeland Security (October 2001) <www.whitehouse.gov/news/releases/2001/10/20011008-2.html>

United States Government, *National Security Strategy* (September 2002) <www.whitehouse.gov/nsc/print/nsall.html>

United States Government, *National Strategy for Combating Terrorism* (February 2003) <www.whitehouse.gov/news/releases/2003/02/counter_terrorism/counter_terrorism_strategy.pdf>

Resources Available on the Web

One of the best resources for students of the Cold War is to be found at the Cold War International History Project. See <www.wilsoncenter.org>

See also the invaluable site at Harvard University on Cold War Studies <www.fas.harvard.edu>

Bibliography

Note: Documentary collections and Web resources can be found at the end of the Further Reading on page 171.

Acheson, Dean (1969), *Present at the Creation: My Years in the State Department* (New York: W.W. Norton).

Acton, Edward (1990), *Rethinking the Russian Revolution* (London: Hodder Headline).

Adler, Selig (1957), *The Isolationist Impulse: Its Twentieth Century Reaction* (New York: Abelard-Schuman), reprinted by Greenwood in 1974.

Adomeit, Hannes (1982), *Soviet Risk-Taking and Crisis Behaviour* (London: Allen & Unwin).

Aldrich, Richard J. (2001), *The Hidden Hand: Britain, America and Cold War Secret Intelligence* (London: John Murray).

Allison, Graham T. (1971), *Essence of Decision: Explaining the Cuban Missile Crisis* (Boston: Little, Brown).

Almond, Gabriel Abraham (1954), *The Appeals of Communism* (Princeton, NJ: Princeton University Press).

Alperovitz, Gar (1985), *Atomic Diplomacy, Hiroshima and Potsdam*, expanded edition, (New York: Penguin).

Alperovitz, Gar and Kai Bird (1994), 'The Centrality of the Bomb', *Foreign Policy*, 3–20.

Amis, Martin (2002), *Koba the Dread: Laughter and the Twenty Million* (New York: Hyperion).

Andrew, Christopher (1995), *For the President's Eyes Only: Secret Intelligence and the American Presidency from Washington to Bush* (London: HarperCollins).

Andrew, Christopher and Oleg Gordievsky (1990), *KGB: The Inside Story of its Foreign Operations from Lenin to Gorbachev* (New York: HarperCollins).

Andrew, Christopher and Vasili Mitrokhin (1999), *The Mitrokhin Archive: the KGB in Europe and the West* (London: Penguin).

Ansari, Ali (2006), *Confronting Iran* (London: Hurst).

Applebaum, Anna (2003), *Gulag: A History* (New York: Doubleday).

Arendt, Hannah (1951), *The Origins of Totalitarianism* (New York: Harcourt).

Armitage, John A. (1982), 'The View from Czechoslovakia', in Thomas Hammond (ed.), *Witnesses to the Origins of the Cold War* (Seattle: University of Washington Press), 210–30.

Armstrong, J. A. (1983), 'W. G. Hahn Post-War Soviet Politics: The Fall of Zhdanov and the Defeat of Moderation', Book Review, *Soviet Studies*, 35/3, 418–19.

Baier, C. W. and R. P. Stebbins (eds) (1953), *Documents on American Foreign Relations 1952* (New York: Harper Brothers).

Bamford, Bradley W. C. (2004), 'The United Kingdom's "War Against Terrorism"', *Terrorism and Political Violence*, 16/4, 737–56.

Barker, Elizabeth (1983), *The British Between the Superpowers, 1945–50* (London: Macmillan).

Baylis, John (1997), *Anglo-American Relations since 1939* (Manchester: Manchester University Press).

Becker, Jasper (1996) *Hungary Ghosts: Mao's Secret Famine* (New York: Free Press).

Beevor, Anthony (1999), *Stalingrad* (London: Penguin).

Beevor, Anthony (2002), *Berlin: The Downfall 1945* (London: Viking).

Beichman, Arnold (2003), 'Roosevelt's Failure at Yalta', *Humanitas*, 16/1, 97–106.

Beschloss, Michael R. (1991), *The Crisis Years: Kennedy and Khrushchev, 1960–1963* (New York: HarperCollins).

Bialer, S. (1987), *The Soviet Paradox External Expansion, Internal Decline* (New York: Vintage Books).

Black, Conrad (2005), *Franklin Delano Roosevelt* (London: HarperCollins).

Blair, Tony (2003), Iraq interview, 6 February, <http://news.bbc.co.uk>

Blight, James G., Bruce J. Allyn and David A. Welch (1993) *Cuba on the Brink; Castro, the Missile Crisis and the Soviet Collapse* (New York: Pantheon).

Bobbitt, Philip (2002), *The Shield of Achilles: War, Peace and the Case of History* (London: Allen Lane).

Bracher, Karl Dietich (1985), *The Age of Ideologies* (London: Methuen).

Brands, H. W. (1989), 'The Age of Vulnerability: Eisenhower and the National Insecurity State', *American Historical Review*, 94, 963–89.

Brodie, Bernard (ed.) (1946), *The Absolute Weapon: Atomic Power and World Order* (New York: Harcourt, Brace & World).

Bruer, William B. (1993), *Race to the Moon: America's Duel with the Soviets* (Westport, CT: Praeger).

Burleigh, Michael (2005), *Earthly Powers: Religion & Politics in Europe from the French Revolution to the Great War* (London: HarperCollins).

Burleigh, Michael (2006), *Sacred Causes: Religion and Politics from the European Dictators to Al Qaeda* (London: HarperPress).

Buzan, Barry (2004), *The United States and the Great Powers: World Politics in the Twenty-First Century* (Cambridge, UK: Polity Press).

Buzan, Barry and Richard Little (2000), *International Systems in World History: Theory Meets History* (Oxford: Oxford University Press).

Campbell, David (1998), *National Deconstruction: Violence, and Identity and Justice in Bosnia* (Minneapolis: University of Minnesota Press).

Carr, E. H. (1939), *The Twenty Years' Crisis, 1919–1939: An Introduction to the Study of International Relations* (New York: St Martin's Press).

Carr, E. H. (1950), *The Bolshevik Revolution 1917–1923*, Vol. 1 (London: Macmillan).

Carr, E. H. (1961), *What is History?* (New York: Vintage).

Caute, David (1978), *The Great Fear: The Anti-Communist Purge under Truman and Eisenhower* (New York: Simon and Schuster).

Chace, James (1998), *Acheson: The Secretary of State who Created the American World* (New York: Simon & Schuster).

Chan, Stephen (2005), *Out of Evil. New International Politics and Old Doctrines of War* (New York: I. B.Tauris).

Chomsky, Noam (2003), *Hegemony or Survival: America's Quest for Global Dominance* (New York: Metropolitan).

Churchill, Winston S. (1962 [1954]), *The Second World War: Triumph and Tragedy* (New York: Bantam).

Clark, Ian (2001), *The Post Cold War Order: The Spoils of Peace* (Oxford: Oxford University Press).

Clemens, Diane (1970), *Yalta* (New York: Oxford University Press).

Cohen, Stephen F. (1985), *Rethinking the Soviet Experience: Politics & History Since 1917* (New York/Oxford: Oxford University Press).

Conquest, Robert (1990), *The Great Terror: A Reassessment* (New York: Oxford University Press).

Conquest, Robert (1991), *Stalin: Breaker of Nations* (London: Weidenfeld & Nicolson).

Cox, Michael (ed.) (1999), *Rethinking the Soviet Collapse: Sovietology, the Death of Communism and the New Russia* (London: Pinter Publishers).

Cox, Michael (2002), 'September 11 and US Hegemony – or Will the 21st Century be American Too?', *International Studies Perspectives*, 3, 53–70.

Cox, Michael and Caroline Kennedy-Pipe (2005), 'The Tragedy of American Diplomacy? The Marshall Plan Revisited', *Journal of Cold War Studies*, 7/1, 97–134.

Crockett, Richard (1995), *The Fifty Years War: The United States and the Soviet Union in World Politics, 1941–1991* (New York: Routledge).

Croft, Stuart (2006), *Culture, Crisis and America's War on Terror* (Cambridge: Cambridge University Press).

Cummings, Bruce (1993), 'Revising Postrevisionism or The Poverty of Theory in Diplomatic History', *Diplomatic History*, 12, 539–69.

D'Agostino, Anthony (1988), *Soviet Succession Struggles: Kremlinology and the Russian Question from Lenin to Gorbachev* (Winchester, MA: Unwin Hyman).

Dallin, D. J. (1962), *Soviet Foreign Policy after Stalin* (London: Methuen).

Danilov, V. P. (1988), *Rural Russia under the New Regime* (London: Hutchinson).

Davis, Joseph (1941), *Mission to Moscow* (New York: Simon & Schuster).

Deakin, F. W. (1962), *The Brutal Friendship – Mussolini, Hitler and the Fall of Italian Fascism* (London: Weidenfeld & Nicolson).

De Groot, Gerald (2004), *The Bomb: A Life* (London: Jonathan Cape).

Deighton, Anne (1990), *The Impossible Peace: Britain, the Division of Germany, and the Origins of the Cold War* (New York: Oxford University Press).

Dershowitz, Alan M. (2006), *Preemption: A Knife that Cuts both Ways* (New York: W. W. Norton).

Deutscher, I. (1996), *Stalin* (London: Penguin).

Di Biagio, Anna (1996), 'The Marshall Plan and the Founding of the Cominform, June–September 1947', in Francesca Gori and Silvio Pons (eds), *The Soviet Union and Europe in the Cold War 1943–53* (London: Macmillan), 208–21.

Doyle, Michael (1986), *Empires* (Ithaca: Cornell University Press).

Duffy, Christopher (1991), *Red Storm on the Reich: The Soviet March on Germany, 1945* (London: Routledge).

Dukes, Paul (1989), *The Last Great Game: USA versus USSR, Events, Conjunctures, Structures* (London: Pinter).

Dukes, Paul (1998), *A History of Russia c.882–1996* (3rd edn) (Basingstoke: Palgrave).

Dumbrell, John (2006), *A Special Relationship: Anglo-American Relations from the Cold War to Iraq* (Basingstoke, Palgrave).

Earl of Avon (Anthony Eden) (1962), *The Eden Memoirs, Vol. 1. Facing the Dictators* (London: Cassell).

Eichengreen, Barry (1970), *Golden Fetters: The Gold Standard and the Great Depression Between the Wars* (Cambridge, MA: Harvard University Press).

Eisenberg, Carolyn (1982), 'US Policy in Post-War Germany: the Conservative Restoration', *Science and Society*, 46/1, 24–8.

Eisenberg, Carolyn (1996), *Drawing the Line: The American Decision to Divide Germany, 1944–1949* (Cambridge: Cambridge University Press).

Erickson, John (1975), *The Road to Stalingrad* (New York: Harper).

Evangelista, Matthew (1999), *Unarmed Forces: The Transnational Movement to End the Cold War* (Ithaca, NY: Cornell University Press).

Evtuhov Catherine, David Goldfrank, Lindsey Hughes and Richard Stites (2004), *A History of Russia: Peoples, Legends, Events, Forces* (Boston/New York: Houghton Mifflin).

Falk, Richard (2002), 'Testing Patriotism and Citizenship in the Global War on Terror', in Ken Booth and Tim Dunne (eds), *Worlds in Collision: Terror and the Future of Global Order* (Basingstoke: Palgrave).

Farnham, Barbara (2000), *Roosevelt and the Munich Crisis: A Study of Political Decision-Making* (Princeton, NJ: Princeton University Press).

Fawcett, Louise (1992), *Iran and the Cold War: The Azerbaijan Crisis of 1946* (Cambridge, MA: Harvard University Press).

Feis, Herbert (1950), *From Trust to Terror: The Onset of the Cold War 1945–1950* (New York).

Feis, Herbert (1960), *Between War and Peace: The Potsdam Conference* (Princeton, NJ: Princeton University Press).

Ferguson, Niall (2004), *Colossus: The Price of America's Empire* (New York: Penguin).

Figes, Orlando (1996), *A People's Tragedy: The Russian Revolution 1891–1924* (London: Jonathan Cape).

Fish, Stephen M. (1986), 'After Stalin's Death: The Anglo-American Debate Over a New Cold War', *Diplomatic History*, 10, 333–55.

Fleming, D. F. (1961), *The Cold War and Its Origins 1917–1960* (New York: Garden City).

Foot, Rosemary (1985), *The Wrong War: American Foreign Policy and the Dimensions of the Korean Conflict, 1950–1953* (Ithaca, NY: Cornell University Press).

Fox, William T. R. (1944), *The Superpowers: The United States, Britain and the Soviet Union–Their Responsibility for Peace* (New York: Harcourt, Brace).

Freedman, Lawrence (1989), *The Evolution of Nuclear Strategy* (2nd edn) (Basingstoke: Macmillan).

Freedman, Lawrence (2000), *Kennedy's Wars: Berlin, Cuba, Laos, and Vietnam* (New York: Oxford University Press).

Freedman, Lawrence (2004), *Deterrence* (Cambridge: Polity).

Freedman, Lawrence (2005), *The Evolution of Nuclear Strategy* (3rd edn) (London: Palgrave).

Freidal, Frank (1952), *Franklin D. Roosevelt: The Apprenticeship* (Boston: Little, Brown).

Gaddis, John Lewis (1972), *The United States and the Origins of the Cold War 1941–1947* (New York: Columbia University Press).

Gaddis, John Lewis (1974), 'Was the Truman Doctrine a Real Turning Point?', *Foreign Affairs*, 52.

Gaddis, John Lewis (1987), *The Long Peace: Inquiries into the History of the Cold War* (Oxford: Oxford University Press).

Gaddis, John Lewis (1990), *Russia, the Soviet Union and the United States: An Interpretive History* (2nd edn) (New York: McGraw-Hill).

Gaddis, John Lewis (1992/93), 'International Relations Theory and the End of the Cold War', *International Security*, 17, 5–58.

Gaddis, John Lewis (1994), *The United States and the End of the Cold War. Implications, Reconsiderations and Provocations* (Oxford: Oxford University Press).

Gaddis, John Lewis (1997), *We Now Know: Rethinking Cold War History* (Oxford: Oxford University Press).

Gaddis, John Lewis (2000), 'On Starting All Over Again: A Naïve Approach to the Study of the Cold War', in Odd Arne Westad (ed.), *Reviewing the Cold War: Approaches, Interpretations, Theory* (London/ Portland, OR: Frank Cass), 27–43.

Gaddis, John Lewis (2002), 'A Grand Strategy of Transformation', *Foreign Policy*, 13, 50–7.

Gaddis, John Lewis (2002), *The Landscape of History: How Historians Map the Past* (Oxford: Oxford University Press).

Gaddis, John Lewis (2004), *Surprise, Security and the American Experience* (New York: Yale University Press).

Gaddis, John Lewis (2005), *The Cold War* (London: Allen Lane).

Garthoff, Raymond L. (1958), *Soviet Strategy in the Nuclear Age* (New York: Frederick A. Praeger).

Garthoff, Raymond L. (1989), *Reflections on the Cuban Missile Crisis* (revised edn) (Washington, DC: The Brookings Institute).

Garthoff, Raymond L. (1994), *Détente and Confrontation:American-Soviet Relations from Nixon to Reagan* (revised edn) (Washington, DC: Brookings Institute).

Garton Ash, Timothy (1989), *The Uses of Adversity: Essays on the Fate of Central Europe* (New York: Random House).

Garton Ash, Timothy (1997), *The File: A Personal History* (London: Harper Collins).

Gati, Charles (2006), *Failed Illusions: Moscow, Washington, Budapest and the 1956 Hungarian Revolt* (Stanford: Stanford University Press).

Gatzke, H. W. (1957–58), 'Russo-German Military Collaboration during the Weimar Republic', *American Historical Review*, 63, 565–97.

Gilbert, Felix (1961), *To the Farewell Address: Ideas of Early American Foreign Policy* (Princeton, NJ: Princeton University Press).

Gleason, Abbott (1995), *Totalitarianism: The Inner History of the Cold War* (New York: Oxford University Press).

Goldstein, Steven M. (1994), 'Nationalism and Internationalism: Sino-Soviet Relations', in Thomas W. Robinson and David Shabaugh (eds), *Chinese Foreign Policy: Theory and Practise* (New York: Oxford University Press).

Gooding, John (1996), *Rulers and Subjects: Government and People in Russia 1801–1991* (London: Edward Arnold).

Gorodetsky, Gabriel (ed.) (1994), *Soviet Foreign Policy 1917–1991: A Retrospective* (London: Frank Cass).

Gorodetsky, Gabriel (1999), *Grand Delusion: Stalin and the German Invasion of Russia* (New Haven, CT/ London: Yale University Press).

Grabbe, Hans-Jurgen (1990), 'Konrad Adenauer, John Foster Dulles, and West German–American Relations', in R. H. Immerman (ed.), *John Foster Dulles and the Diplomacy of the Cold War* (Princeton, NJ: Princeton University Press).

Graubard, Stephen (2004), *The Presidents: The Transformation of the American Presidency From Theodore Roosevelt to George W. Bush* (London: Allen Lane).

Gray, Colin S. (2002) *Strategy for Chaos: Revolutions in Military Affairs and the Evidence of History* (London/Portland, OR: Frank Cass).

Gray, John (2003), *Al-Qaeda and What it is to be Modern* (London: Granta Books).

Hahn, W. (1982), *The Fall of Zhdanov and the Defeat of Moderation, 1946–53* (New York: Cornell University Press).

Halle, Louis B. (1967), *The Cold War as History* (New York: Harper & Row).

Halliday, Fred (1983), *The Making of the Second Cold War* (London: Verso Press).

Halliday, Fred (1996), *Islam and the Myth of Confrontation; Religion and Politics in the Middle East* (London: I. B.Tauris).

Halper, Stefan and Jonathan Clarke (2004), *America Alone: The Neo-Conservatives and the Global Order* (Cambridge: Cambridge University Press).

Harper, John Lamberton (1996), *American Visions of Europe: Franklin D. Roosevelt, George F. Kennan and Dean G. Acheson* (Cambridge: Cambridge University Press).

Harriman, W. Averell (1982), 'Stalin at War', in G. R. Urban (ed.), *Stalinism: Its Impact on Russia and the World* (London: Maurice Temple Smith).

Harriman, W. A. and E. Abel (1976), *Special Envoy to Churchill and Stalin 1941–1946* (London: Hutchinson).

Harris, T. (1976), 'The Origins of the Conflicts Between Malenkov and Zhdanov 1939–1941', *Slavonic Review*, 35/2, 296–7.

Haslam, Jonathan (1984), *The Soviet Union and the Struggle for Collective Security in Europe, 1933–39* (New York: St Martin's Press).

Haslam, Jonathan (1997), 'Russian Archives and Our Understanding of the Cold War', *Diplomatic History*, 21/2, 217–28.

Haynes, John E. (1990), *Red Scare or Red Menace? American Communism and Anti-Communism in the Cold War Era*, American Ways Series (Chicago, IL: Ivan R. Dee).

Heikal, Mohammed (1978), *The Sphinx and the Commissar: The Rise and Fall of Soviet Influence in the Middle East* (New York: Harper Row).

Heretz, L. (1997), 'The Psychology of the White Movement', in V. N. Brovkin (ed.), *The Bolsheviks in Russian Society: The Revolution and Civil Wars* (New Haven, CT: Yale University Press).

Herring, Eric and Glen Rangwala (2006), *Iraq in Fragments: The Occupation and its Legacy* (London: Hurst).

Herring, G. C. (1973), *Aid to Russia 1941–1946. Strategy Diplomacy. The Origins of the Cold War* (New York: Columbia University Press).

Hershberg, James G. (2003), 'Where the Buck Stopped: Harry S. Truman and the Cold War', *Diplomatic History*, 27/5, 735–9.

Herschberg, James G. and James B. Conant (1993), *Harvard to Hiroshima and the Making of the Nuclear Age* (New York: Knopf).

Heuser, Beatrice (1989), *Western 'Containment' Policies in the Cold War: The Yugoslav Case, 1948–53* (New York: Routledge).

Heuser, Beatrice (1991), 'NSC 68 and the Soviet Threat: A New Perspective on Western Threat Perceptions and Policy Making', *Review of International Studies*, 17, 17–40.

Hobsbawm, Eric (1994), *The Age of Extremes: A History of the World, 1914–1991* (London: Michael Joseph).

Hogan, Michael J. (1987), *The Marshall Plan: America, Britain and the Reconstruction of Western Europe, 1947–1952* (Cambridge: Cambridge University Press).

Hogan, Michael J. (1998), *A Cross of Iron: Harry S. Truman and the Origins of the National Security State 1945–1954* (Cambridge: Cambridge University Press).

Holloway, David (1983), *The Soviet Union and the Arms Race* (New Haven, CT/ London: Yale University Press).

Holloway, David (1993), 'Soviet Scientists Speak Out', *Bulletin of the Atomic Scientists*, 49, 18–19.

Holloway, David (1994), *Stalin and the Bomb: The Soviet Union and Atomic Energy, 1939–1954* (New Haven: Yale University Press).

Hopkins, Harry L. (1949), *The White House Papers of Harry Hopkins*, ed. R Sherwood (London: Eyre & Spottiswoode).

Hull, C. (1948), *The Memoirs of Cordell Hull* (London: Hodder & Stoughton)

Hulse, J. W. (1959), *The Forming of the Communist International* (Stanford, CA: Stanford University Press).

Hunt, Michael H. (1992), 'The Long Crisis in US Diplomatic History: Coming to Closure', *Diplomatic History*, 16/1, 115–42.

Huntington, Samuel P. (1996), *The Clash of Civilizations: And the Remaking of World Order* (New York: Simon & Schuster).

Husband, William B. (2000), *Godless Communists: Atheism and Society in Soviet Russia, 1917–1932* (De Kalb: Northern Illinois University Press).

Ikenberry, G. John (2000), *After Victory* (Princeton, NJ: Princeton University Press).

Inglis, Fred (1991), *The Cruel Peace Everyday Life in the Cold War* (New York: Basic Books).

Jackson, Robert J. and Philip Towle (2006), *Temptations of Power: The United States in Global Politics after 9/11* (Basingstoke: Palgrave).

James, Harold (1988), *The German Slump* (Oxford: Oxford University Press).

Johnson, Chalmers (2002), *Blowback: The Costs and Consequences of American Empire* (New York: Time Books).

Jones, Dorothy (1992), *Code of Peace? Ethics and Security in the World of the Warlord States* (Chicago: University of Chicago Press).

Kagan, Robert (2003), *Paradise and Power America and Europe in the New World Order* (London: Atlantic Books).

Kaplan, Fred (1983), *The Wizards of Armageddon* (New York: Simon & Schuster).

Kaplan, S. S. (1981), *Diplomacy of Power: Soviet Armed Forces as a Political Instrument* (Washington, DC: The Brookings Institute).

Keeble, C. (ed.) (1985), *The Soviet State: The Domestic Roots of Soviet Foreign Policy* (Aldershot: Gower).

Keep, John (1996), *Last of the Empires: A History of the Soviet Union 1945–1991* (Oxford: Oxford University Press).

Kennan, George F. (1947), 'Sources of American Conduct', *Foreign Affairs*, 25, 566–82.

Kennan, George F. (1951), *American Diplomacy: 1900–1950* (Chicago: Chicago University Press).

Kennan, George F. (1961), *Russia and the West under Lenin and Stalin* (Boston: Little, Brown).

Kennedy, Paul (1987), *The Rise and Fall of the Great Powers: Economic Change and Military Conflict from 1500–2000* (New York: Random House).

Kennedy-Pipe, Caroline (1995), *Stalin's Cold War* (Manchester: Manchester University Press).

Kennedy-Pipe, Caroline (1998), *Russia and the World* (London: Edward Arnold).

Kennedy-Pipe, Caroline (2000), 'International History and International Relations Theory: A Dialogue beyond the Cold War', *International Affairs*, 76/4, 741–54.

Kennedy-Pipe, Caroline and Nicholas Rengger (2006), 'Apocalypse Now: Continuities and Disjunctions in World Politics after 9/11', *International Affairs*, 82/3, 539–52.

Keohane, Robert O. (ed.) (1986), *Neorealism and Its Critics* (New York: Columbia University Press).

Keohane, Robert O. and Joseph S. Nye (2000 [1977]), *Power and Interdependence: World Politics in Transition* (3rd revised and expanded edn) (Boston: Little, Brown).

Keppel, Gilles (2005), *The Roots of Radical Islam* (Paris: Saqi Books).

Kersten, Krystyna (1994), '1956 – The Turning Point', in Odd Arne Westad, Sven Holtsmark and Iver B. Neumann (eds), *The Soviet Union in Eastern Europe, 1945–89* (New York: St Martin's Press).

Khrushchev, Nikita (1970), *Khrushchev Remembers*, trans. and ed. Strobe Talbott (Boston: Little, Brown).

Khrushchev, Nikita (1974), *Khrushchev Remembers: The Last Testament*, trans. and ed. Strobe Talbott (Boston: Little, Brown).

Khrushchev, Nikita (1990), *Khrushchev Remembers: The Glasnost Tapes*, trans. and ed. Jerrold L. Schecter with Vyacheslav V. Luchkov (Boston: Little, Brown).

Kimball, Warren F. (1991), *The Juggler: Franklin Roosevelt as Wartime Statesman* (Princeton: Princeton University Press).

Kindleberger, Charles P. (1973), *The World in Depression: 1929–1939* (Berkeley/Los Angeles: University of California Press).

Kirkpatrick, Jeane (1982), *Dictatorships and Double Standards: Rationalism and Reason in Politics* (New York: Simon & Schuster).

Kissinger, Henry (1969), *Nuclear Weapons and Foreign Policy* (New York: Norton).

Kissinger, Henry A. (1994), *Diplomacy* (New York: Simon & Schuster).

Kissinger, Henry (1999 [1954]), *A World Restored: Metternich, Castlereagh and the Problems of Peace 1812–22* (London: Weidenfeld & Nicolson).

Klehr, H., J. Haynes and F. Firsov (1995), *The Secret World of American Communism* (New Haven, CT: Yale University Press).

Knight, Amy (1993a), *Beria: Stalin's First Lieutenant* (Princeton, NJ: Princeton University Press).

Knight, Amy (1993b), 'The Fate of the KGB Archives', *Slavic Review*, 52, 582–6.

Knock, Thomas (1992), *To End All Wars: Woodrow Wilson and the Quest for a New World Order* (New York: Oxford University Press).

Koestler, Arthur (1979 [1940]), *Darkness at Noon* (London: Penguin).

Kramer, Mark (1992), 'New Sources on the 1968 Soviet Invasion of Czechoslovakia', *Cold War International History Project Bulletin*, 2.

Kramer, Mark (1993), 'Archival Research in Moscow: Progress and Pitfalls', *Cold War International History Bulletin*, 31–4.

Kramer, Mark (1995), 'Hungary and Poland, 1956: Khrushchev's CPSU CC Presidium Meeting on East European Crises, 24 October 1956', *Cold War International History Project Bulletin*, 5, 50–1.

Kramer, Mark (1996/97), 'New Evidence on the 1956 Polish and Hungarian Crisis', *Cold War International History Project Bulletin*, 8–9.

Krasner, Stephen D. (ed.) (1983), *International Regimes* (Ithaca, NY: Cornell University Press).

Kratochwil, Fritz (1989), *Rules, Norms, Decisions* (Cambridge: Cambridge University Press).

Kyle Keith, (1991) *Suez* (New York: St Martin's).

Lacqueur, Walter (1990 [1965]), *Russia and Germany: A Century of Conflict* (New Brunswick, NJ/London: Transaction Publishers).

Lane, Christel (1981), *The Rites of Rulers Ritual in Industrial Society – the Soviet Case* (Cambridge: Cambridge University Press).

Lebow, R. N. and J. G. Stein (1994), *We All Lost the Cold War* (Princeton, NJ: Princeton University Press).

Lebow, Richard Ned (1983), 'The Cuban Missile Crisis: Reading the Lessons Correctly', *Political Science Quarterly*, 98/3, 431–58.

Lebow, Richard Ned and Thomas Riesse-Kappen (eds) (1995), *International Relations Theory and the End of the Cold War* (New York: Columbia University Press).

Leffler, Melvyn P. (1992), *A Preponderance of Power: National Security, the Truman Administration, and the Cold War* (Stanford, CA: Stanford University Press).

Leffler, Melvyn P. (1994), *The Specter of Communism: The United States and the Origins of the Cold War, 1917–1953* (New York: Hill & Wang).

Leffler, Melvyn P. (1996), 'Inside Enemy Archives: The Cold War Reopened', *Foreign Affairs*, 75, 120–35.

Leffler, Melvyn P. (2000), 'Bringing it Together: The Parts and the Whole', in Odd Arne Westad (ed.), *Reviewing the Cold War: Approaches, Interpretation, Theory* (London/ Portland, OR: Frank Cass), 43–63.

Lenin, V. I. (1964), 'On the History of the Question of the Unfortunate Peace', in *Collected Works*, vol. 26 (Moscow: Progress Publishers), 442–6.

Light, Margot (1988), *The Soviet Theory of International Relations* (Brighton: Wheatsheaf).

Lippmann, Walter (1943), *US Foreign Policy: Shield of the Republic* (Boston: Little, Brown).

Lippmann, Walter (1947), *The Cold War* (New York: Harper).

Loth, Wilfried (1988), *The Division of the World 1941–1955* (London: Routledge).

Loth, Wilfried (1998), trans. Robert F. Hogg, *Stalin's Unwanted Child: The Soviet Union, the German Question and the Founding of the GDR* (New York: St Martin's Press).

Lundestad, Geir (1986), 'Empire by Invitation? The United States and Western Europe, 1945–1952', *Journal of Peace Research*, 23, 263–77.

McCagg, W. O. Jr (1977), 'Domestic Politics and Soviet Foreign Policy at the Cominform Conference in 1947', *Slavonic and Soviet Series*, 2/1, 3–30.

McCagg, W. O. (1978), *Stalin Embattled, 1943–1948* (Detroit, IL: Wayne State University Press).

McDonald, D. J. (1995), 'Communist Bloc Expansion in the Early Cold War: Challenging Realism, Refuting Revisionism', *International Security*, 20/3, 152–78.

MccGwire, Michael (1991), *Perestroika and Soviet National Security* (Washington, DC: The Brookings Institute).

Mackintosh, J. M. (1962), *Strategy and Tactics of Soviet Foreign Policy* (London: Oxford University Press).

MacMillan, Margaret (2002), *Paris 1919: Six Months that Changed the World* (New York: Random House).

Mann, Thomas E. (2002), 'What Bush Can Learn from Truman', *New York Times Week in Review*, 6 October.

Mark, Edward (1997), 'The War Scare of 1946 and Its Consequences', *Diplomatic History*, 21/3, 383–416.

Marolda, Edward J. (ed.) (1998), *FDR and the US Navy* (London/Basingstoke: Palgrave Macmillan).

Mastny, Vojtech (1979), *Russia's Road to the Cold War: Diplomacy, Warfare and the Politics of Communism, 1941–1945* (New York: Columbia University Press).

Mastny, Vojtech (1996), *The Cold War and Soviet Insecurity: The Stalin Years* (New York: Oxford University Press).

Mazower, Mark (1998), *Dark Continent: Europe's Twentieth Century* (New York: Knopf).

Mead, Walter Russell (2001), *Special Providence: American Foreign Policy and How it Changed the World* (New York: Knopf).

Medvedev, R. (1982), *Khrushchev* (English trans.) (Oxford: Basil Blackwell).

Merridale, Catherine (2000), *Night of Stone: Death and Memory in Russia* (London: Granta, 2000).

Miller R. F. and F. Feher (1984), *Khrushchev and the Communist World* (London: Croom Helm).

Montefiore, Simon Sebag (2003), *Stalin The Court of the Red Tsar* (London: Phoenix).

Mueller, John (1989), *Retreat From Doomsday: The Obsolescence of Major War* (Oxford: Oxford University Press).

Mueller, John (1995), *Quiet Cataclysm: Reflections on the Recent Transformation of World Politics* (New York: HarperCollins College Publishers).

Mueller, John (2004), *The Remnants of War* (Ithaca, NY: Cornell University Press).

Naimark, Norman M. (1995), *The Russians in Germany. A History of the Soviet Zone of Occupation, 1945–1949* (Cambridge, MA: Belknap Press).

Narinskii, Michail M. (1996), 'The Soviet Union and the Berlin Crisis, 1948–9', in Francesca Gori and Silvio Pons (eds), *The Soviet Union and Europe in the Cold War, 1943–53* (Basingstoke, UK: Palgrave Macmillan), 37–56.

Nation, R. Craig (1992), *Black Earth, Red Star, A History of Soviet Security Policy, 1917–1991* (Ithaca, NY/London: Cornell University Press).

Nelson, Anna Kasten (1985), 'President Truman and the Evolution of the National Security Council', *Journal of American History*, 72/2, 360–78.

Neumann, Iver B. (1996), *Russia and the Idea of Europe* (London: Routledge).

Offner, Arnold A. (1999), 'Presidential Address "Another Such Victory": President Truman, American Foreign Policy, and the Cold War', *Diplomatic History*, 23/2, 127–55.

Overy, Richard (1997), *Russia's War* (London: Allen Lane).

Parmar, Inderjeet (2005), 'Catalysing Events, Think Tanks and American Foreign Policy Shifts: A Comparative Analysis of the Impacts of Pearl Harbor 1941 and 11 September 2001', *Government and Opposition*, 40/1, 1–25.

Parrish, Scott D. (1994), 'The Turn toward Confrontation: The Soviet Reaction to the Marshall Plan, 1947', in 'New Evidence on the Soviet Rejection of the Marshall Plan, 1947: Two Reports', Working Paper No. 9, *Cold War International History Project* (Woodrow Wilson International Center for Scholars).

Perkins, Francis (1946), *The Roosevelt I Knew* (New York: Viking).

Potter, William C. and Lucy Kearner (1988), 'Soviet Decision-Making for Chernobyl: An Assessment of Ukrainian Leadership Performance', *Studies in Comparative Communism*, 21/2, 203–20.

Preston, Paul (1993), *Franco* (London: HarperCollins).

Preston, Paul (1996), *A Concise History of the Spanish Civil War* (London: Fontana).

Raack, R. C. (1993), 'Stalin Plans his Post-War Germany', *Journal of Contemporary History*, 28, 53–73.

Raack, R. C. (1995), *Stalin's Drive to the West 1938–1945: The Origins of the Cold War* (Stanford, CA: Stanford University Press).

Ra'anan, G. D. (1983), *International Policy Formation in the USSR: Factional Debates during the Zhdanovshine* (Hamden, CT: Archon Books).

Rashid, Ahmed (2001), *Taliban: Islam, Oil and the New Great Game in Central Asia* (London: I. B.Tauris).

Rengger, Nicholas (2003), 'Eternal Return? Modes of Encountering Religion in International Relations', *Millennium: Journal of International Studies*, 32/2, 327–36.

Reynolds, David (2000), *One World, Divisible: A Global History Since 1945* (London: Penguin).

Roberts, Geoffrey (1994), 'Moscow and the Marshall Plan: Politics, Ideology and the Onset of the Cold War, 1947', *Europe-Asia Studies*, 46, 1371–96.

Roberts, Geoffrey (1995), *The Soviet Union and the Origins of the Second World War: Russo-German Relations and the Road to War, 1933–1941* (Houndmills, Basingstoke: Macmillan Press).

Roberts, Geoffrey (2006), *Stalin's Wars: From World War to Cold War, 1939–1953* (New Haven and London: Yale University Press).

Robinson, Paul (2002), *The White Russian Army in Exile 1920–1941* (Oxford: Oxford University Press).

Rodrigo, Robert (1960), *Berlin Airlift* (London: Cassell).

Rosenstone, Robert (1990), *Romantic Revolutionary: A Biography of John Reed* (Cambridge, MA: Harvard University Press).

Rostrow, W. W. (1982), *Europe after Stalin: Eisenhower's Three Decisions of March 11, 1953* (Austin, TX: University of Texas Press).

Savranskaya, Svetana V. (2005), 'New Sources on the Role of Soviet Submarines in the Cuban Missile Crisis', *Journal of Strategic Studies*, 28/2, 233–60.

Schelling, Thomas (1980), *The Strategy of Conflict* (Cambridge, MA: Harvard University Press).

Schroeder, Paul W. (1994), *The Transformation of European Politics 1763–1848* (Oxford: Clarendon Press).

Service, Robert (1997), *A History of Twentieth Century Russia* (London: Allen Lane).

Sfikos, T. D. (2001), 'War and Peace in the Strategy of the Communist Part of Greece, 1945–1949', *Journal of Cold War Studies*, 3/3, 5–30.

Sharp, Tony (1975), *The Wartime Alliance and the Zonal Division of Germany* (Oxford: Oxford University Press).

Sherry, Michael (1997), *In the Shadow of War* (New Haven: Yale University Press).

Shlaim, Avi (1983), *The United States and the Berlin Blockade 1948–1949: A Study in Crisis Decision Making* (Berkeley/Los Angeles: University of California Press).

Shukman, Harold (ed.) (1997), *Stalin's Generals* (London: Phoenix).

Shulman, Marshall D. (1963), *Stalin's Foreign Policy Reappraised* (London: Oxford University Press).

Sick, Gary (1985), *All Fall Down: America's Fateful Encounter with Iran* (London: Tauris).

Skidelsky, Robert (1992), *John Maynard Keynes: The Economist as Saviour 1920–1937* (London: Macmillan).

Small, Melvin (1996), *Democracy & Diplomacy The Impact of Domestic Politics on U.S. Foreign Policy, 1789–1994* (Baltimore/London: The John Hopkins University Press).

Stalin, Joseph and H. G. Wells (1937), 'Marxism vs Liberalism: An Interview', Exhibit no. 44 (New York: New Century Publishers; repr. October 1950) at http://www.rationalrevolution.net/special/library/cc835_44.htm.

Steel, Ronald (1980), *Walter Lippmann and the American Century* (London: The Bodley Head).

Steiner, Zara (1997), 'On Writing International History: Chaps, Maps and Much More', *International Affairs*, 73/3, 531–46.

Stevenson, David (1988), *The First World War and International Politics* (Oxford: Clarendon Press).

Stueck, W. (1976), 'The Soviet Union and the Origins of the Korean War', *World Politics*, 28/4, 622–35.

Stueck, William (2002), *The Korean War. An International History* (Princeton: Princeton University Press).

Swearer, H. R. (1964), *The Politics of Succession in the USSR: Materials on Khrushchev's Rise to Leadership* (Boston: Little, Brown).

Taubman, W. (1982), *Stalin's American Policy From Entente to Detente to Cold War* (Ontario: Penguin).

Taubman, William (1996), 'How much of the Cold War was inevitable? A Comment on Chapters 4, 6, 8 and 9', in Francesca Gori and Silvio Pons (eds), *The Soviet Union and Europe in the Cold War 1945–1953* (London: Macmillan, 1996).

Taylor, A. J. P. (1954), *The Struggle for Mastery in Europe 1848–1918* (Oxford: Oxford University Press).

Thomas, Scott (2005), *The Global Resurgence of Religion and the Transformation of International Relations* (Houndmills, Basingstoke: Palgrave).

Thucydides, tr. Rex Warner (1972), *History of the Peloponnesian War* (London: Penguin).

Toolis, Kevin (2006), 'Compare Bloodshed. Saddam is then the moral victor, not Bush', *The Times*, 11 November.

Toynbee, Arnold (1954), *A Study of History* (Oxford: Oxford University Press).

Truman, H. S. (1955), *Memoirs, Vol. 1 Year of Decisions* (New York: Doubleday).

Truman, H. S. (1956), *Memoirs, Vol. 2 Years of Trial and Hope* (New York: Doubleday).

Tucker, Robert (1990), *Stalin in Power: The Revolution from Above* (New York: Norton).

Ulam, Adam (1971), *The Rivals: America and Russia Since World War II* (New York: Viking).

Ulam, Adam B. (1973), *Stalin: The Man and His Era* (London: Allen Lane).

Ulam, Adam B. (1974), *Expansion and Co-existence: Soviet Foreign Policy 1917–73* (2nd edn) (New York: Praeger).

Vaksberg, Arkady (1994), *Stalin Against the Jews* (New York: Knopf).

Varsori, Antonio (2000), 'Reflections on the Origins of the Cold War', in Odd Arne Westad (ed.), *Reviewing the Cold War: Approaches, Interpretation, Theory* (London/Portland, OR: Frank Cass), 281–302.

Volkogonov, Dmitri (1991), ed. and trans. Harold Shukman, *Stalin: Triumph and Tragedy* (London: Weidenfeld & Nicholson).

Volkogonov, Dmitri (1998), trans. Harold Shukman, *The Rise and Fall of the Soviet Empire Political Leaders from Lenin to Gorbachev* (London: HarperCollins).

Walker, William (2004), *Weapons of Mass Destruction and International Order*, Adelphi Papers No. 370 (London: Oxford University Press for International Institute for Strategic Studies).

Walt, Stephen (1986), *Origins of Alliances* (Ithaca, NY: Cornell University Press).

Waltz, Kenneth N. (1979), *Theory of International Relations* (New York: Random House).

Weathersby, Kathryn (1993), 'New Findings on the Korean War', *Cold War International History Project Bulletin*, 3.

Wendt, Alexander (2001), *Social Theory of International Politics* (Cambridge: Cambridge University Press).

Westad, Odd Arne (1988), *Brothers in Arms: the Rise and Fall of the Sino-Soviet Alliance 1945–1963* (Stanford, CA: Stanford University Press).

Westad, Odd Arne (1993), *Cold War and Revolution: Soviet–American Rivalry and the Origin of the Chinese Civil War, 1944–1946* (New York: Columbia University Press).

Westad, Odd Arne (1997), 'Secrets of the Second World: The Russian Archives and the Reinterpretation of Cold War History', *Diplomatic History*, 21/2, 259–71.

Westad, Odd Arne (1998), *Brothers in Arms: The Rise and Fall of the Sino-Soviet Alliance 1945–1963* (Stanford: Stanford University Press).

Westad, Odd Arne (2003), *Decisive Encounters: The Chinese Civil War, 1945–1950* (Stanford: Stanford University Press).

Westad, Odd Arne (2006), *The Global Cold War: Third World Interventions and the Making of Our Times* (Cambridge: Cambridge University Press).

White, Hayden (1975), *Metahistory: the Historical Imagination in Nineteenth-Century Europe* (Baltimore, MD: The Johns Hopkins University Press).

Wight, Martin (1977), *Systems of States* (Leicester: Leicester University Press).

Williams, William Appleman (1962), *The Tragedy of American Diplomacy* (New York: World Publishing).

Willkie, Wendell (1943), *One World* (New York: Simon and Schuster).

Woff, Richard (1997), 'Stalin's Ghosts', in Harold Shukman (ed.), *Stalin's Generals* (London: Phoenix).

Wohlforth, William C. (1993), *The Elusive Balance: Power and Perception during the Cold War* (Ithaca, NY: Cornell University Press).

Wohlforth, William C. (2000), 'A Certain Idea of Science: How International Relations Theory Avoids Reviewing the Cold War', in Odd Arne Westad (ed.), *Reviewing the Cold War: Approaches, Interpretation, Theory* (London/Portland, OR: Frank Cass), 126–48.

Wohlstetter, Roberta (1962), *Pearl Harbor: Warning and Decision* (Stanford, CA: Stanford University Press).

Wolfe, T. (1970), *Soviet Power and Europe 1945–1970* (Baltimore, MD: The Johns Hopkins Press).

Wright, Lawrence (2006), *The Looming Tower* (London: Allen Lane).

Young, John W. (1997), *Britain and the World in the Twentieth Century* (London: Edward Arnold).

Young, John W. (2001), 'Churchill and East–West Détente', *Royal Historical Society Transactions*, 11, 373–92.

Zhang, Shu Guang (2000), 'China's Strategic Culture and the Cold War Confrontations', in Odd Arne Westad (ed.), *Reviewing the Cold War: Approaches, Interpretation, Theory* (London/Portland, OR: Frank Cass).

Zhisui Li (1994), trans. by Tai Hung-chao, *The Private Life of Chairman Mao: The Memoirs of Mao's Personal Physician* (New York: Random House).

Zubkova, Elena (1998), *Russia after the War: Hopes, Illusions and Disappointments, 1945–1957* (New York: M. E. Sharpe).

Zubok, Vladislav and Constantine Pleshakov (1996), *Inside the Kremlin's Cold War: From Stalin to Khrushchev* (Cambridge, MA: Harvard University Press).

Index

189